# AMERICAN ARTERY

## *A Pan American Journey*

FROM WINNIPEG TO PANAMA ON AMERICA'S LONGEST ROAD

## JERRY WILSON

*11-21-00*

*Jerry Wilson*

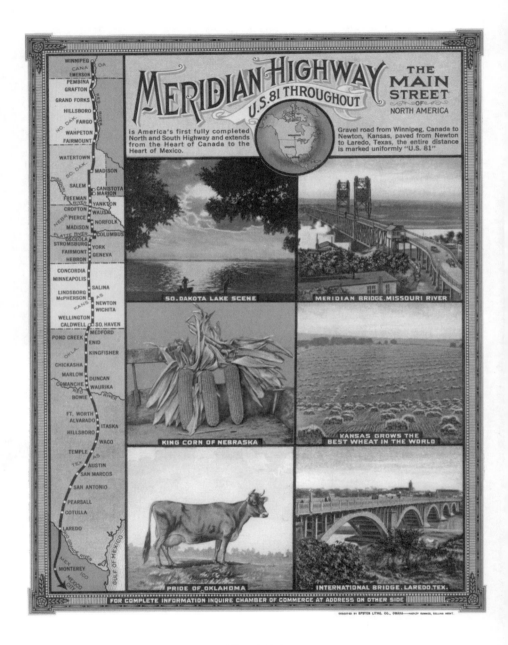

1930s Meridian Highway poster,
Courtesy of Rexford M. Shield.

# American Artery
## A Pan American Journey

*Jerry Wilson*

Cover photo by Clarence Pederson
All other photos by the author

> "There are no worlds beyond our own. There is one
> world everywhere, waiting for us to find it."
>
> ~ Jacques Cousteau ~

South Dakota Magazine
Nebraska Life Magazine

ISBN: 1-57579-199-4

LCCN: 00-092233


Printed in the United States of America
Pine Hill Press
4000 West 57th Street
Sioux Falls, S.D. 57106

# ACKNOWLEDGEMENTS

MANY PEOPLE contributed, directly or indirectly, to the completion of this work; I appreciate all who patiently endured my single-minded preoccupation with this highway and the continent it traverses. I am grateful to my wife, Norma, and to our children, Walter and Laura, for the freedom to travel, and for welcoming me home.

I am indebted to those who read all or parts of the manuscript or made helpful suggestions, not to mention saving me embarrassment by discovering errors which had escaped my attention. Those readers include Norma Wilson, Bob Lewis, Art Huseboe, Sr. Eileen Neville, Bruce and Betsy Noll, Barbara and Bob Schmitz, Alice and Tom Gasque, Sr. Consuelo Chavez, Richard Stinshoff, Jean Dederman, Pat Keating, Nancy Scott, Frank Parman, Larry Griffin, Karen Cardenas, Phil Smith, Charles Hall, Bernie Hunhoff, Mary Johnson, Roger Holtzmann and Kim Johnson. For any errors which might remain I must take credit, and I regret them in advance.

Most of all, I wish to thank the scores of people who shared their time, a cup of coffee or a beer, a meal or a roof – people from Canada to Panamá who revealed their insights and visions, fears and dreams, knowledge and hope. Without these people, many of whom appear in the book, there would be no book, at least not this book. The people who live and work, who love and dream along the Pan American Highway are the links in a chain binding Canada to Panamá, connecting the peoples of North America, sustaining the life of our continent. They are the life blood of the American Artery. It is to them that I dedicate this book.

*The author would also like to acknowledge the assistance of his trusty 1980 Dodge Omni, without which this book would not have been possible.*

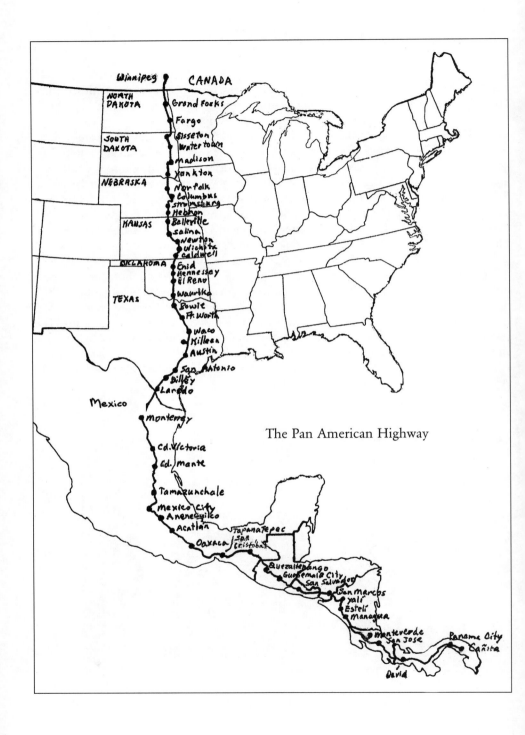

The Pan American Highway

# CONTENTS

# SOUTH FROM WINNIPEG

*"There are no worlds beyond our own. There is one
world everywhere, waiting for us to find it."*

~ *Jacques Cousteau*

I stood at the intersection of Canada 1 and the Pan American Highway, scanning the southern horizon.

"Looking for something?" It was a kind voice, a small gray-suited man.

"Oh, no," I said, dropping my gaze. "No thanks."

Who knows? Maybe he had answers. But how do you tell a stranger on a street corner that it's not something as simple as a restaurant or a bar you're looking for. Not a street or a neighborhood, not even a country or a place on a map. If I'd said I was looking for America, he'd probably have pointed south down the Pembina Highway toward North Dakota.

The light turned green. The stranger nodded, stepped off the curb and strode west. I resumed my survey of the southern constellations. The top star of Crux Australis, the Southern Cross, would not appear until 30 degrees latitude, about San Antonio. The entire constellation should be visible by Monterrey, Mexico. That touchstone of southern navigation would lead me to the end of the road. Down Pembina Highway and U.S. 81, through Mexico on 85 and 190, all the way to the end of Central America 1 at Cañita, Panamá.

But those are only highway signs along 5,000 miles of concrete and asphalt. Besides, it wasn't just the road itself that drew me. What I sought was something more ephemeral. The truth is, I wasn't sure how to put into words what had set me on this journey. Perhaps it was a quest for hints of hope that the continent's future could be carried forward.

I knew that in 50 years of living, I'd witnessed degradation of both people and the natural environment. But I'd also seen people in all walks of life remembering the best in our past, and seeking some formula to keep the planet spinning. The word that came to mind was "sustainability." Strangely enough, the word wasn't even in my dictionary, even though it perhaps best describes the creative principle of life itself, not to mention our age-old struggle to leave for our children what we value most.

Clearly all was not well in the sustainable universe. But how badly damaged were our rivers and forests and land? How many people were eating well, and how many hardly at all?

I knew there were no easy answers to any of these questions, but nevertheless, the questions needed to be asked. And I knew only one way to do it. Get in a car and drive down the Pan American Highway – the one that goes all the way, from Canada to Panamá, the one that links the peoples of our continent. I would stop in every city and town, walk in the forests, talk to people on countless streets. I wanted to know their vision for the future, their fears for their children and the Earth. Perhaps it was the soul of the continent I sought, the heartbeat of America, throbbing with life along the great American artery.

On New Year's Day of 1994, the North American Free Trade Agreement linked the economies of Canada, the United States and Mexico. At dawn, Maya Indians in the Southern Mexican state of Chiapas moved up the Pan American Highway, seizing four towns including the regional city of San Cristóbal. The Zapatistas were protesting NAFTA and the Mexican government's indifference to their oppression and hunger. I was with my family in the neighboring state of Yucatán that day, marveling at the timeless pyramids of Uxmal. Life went on as usual there: Beside the ruins of ancient cities of their ancestors, modern Mayas toiled under a punishing sun, planting, harvesting, building, bearing burdens of every sort, putting tortillas on the table one more day.

The Mexican government sent troops to quell the rebellion, and to halt the flood of refugees from Central America. Tens of thousands had already crossed from Guatemala, and thousands more were coming. From Nicaragua, Honduras and El Salvador, from Guatemala and Mexico, people were moving north – to refugee camps in Chiapas, to oil fields in Oklahoma and beet fields in North Dakota, even to this far north star of Winnipeg. They'd fled their homelands seeking safety, work, a better life. Their major route: The Pan American Highway.

The U.S. stretch of the highway began as an Indian trade route, marked in 1861 by Delaware scout, Black Beaver. In 1863 it took the name of Jesse Chisholm, a Cherokee-Scotch freighter. In the 1870's more than a million cattle trod the fabled Chisholm Trail from Texas through Indian Territory to railheads in Kansas. By 1924 the Meridian Road was graveled from Mexico to Canada. It was completed that year by a bridge across the Missouri River at Yankton, South Dakota. In 1927 the road became U.S. 81, and in 1936 it was named the U.S. link of the Pan American Highway.

I was born a thousand miles down this road in the farm town of Okeene, Oklahoma. Okeene's name was coined from the first letters of Oklahoma and the last letters of Cherokee and Cheyenne. In 1867 the federal government had uprooted the Cheyenne and Arapaho tribes from ancestral lands to the north and west and dumped them together in this corner of Indian Territory on land that was to be theirs as long as the grass should grow. A generation later the same government declared most of the land "surplus" and gave it to white settlers in the land run of 1892. Two of my great grandfathers made the run, staking claims on the Cimarron River bluff.

Four wheat elevators, the first of which my father helped build in 1938 for 30 cents an hour, tower over the town. Like their Bermuda grass lawns and

Chinese elms, the lives of Okeene's 1,600 residents are rooted in hard red earth.

As a school boy I traced the Pan American Highway, a long black thread down a yellowed classroom map. Dusky eyes peered from Mexican cacti, shaded by broad sombreros. Iridescent birds flickered in the margins of Central America.

Mention Okeene, and folks think Rattlesnake Roundup. West of town, wheat fields yield to the buttes of the Glass Mountains. In April, diamond-backed rattlers crawl from the selenite and gypsum-creviced hills, hungry from their winter's sleep. Even before city fathers saw that serpents could lure visitors to town, the annual rite had begun. Embrace the coming spring, perform a preemptive strike at the poisonous viper, devour a slab of snake. When you finish, you can pick your teeth with a rib. There was even a carnival for the kids.

The carnies, Uncle Melvin called them, were peculiar to the local folks. The somber eyes of the ferris wheel man peered from a shadowy face like those on the map. His words were strange. He took my quarter and whirled me high over Main, a blacktop ribbon shimmering toward infinity.

The passion to see beyond the next hill must be in the blood. As a boy I heard the tales of my ancestors' treks. Each generation inched westward from their birthplace to somewhere else – from Virginia to Tennessee, from Missouri to Kansas, finally to Oklahoma Territory in the run of 1892.

But Great Grandpa Bedwell still had itchy feet. When his 21st and final child was three days old, he left his homestead and caught a train for Mexico. Eventually he returned, bringing a parrot that Grandma said finally learned to talk American, but never stopped singing in Spanish.

While many of the next generation of Okies fled to California in the 1930s, my folks outlasted the Dust Bowl in rattlesnake country. But me – the rattlers wouldn't let me stay. Surely my birthplace was not the only town with bizarre and exotic ways. If not taunting and consuming the deadly symbol of evil, then what? Lured by the serpentine highway vanishing in the cosmic mirage, I knew even as a boy squinting south from atop the ferris wheel, there had to be more.

My teenage years passed on the family farm, next to the wheat and oil town of Hennessey. Main Street is U.S. 81. Pounded hard by millions of hooves, the Chisholm Trail had been paved through town by the thirties. Wheat trucks rumble down Main in the summer heat, whipping red dust brought by oil rigs in mud time.

On Saturday nights we "drug Main," not with a needle or a pipe, but in a '54 Mercury, two-door hardtop, busted right tail light. From the high school on the south to the Farmers' Co-op on the north, a good eight blocks, around and around. Once Mrs. Ortman's pink '57 T-bird pulled away from the theater, everything was shut down for the night except the Sooner Grill. Great greasy burgers for 50 cents.

I left the highway for a time, first to college in Shawnee, then to the army in New Jersey. But fortune's magnet drew me back to the path of my destiny, to Fort Hood, Texas, just off 81. That was 1967, the year I first ventured into Mexico, down the Pan American Highway through Austin and San Antonio, across the Rio Grande to Nuevo Laredo, once as far as Monterrey. I planned a trip to Mexico City for the 1968 Olympics, but on October 2 the Mexican government massacred 300 students at Tlatelolco Plaza, and the army canceled my leave. The great city had to wait until Uncle Sam turned me loose.

When Norma and I married in 1973, our wedding trip was down Highway 81 again to Mexico. Later we looked west for work, but found it north instead in South Dakota. For 17 years I taught at Mount Marty College, and now I'm an editor of *South Dakota Magazine*, both in the Dakota Territorial Capital of Yankton – on Highway 81, the inescapable axis of my life. One summer we took the kids north up 81 to Winnipeg, this tranquil northern star of my solar plexus.

Just 65 miles north of the U.S. on Canada 75, Winnipeg is the logical northern terminus of the Pan American Highway. Farther north there are few people, fewer towns, and even fewer roads. Canada 6 continues north to Thompson, the only town of a thousand residents north of Winnipeg. The Red River flows north to Lake Winnipeg, as it has since the great Valders Glacier melted at the end of the last ice age, draining the vast and ancient Lake Agassiz that is now the Red River valley northward. The Nelson River empties Lake Winnipeg into Hudson Bay and the Atlantic Ocean, connecting Winnipeg by water to the "old world." Canada's major east-west highway, Canada 1, intersects the Pan American Highway where I stood.

As a modern international artery, the Pan American Highway runs south between the 97th and 98th meridians from Winnipeg through the Dakotas, Nebraska, Kansas, Oklahoma and Texas on U.S. 81. At San Antonio the route leaves the Chisholm Trail and veers southwest on the Spanish Upper Presidio Road to the border at Laredo.

From the Rio Grande, the highway is Mexico 85 to Mexico City, then 190 to the Guatemala border. All the way through Central America – through Guatemala, El Salvador, Honduras, Nicaragua, Costa Rica and Panamá – the route is Central America 1, and for much of the way, it is the only paved north-south road. The highway turns to gravel at Cañita, Panamá, 5,000 miles from Winnipeg. An unsigned path snakes on through the swamps of Darién to South America, passable on foot in the drier season. Central America's borders were blocked by war when I was there in the 1980s. The highway crumbled in the nineties. And in 1998 Hurricane Mitch washed out bridges and buried the great American artery in mud. But tonight the route was open. I was eager to hit the road.

In Canada and the United States, the most important roads run east to west, like the Trans-Canadian Highway whose traffic flowed like a river at my back. Highways parallel the westward movement of millions of Europeans, including my forebears. But the east-west road is the black road in the vision of Lakota holy man Black Elk, the road which brought white people and destruction, the road of Native American flight. The north-south road is Black Elk's good red road, the road toward the sun.

East-west roads are secondary in Central America. In fact, in Nicaragua no paved road links the nation's Atlantic and Pacific shores. And only the Pan American Highway traverses the continent longitudinally, binding nine nations, bearing our products of trade, transporting migrants north and south. Now more than half a century old, this highway links the capitals of six North American nations. Some day the road may bridge the Darién Gap, tying North America to another 5,000 miles of Pan American Highway through South America, hugging the Pacific on its journey through Colombia, Ecuador, Peru and Chile, connecting Winnipeg to Tierra del Fuego. Destined to increasing prominence in a free-trading 21st century, the Pan American Highway is the longest, and continentally-speaking, the most important road in the Americas.

The traffic light at the intersection of two great highways cycled green for the third or fourth time, waking me from my reverie. The day had been long and delicious — tramping across the city in the August heat, sampling Folklorama, Winnipeg's annual celebration of her diverse cultures. But the hour was late. I ambled south toward my $14 room at the Guest House International.

But when I got there I couldn't stop. It was just a couple more blocks to the Assiniboin, and just a short stroll down the river to what the French call La Fourche, and the British, The Forks. Maybe my feet had that much life left.

By starlight it was easy to imagine the confluence of the Red and Assiniboin Rivers as the meeting place it had been for the Cree and the Assiniboin long before the French came — and as the scene of violence once Europeans arrived. When French trappers and traders arrived almost three centuries ago, they and the native women they married established the Métis culture along the rivers.

Of course the French quickly built forts to keep themselves in and others out, beginning with Fort Rouge, constructed by Pierre Gaultier de Varennes in 1736. But it was when fellow Europeans arrived at the Forks in the next century that the real conflict began. The Northwest Company, whose "trading post" still stands just north of the Forks, built Fort Gibraltar at the confluence in 1806, and in 1812 Lord Selkirk brought Scotch and Irish settlers to Fort Douglas to bolster the trade of the rival Hudson's Bay Company.

By then the Métis had been living around the forks for decades, trading with the Hudson's Bay Company, which established itself on the continent in 1670 and moved west with the trade. By 1812 the Métis had a settled lifestyle, trapping, trading, building and managing canoes and ox carts, harvesting wood and hay.

Numerous clashes ensued between the Métis and the Selkirk settlers. This vast territory, all the land that drained into the Hudson Bay, had been chartered in 1670 to Prince Rupert, grandson of King James I of England. Two centuries later, the British North America Act of 1867 provided for the admission of "Rupert's Land and the North-western Territory" into Canada.

In 1869, without consulting the people at Red River (now Winnipeg), the

Dominion of Canada negotiated with the Hudson's Bay Company for the transfer of Rupert's Land to British colonists of the Orange Order. Under the leadership of poet and Member of Parliament Louis Riel, "the Che Guevara of the prairies," biographer Maggie Siggins calls him, the Métis resisted, taking possession of Fort Gary and setting up a provisional colonial government. The Canadian government eventually acceded to some of the Métis' demands, the rebellion was subdued, and Manitoba, then a relatively small area around present Winnipeg, became a province of Canada in 1870.

For leading the rebellion, Riel was hanged in 1885. In his last will and testament he asked pardon for the "scandal" he had created by resisting civil and religious authority. Riel lies just across the Red River from the Forks, next to orthodox Catholic founders in the churchyard of the 1818 St. Boniface Cathedral. In the centennial of his execution, Métis descendants formally petitioned the government for his pardon.

Many of the Métis were pushed west to what is now Saskatchewan, and French Canadians moved in to occupy abandoned Métis lands, forming a substantial French-speaking community. St. Boniface was its center. By 1900 St. Boniface was one of the largest towns in the Canadian west, a formidable rival of Red River.

In the afternoon I'd visited the French Quarter, centered along Avenue Tache around the St. Boniface Cathedral and the convent of the Soeurs Grises, the Gray Nuns, the first four of whom arrived in 1818 after a 58-day canoe trip from Montreal to "teach school, care for the sick, sew, spin, weave, cook and sing." The massive cathedral burned in 1968, but its hulk dimly lurked across the river. Within those walls stands a modern steel edifice, a virtual parody of the earlier church. But the community is still clearly French; its streets are rues, with names like Darveau, La Vérendrye, Notre Dame, and Goulet.

French influence continues to rival English throughout the region; most public signs communicate in both English and French, and both languages are studied by every Canadian student. But to their credit, when Red River and St. Boniface eventually merged, these dominant peoples adopted indigenous names for both city and state. Winnipeg is Cree for "muddy water," and the province became Manitoba, named for "Manitou," the Great Spirit.

Thunder clouds rumbled in the western sky; when lightning flashed I headed for the International, reaching the door as the first drops splashed.

The International was a hostel in an aging and slightly decrepit three-story house on Maryland Street. As rain pounded outside, dripping travelers from several continents – a virtual United Nations – took refuge around a battered table in the dining room. Our host Jean poured cups of coffee and glasses of wine.

Most of the International's guests were there for Folklorama. Forty ethnic groups set up pavilions to entertain each other and guests with their music and dance, crafts and history, food and drink. Jean bragged that Folklorama simply epitomizes Canada's and Winnipeg's long tradition of welcoming refugees, beginning when the Cree and the Assiniboin accepted the French as neighbors. But Winnipeg has since harbored newcomers from around the world: hunted Indians, persecuted Hutterites, refugees from political violence in Eastern Europe and Latin America, even soldiers AWOL from war in Vietnam.

"But what is it about Canada that makes living in harmony possible," I asked. "Why can people get along here who couldn't get along where they came from?"

"Maybe it's the cold," Jean joked. "Even wild animals are more sociable in the cold. But seriously," he added, "it has something to do with respect. People can't find peace unless there is justice and respect."

I had visited three of Winnipeg's peoples that day, the Greek Islands first. What could be more stabilizing, I reasoned, than lunch with people from a 3,000-year-old culture? Anyway, I would follow that with visits to cultures in turmoil, the Ukrainians and the Serbs, peoples from two countries which had ceased to exist since my earlier visit to Winnipeg.

The Greek celebration, held at the University of Winnipeg, was everything I anticipated. Nickolas, the chef, told me the secrets of his mouth-watering souvlaki. The bazouki music and dancing reminded me of Zorba's message – how essential pleasure is to staying alive. A big banner behind the stage proclaimed that "in Greece, dancing and wine are as necessary as breath."

The Ukrainian pavilion was lively and upbeat too. Like the peoples of the former Yugoslavia, the Ukrainians and other republics of the former Soviet Union had parted ways since I first visited Folklorama in 1988. But unlike the Croats, Bosnians, Kosovars and Serbs, the Ukrainians avoided a death struggle, and their music and dance brandished optimism and vitality. The Ukrainians had chosen for their pavilion the historic hall of the IWW, the International Workers of the World. Over the door, chiseled in stone, is the admonition, "Workers of the World Unite!" The Soviet Union is dead, but perhaps the collectivist dream lives on.

Following the exuberant celebration of cultural life with the Greeks and the Ukrainians, I headed up McGregor Street to meet the Serbs. When my family and I had visited the Croatian pavilion in 1988 they were clamoring for Croatian independence from the communists and Serbs. I had hoped to talk again with Croatian people, to ask whether independence had been worth the price paid by all the peoples of the former Yugoslavia. Had they found ethnic identity a higher good than cooperative nationhood? But Folklorama's success had required expansion to two weeks, and I had missed Croatia. This was the week of the Serbs, so this time I would hear their story.

Given the horrible atrocities experienced by former countrymen in Bosnia and by ethnic Albanians in Kosovo, mostly attributed to Serbs, what would Serbian-Canadians feel? I entered the Parish Hall of the St. Vladimir and Olga Cathedral, a Catholic hall rented to Greek Orthodox Serbs for the occasion.

At the center of a little circle was Risto Pajic, official Serbian Ambassador to Folklorama. A tanned and fit working man, a machinist for the Canadian

National Railway, Risto had come to Canada 35 years earlier, after his father was jailed by Marshall Tito for opposing the Communist government. He married a Croatian woman, and they and their children returned from time to time to visit family and friends in Bosnia where he was born, as well as other parts of Yugoslavia. When I approached Risto, he was reading the latest bloody news from his homeland.

Risto told me that including recent arrivals, there were about 200 Serbian families in Winnipeg, and perhaps a larger number of Croats. I asked whether Serbs and Croats in Winnipeg got along. "My friends are still friends," he said, "but I guess it's a little changed." He said that in order to avoid conflict, the Croats and Serbs no longer attended each other's Folklorama pavilions as in the past.

Risto offered no defense of the war. Though he was critical of the "iron fist" with which Tito had held the Yugoslav nation together, he said the division of the republics was a mistake. Under communist unity, he said, people labored together to build a modern country. How would it work if the 50 U.S. states separated, he asked. Or if the states of Europe didn't cooperate. "Germany produces Volkswagens and Mercedes cars, but can they eat them? No, people must cooperate and trade," Risto said. "If division is good, why would Germany get united?"

Risto was frustrated that the international community had thus far done so little to stop the conflict. He resented the Vatican and Germany's quick recognition of Croatia and the other break-away republics. He said his Bosnian homeland is a geographic rather than an ethnic region, the place where three worlds meet: Catholic Croatians, Greek Orthodox Serbs, and Muslims. Ironically, the perennial conflict has pitted virtually indistinguishable Christian Europeans, who speak the same language and share the cultural traditions displayed at Folklorama.

After a lifetime of trying, Risto still couldn't understand why the two peoples must kill each other. But he told a bitter joke which put the blame for historic enmity on others. When Marshall Tito died and went to Hell, he found other Yugoslavians of all ethnic groups represented. "How is it here?" Tito asked.

"The same," came the reply. "It's just like on Earth. We're all still working for the Germans."

The rain continued, but the stories and the wine came to an end. Very late I climbed the stairs to my little room. I laid my head by the bay window that first night of my journey, peering out into the darkness of a prairie thunderstorm. As in *Stone Angel* by Canadian novelist Margaret Laurence, lightning tore the sky "like an angry claw at the cloak of God." The battering rain lulled me to sleep, awash in a bountiful cultural sea.

When light returned, a more profound change had come. Rain continued to fall, but now the air was cool. It was time to head south, ahead of the geese, who needn't stop for conversations and who see all they need from their own lofty highway. They know what is to be known from ancestral times about migrations and the reasons to go.

I made one last stop before hitting the road, at the Living Prairie Museum on the western edge of the city. A small building shelters prairie exhibits and an interpretive center, but the "living museum" is 32 acres of virgin prairie, preserved so modern city builders and wheat planters can experience the plains of Manitoba as they were when the sacred Manitou whispered to the Cree through the narrows of Lake Manitoba.

I have lived most of my life on prairie and former prairie, and have even replanted native grasses on my South Dakota hills. So I felt at home, strolling through big blue stem, Indiangrass and buffalo grass, meadow roses and blazing star, gumweed and smooth asters, goldenrod and sage, ancient survivors of this native prairie culture. What better harbor from which to launch a journey of continental exploration?

A light mist still fell, and thunder promised more when I returned to my car. I said good-bye to the northern pole of my solar plexus and headed for Panamá, hoping to find along my way what I had sensed in Winnipeg – ties that bind the peoples of our continent as one.

Driving out of Winnipeg on the Pan American Highway (Pembina Highway, or Canada 75), I forgot for a moment that this was not a U.S. city. McDonald's, Honda and Shell – U.S., Japanese and Dutch corporations – announce themselves as garishly in Winnipeg as they do in Wichita or Fort Worth. In fact I had come to Winnipeg expecting an extension of the American Midwest, but I had discovered a rich salad bowl. Would I find such diversity again in any of the nine countries linked by this great road?

Along the U.S. portion of the Pan American Highway, cities creep out across the prairies and fields in a phenomenon we call urban sprawl. In much of Mexico and Central America, one finds people virtually everywhere. But in Canada that is not the case. A glance at the Winnipeg map shows a clear line of demarcation. At a definable point, the city abruptly stops. One moment I was negotiating city traffic lights, and the next my eye embraced limitless fields of grain. Within a mile one leaves the city behind, plunging into wheat and flax, rape seed, barley and oats. McDonald's and Shell give way to grain elevators and combines.

I flipped on the radio and scanned both AM and FM bands. I found country and western, farm market reports, various stripes of rock and roll, and a collection of oldies. Strangely, the cultural and linguistic medley which so characterizes this city hadn't found its way to the air-waves. Not even a word of French did I hear, let alone the music of the Caribbean or Eastern Europe. The rain intensified, and I turned off the noise and headed up the Red River to its origin 300 miles south, lulled by the slap of the wiper blades, anticipating the long journey ahead, reliving former journeys.

In 1985 I had ventured south of Mexico for the first time into Central America. Saddened that Cold War had turned peasant peoples to pawns, I picked my way down the land-mined American artery through Nicaragua, part of a band of North Americans who wanted to stop the killing. I came home inspired by the Nicaraguan determination to forge a future free of external control. But I came home with more questions than answers. What had I really learned?

Three years later, I caught a bus in Mexico City, bound for the Instituto Tecún Umán in Antigua, Guatemala, the Spanish colonial capital. I was going there to study Spanish, but also to experience the Maya culture. I wanted to see the beauty of Guatemala, to meet a few of her people, to explore the jungle-shrouded Maya capital of Tikal.

By then I was determined to better understand the political struggles, which in Guatemala had taken 100,000 lives in a decade. What were the roots of this generation of violence, fueled with my tax dollars? Where was the logic in arming anti-government rebels in Nicaragua, while supporting government repression of rebels in Guatemala and El Salvador?

From South Dakota to Mexico City by jet took five hours. From there down the Pan American Highway to the Guatemalan border by bus required two days, first-class to Tehuantepec, second-class to Comitán, hand-me-down school bus to the frontier. From the Guatemala border south was a question mark.

Behind me was the so-called Third World, impoverished and reeling, stripped of ancient forests, clinging to threads of hope. Ahead must be the Fourth, the highlands of Guatemala. I paid $2 for a passport stamp and walked across the line. I edged my way through a multitude of Maya refugees, desperate to cross the other way to Mexico. In my backpack was everything I'd need for a month's sojourn in Central America. On their backs in gunny sacks and ponchos were all their possessions, everything with which they had fled, besides their lives.

At last a smoking Ford van arrived. I tossed my pack on top and climbed in. It was an aging nine-passenger model with an extra bench. I was glad to have a seat – until I realized that in Guatemala there is no such thing as a full bus. The van was crammed with 25 people, I in the bottom layer, when it groaned away from La Mesilla.

Through the Guatemalan mountains the great American artery had crumbled to potholes and gravel, a parody of the smooth northern stretch I now hydroplaned through lashing Canadian rain. But at last we arrived in Antigua, whose name means ancient. Founded in 1542 after Agua Volcano destroyed the first conquistador capital of Ciudad Viejo (old city) in 1541, Antigua was built a few miles farther from the volcano. But it too was destroyed, by earthquake in 1773. The capital was moved yet farther east to the present site of Guatemala City, which in turn was leveled by earthquake in 1917, but rebuilt once again.

Once the most important Spanish site between Mexico City and Lima, Peru, I found Antigua to be a semi-modern, one-story town, still crouched below the steaming mouth of Volcán de Agua. The city center lay in fragments, gigantic cathedral columns and palace walls resting where they had fallen two centuries before. The ruins draw tourists from around the world.

I wandered among the fallen monuments, wondering why in 200 years before the tourists came, no one had bothered to move the debris. Instead they simply built around it and went on with their lives. Perhaps the massive stones became as much a part of the landscape as the volcano itself. Anyway, if the stones must be moved, another generation could do it. They weren't going anywhere.

Those ancient stones got me thinking about time. I realized that in all sorts of ways, the farther south I'd traveled, the less that time as measured by clocks seemed to matter. I remembered Jeremy Rifkin's observation about people and the watches they choose. Those with modern digitals live in the present moment, he said, disconnected from past and future; those with analogical time-pieces see the present as part of a continuum, their watch dials analogous to the earth in the solar system, to our relations in space and time.

Astonishingly, nowhere in Antigua had I seen or heard a public time-piece of any sort. There were no church bells to toll the hours as at St. Boniface Cathedral back in Winnipeg. No noon whistle signaled a break from work, as in farm towns along U.S. 81. No, in Antigua there was not so much as a bank temperature and time. In that ancient place, where the Maya developed an accurate calendar before the eminence of Rome and where every day of the year had significance, one could see that until recently the hours and minutes of Europeans and North Americans had passed without note.

But change was underway. Young men's wrists were now cuffed with digital plastic watches from Asia. Where Europeans had failed for four and a half centuries, entrepreneurs from the Far East had succeeded in a decade in saddling Guatemala with time. Perhaps in some mechanistic way, peoples far distant on the American artery now felt some common pulse. In fact, the Manitoba central standard time on my watch read the same as in Antigua, though separated by 3,000 miles. And yet, I wondered if this synchronization of time could begin to offset some impalpable, but inevitable loss.

One morning I rode a local bus as far as it went, then walked until a manure-splattered pickup truck offered me a ride to the village of Santa María de Jesús, perched precariously on the slope of Volcán de Agua as only a town with such a name would dare to be. I strolled around the dusty plaza, polling local residents about the departure time of the afternoon bus, which I hoped would return me to Antigua after my climb. Some said noon, others 1:00 or 1:30. I settled on noon, checking my own analogical Timex and calculating the half-way point in time at which I'd need to turn around and start back down the mountain.

I was nearing the crater of the volcano, and running out of time, when I met a grizzled, wiry man, bent low by an immense bundle of firewood. As we met he squatted on a rock and unshouldered his burden. I figured one more opinion about the bus wouldn't hurt, so I asked him when it went. "Hoy," he said. Today. A flash of light burned away centuries-old illusions of time. The ancient city, the ruins, the timeless lifestyle, the ability to wait without fretting, the recognition of mañana. The bus goes today. And if you miss it, again tomorrow.

A few days later I was alone in the sanctuary atop Temple IV at Tikal, the tallest aboriginal structure in the Americas. A thunderstorm was pounding the jungle below, howler monkeys wailing their replies to the thunder claps. Peering through the deluge at 20-century-old temples protruding from the forest, I began to see why those aging columns lay unmolested in Antigua. There hadn't yet been time to move them. After all, Tikal was two millennia old; it had been deserted for most of a thousand years. The stones of Antigua had fallen only yesterday, and the business of today was survival. Guatemalans had endured three decades of struggle against military dictatorship and official murder; yet the longest-running war in the Americas showed no sign of abatement. A whole generation and more had lived, thousands had died, and the conflict continued. But who could tell what mañana might bring?

I had come a long way south. A mere 3,000 miles as the jet flies, time enough to hike to the crater of the volcano and down again. But in ways not measurable by instruments of modern man, I had arrived in a different world, a world with much to understand. If we Americans had such gaping divergence in our perceptions of time, then what else? In what other ways are we so very different, I wondered, and how, at the core, are we the same? I stood atop the ancient temple, and questions poured down with the rain.

Now a decade later, traveling south once more through rain, I pondered those questions and more. What of the North American continent itself? What about this Turtle Island is unique, and what is the state of its health? Where lie the tentacles that connect the histories of the American peoples? What can we learn from each other, and from our past, that might sustain our collective future? What American values and practices have preserved life, have made us brothers and sisters, and still give us hope?

I had known life nourished by ancient traditions, by social intercourse, by protection of our shared environment. I had seen peace thrive in a climate of justice. Yet, along-side human cooperation leers the face of exploitation, sneering at community, denying respect for the "other," and for the planet.

I knew that half the topsoil of the Great Plains had washed or blown away. I had witnessed the shriveling of heartland towns. And though not destitute like the peasant farmers of Guatemala, diversified farmers across the plains were going broke. I'd read about disappearing forests in Mexico and Central America. I'd met people whose choices were starve or fight. In fact, the future and vitality of the continent itself seemed at risk.

But these are generalizations. I knew that my perceptions of my own region, let alone of the continent, were sketchy at best – the perspective of the insulated traveler, life glimpsed through the rain-streaked windows of a speeding car. Even across the plains from South Dakota to Texas, down the highway I thought I knew, what I really knew was the order and the names of towns, where the road jogs, the crops the farmers grow. What's more, the few places I'd really known, I didn't necessarily know anymore, for they had changed and so had I.

In Winnipeg I had seen immigrants from 40 cultures live in apparent harmony. Was that achievable elsewhere? I was eager to talk with farmers from Manitoba to Texas about the future of family farms. I wanted to hear from the Zapatistas in Chiapas about their fight for justice. I yearned to visit war-time friends in the Nicaraguan mountains, to see how they are forging peace. I longed to learn from fellow Americans what they hold dear, the truths that keep them afloat in a tumultuous sea.

It was my 50th year on Earth, a good year to listen, to think, to write, a good year for a journey across the strata of North America. I would walk in ancient footsteps, seek my brothers and sisters, observe the state of the Earth. I would listen to the pulse of the continent along the great American artery. Where there was progress toward justice and sustainability, I wanted to celebrate it. And where the scales had tipped, I had to know that too.

As I approached St. Norbert 10 miles south of Winnipeg, the downpour slacked and I pulled off. A Métis community of fur traders on La Salle River near its confluence with the Red, St. Norbert was named in the 1820s for Bishop Norbert Provencher. Gradually it evolved into a French-Canadian agricultural community. I took a quick, dripping walk among the 1870s buildings in what is now a provincial heritage park, and got back on the road.

I cruised past Ste. Agathe, a tiny town whose only discernible feature from the highway was the grain elevator against a roiling sky. Ste. Agathe, a mere 15 miles from Winnipeg, could be in the middle of Kansas, except the elevator was steel instead of concrete, and not as tall.

Most towns in Manitoba have English or French names. South of Winnipeg, four of the five are French. Only the largest, Morris, is English, named for an early lieutenant governor. On the outskirts of town, the clouds burst once more. I turned the radio on again and heard that 150 millimeters, or six inches of rain had fallen, and they were getting more. But a cheery red sign beamed through the deluge, the Wilson Grill. I couldn't have passed a cafe with my name on it, even if I hadn't been hungry and seeking shelter from a storm.

On the north side of the aging white frame building a big red-lettered sign reads "We love Canadians. Breakfast, Mennonite dishes, homemade pies, Wimpy burgers." But the Wilsons don't discriminate. On the south side, it is Americans the Wilsons love. I pulled up as close as I could on the south and splashed my way to the door.

The little dining room was steamy with people and talk. Whether it is always this popular, when not a refuge from rain, I don't know. The Mennonite food was perogies, dough filled with cottage cheese or potato salad, then fried or boiled. I decided to forego the ethnic experience just this once and have some homemade cherry pie.

Looking up from a second bite I realized that every guy in the place, man and boy, had a cap, and that only I had removed mine at the door. But then mine

*Ukrainian dancers at Folklorama in Winnipeg (top), and Wilson's Grill in Morris, Manitoba.*

was plain white and rather dull. One fellow had an Esso Oil cap advertising the Morris Stampede, which I took to be a rodeo. Another advertised NIX Equipment of Lamesa, Texas. A third sported a fish from somewhere in North Carolina. All had seen better days. Actually it was hard reading the caps; all were pointed toward the windows, watching the rain, waiting for it to stop.

In came a young guy with a long pony tail and a dripping black western hat. "How's the cowboy this afternoon?" the waitress asked.

"It's a beautiful day," he replied. He grabbed her arm, steered her to a booth, and plopped down beside her.

The place was run by Pat Braun. "I started working here when I was 12," Pat told me, "30 years ago."

"You must enjoy it," I said.

"It's in the genes," Pat replied. "The waitress with the cowboy is my daughter, and in about 11 years, her baby will work here too."

"So you're Pat Wilson," I asked, introducing myself as if to a new-found cousin.

"Nope. Mrs. Wilson ran the place from 1948 'til she the day she died in 1984," Pat said. "I kept the name for sentimental reasons, out of respect." Pat made great cherry pie.

The rain let up, and the farmers ventured out to check the sky. I followed, and headed for St. Jean Baptiste.

As in the French quarter of Winnipeg, St. Jean has rues instead of streets. The old folks' home is the Paradis des Pionniers. But I didn't realize just how French the town is until I entered the St. Jean Hotel and Bar.

Around a long table in the center of the room, 15 people were gathered, including a scattering of women. Half a dozen animated conversations were in progress, mostly related to farming and rain. There were passing phrases of English, but the premier tongue was French. A somewhat drunken farmer in soiled overalls dominated the conversation at the head of the table. His companions addressed him in both English and French, but his replies were booming and forceful, strictly French.

A guy playing video slots returned to the bar for another $10 in quarters. His jacket said "Romeo's Bar, Cordell, Oklahoma," not far from my birthplace. Small world. After watching him lose that 10, I sidled over and asked if he was from Oklahoma. No, Gregory said. He was from St. Jean, but he has a friend in Cordell, Romeo himself. Gregory raises wheat, flax, oats and rape seed on his farm, but he heads down U.S. 81 for several months every winter, to Oklahoma, Texas, even Mexico.

Gregory said there are 250 families in St. Jean, "98 percent French. It used to be 99.9," he said, "but recently some folks moved out from the city." School is taught in both languages, and everybody is bilingual. "We're not separatists like the people in Quebec," he wanted me to understand. "We just like things the way they are, including being French."

Gregory said times were hard on the local farms. Even though wheat prices were good that year, thanks in part to the misfortunes of farmers whose crops were damaged by spring rains in Oklahoma and Kansas, he said it was hard to make ends meet. The cost of fertilizer and chemicals was skyrocketing. "So is rent," Gregory's neighbor at the slots put in, "especially with the English and Japanese buying up the land." And now, both men were worried there might not be a harvest. After yesterday's heat, today there was too much rain. And fall always comes early in Manitoba. Could this be it? The men joked about snow that late August night, but behind the joke was the knowledge that winter was coming soon, too soon. Gregory was worried about the weather, his crops, and finances. But as we talked, this man whose occupation is at least as risky as that of a professional gambler dropped another $20 in the one-armed bandit, with no return.

When the rain lightened again I said good-bye and headed on down 75 to Letellier. I got a room at the Letellier Hotel, a peeling frame building on the one-block main street. There was a small cafe and Oscar's bar downstairs, and four rooms to rent on the upper floor. Oscar showed me to my room, apologizing about raising his rent from $15 to $25 because he'd put in air-conditioners and color TV. He invited me down to the bar to watch the Winnipeg Bombers take on Vancouver at 8:00. I unpacked, went down for a quick burger just as the cafe was closing, and then the cook and I stepped next door to Oscar's for a beer.

Oscar said that though Letellier is French, the people there aren't "fanatics like up in St. Jean. We speak English here," he said just as proudly as Gregory had announced his preference for French. "Just like up in Morris, even though we all understand French and can talk it if we want to." Oscar said that in the next town west, Altona, the Mennonites still speak German, and in the reserve just north-east of town the Indians speak Cree. Four languages spoken within 20 miles.

Before my second sip of beer an argument broke out between two men at a table near the bar. One guy was sticking his finger in the other's face, offering to punch out his lights for bringing up something that happened 10 years back. The second man stayed cool, and soon the drunk stomped out, leaving in his wake a funereal calm. Nobody but the cook was watching the Bombers, and he, half-heartedly, like he seemed to do everything, including frying burgers. Mercifully the sound was off, replaced by country music on the juke box. "Mama gets crazy when I do this." Then the song ended and it was deathly still. One of the half dozen people left around the table reminded his companions it was supposed to be happy hour, but it was obvious they didn't believe it.

The burger flipper, a long-haired skinny fellow in his early 20s, slipped an occasional quarter into the slot machine. I couldn't decide if he was rationing his meager wages, or if lack of enthusiasm was his way of life. But he paced himself. He didn't expect to win, and he didn't. He talked to nobody and nobody talked to him. He finished his beer and went out into the rain.

Three deer heads stared down from Oscar's walls. But no moose, as in the St.

Jean Hotel. I was close to the United States, and Coors was on tap. A couple of kids showed up, 16 or 17 years old. They threw a few darts, then climbed up on stools by the slots. They couldn't wait to be old enough to pour their money in. I'd had enough of Oscar's. I climbed the creeky stairs and went to bed.

I woke up early and was on the road before Oscar opened his eyes. Letellier looked beautiful in the early morning sun. Everything was fresh and clean. People were moving about, picking up limbs that had fallen, bringing in the paper, gossiping across lawns. Yes, small towns, whether in Canada, South Dakota, or Mexico, can be depressing – and to some denizens of great cities, perhaps laughable. But in spite of the limitations, small-town people with their cafes and bars, schools, churches, and ball games, know a kinship that could only be imagined in the cities. Everybody may know what you did that night 10 years ago, but at least they know you, and you know them. And in the end, whether your language is English or French or Spanish or German or Cree, you speak the language of community.

A historical marker said Letellier was the crossroads of an east-west French route and the "War Road" of the Sioux to the Lake of the Woods. I headed for Sioux country, south through another 15 miles of flatness to the border. It was my third day on the road, and the third climate. The first was a sauna, the second monsoon, and today was crisp and cool, a Great Plains sky so blue and distant the horizon tugged at the eyeballs. The cool north breeze was an inescapable reminder to Canadians that winter was coming, very soon. The geese and I knew that it was time to go. I passed a first field of corn, and in a few minutes arrived at the United States border, the second of nine countries on my journey.

# North Dakota

*"I am happy enough to be here, where Dakota
drifts wild in the universe, Where the prairie is starting
to shake in the surf of the winter dark."*

~ Thomas McGrath, "Beyond the Red River"

At the border I joined Highway 81. New Jersey sociologists Frank and Deborah Popper suggested a few years ago that North Dakota, and the upper Great Plains in general, might revert to a "Buffalo Commons." Most of the people would emigrate, allowing restoration of the native flora and fauna – the native prairies, the bison, the wolf and the grizzly bear. Ernest Callenbach's more recent book is entitled, *Bring Back the Buffalo: A Sustainable Future for America's Great Plains.*

Though the buffalo are returning, both to Indian reservations and to cattle ranches, North Dakotans and other plains people tend to scoff at the notion of being replaced by buffalo. But they are looking for sustainability. What 19th century traditions should we value, they ask. What 20th century practices, and what 21st century innovations can help sustain life in middle America – for buffalo, for people, and for the planet? North Dakota poet Thomas McGrath wanted to know that, and so did I.

On both sides of the U.S.-Canada border, tourists, locals, and small-time entrepreneurs can pick up liquor and cigarettes and other commodities of vice at duty-free shops. Cigarettes are heavily taxed in Canada, so they're a favorite item to take north. When I mentioned to a Canadian that I might have financed my stay in Winnipeg by importing my limit of tobacco, he agreed, but said I'd be competing with people with guns, that smuggling cigarettes was big business in Canada. The border towns did seem slightly tacky compared to their inland neighbors, but the U.S.-Canada boundary is celebrated at the International Peace Garden a few miles west as the longest peaceful and unguarded frontier in the world.

In the northeast corner of North Dakota lies historic Pembina, oldest town in the Dakotas. In fact, for several decades in the 19th century, much of the former Rupert's Land was known as "Pembina Country." The name is from the Chippewa *anepemian*, the local high-bush cranberries which were mixed with dried buffalo meat and fat to make pemmican, a staple food of Indians and European trappers and traders. Located at the confluence of the Pembina and

Red Rivers, Pembina was important as a fur-trading town. In its second century, Pembina became a major port of entry.

In 1797 Charles Baptiste Chaboillez built Fort Panbian on the south bank of the Pembina to protect the North West Company's fur-trading post. In 1801 the rival Hudson's Bay Company built just across the river. In 1812 the Selkirk settlers erected Fort Daer just above the mouth of the Pembina. Fort Pembina was built here in 1870, and occupied until 1895. An 1860s cottonwood log house, home of military officers and a school for their children, still stands.

That Pembina had recognized its tourist potential was clear; the town was pouring all its downtown streets in concrete. That Pembina remains a very small town is also clear; they were doing the entire downtown at once. Flooding is a frequent problem in this flat valley, especially now that the river beds are silted and shallow. As in the river towns of southern Manitoba, an eight-foot dike protected Pembina from its two rivers – until the great flood of 1997.

Just outside Pembina, a historical marker is all that remains of Dakota Territory's first pioneers, buried at Dumoulin Church, founded somewhere in the vicinity in 1818 by Father Sévere Dumoulin. The cemetery has been "lost to progress," the sign says.

South of Pembina, U.S. 81 jogs west 10 miles to the little town of Hamilton. The present route of Interstate 29 is more logical; straighter and shorter, it hugs the Red all the way to Grand Forks, continuing straight south where the river chose to meander. When the Meridian Highway route was sketched in the 1920s, the railroad towns west of the river had the political magnetism to attract the new highway, but in the modern age they lacked the power to keep it. Thus, for the next 65 miles, old 81 is a local road. Passing up the interstate, I headed for Hamilton.

Among the migrants on 81 every summer and fall are the wheat harvesters. They begin in Texas in late May, hop-scotching their flatbed trucks and combines field by field to the north, following the ripening wheat. In June they rumble through Oklahoma and Kansas, in July through Nebraska and South Dakota, and in August and September through North Dakota and Manitoba. Every year they follow the same routes, often cutting the same fields many years running. They hope that before the snow flies they'll load the combines on the wheat trucks and roll back south to await another spring. I was meeting the first wave, though this day they would cut no wheat. Rain means a holiday for harvest gypsies.

The principal attraction in Hamilton is the Pembina County Fair, which the sign boasts is the Harness Racing Capital of North Dakota. Though the graveled main street is somewhat humorously named "Wall Street," and an abandoned building on Wall Street sports an impressive mural of what appears to be the Manhattan skyline, real estate must be considerably more affordable here than in the Big Apple; the town is clearly dying. Yet, this looks like healthful country. North Dakotans didn't have video gambling, at least not yet. There were as many churches as bars. And the farm land is good rich earth so flat there is no relief in sight.

What is flat? The Red River "valley," as they call it, sets the standard for flatness. It is of course a valley in the sense of an extensive land area drained by a river system, but to the eye, this valley lacks contour. A cup of water poured on the ground would flow equally in all directions. An egg would hardly know which way to roll. Emergency brakes on cars are a superfluous invention, which should be a buyer option, like cigarette lighters for non-smokers or heaters in Panamá. With a favorable wind and good bearings, all one would need to roll for miles down this valley would be momentum, the only antagonist friction.

Having lived in southwestern Oklahoma, I know flat. In the front yard of a house Norma and I once bought on the edge of the little town of Martha were the stumps of two large cedar trees. Delaware, who sold us the house, explained that his daughter cut the trees down because she wanted a 360 degree panorama of the cotton fields and plains; the two trees restricted her view.

Look in any direction in eastern North Dakota. Wheat or other food crops stretch to infinity – or to the next grove of trees which farmers have wisely planted here for over a century. The windbreaks have limited wind erosion, and the land is too flat for major water erosion, so unlike some hillier parts of the Midwest and the Great Plains, the soil remains rich and potent.

Unfortunately, the luxuriant crops produced here come at a price. A crop duster in a yellow bi-plane swooped down over the highway, dumping a load of pesticide on a field of potatoes. I'd heard on the radio that morning that much of North Dakota's ground water is already too contaminated with nitrates for humans to drink. What was this fellow adding to it?

I passed Glasston, and rolled down another seven miles of flat to St. Thomas, a pleasant town of 400 people, one bar, a shady town park, and three churches: Catholic, Lutheran, and Methodist, pretty much standard for the territory. Most of what they grow here is for human consumption: wheat, pinto beans, potatoes and sugar beets. The crops were well-watered yesterday, too well in some places.

For farmers, as for harvesters, rain means the chance for a holiday, and St. Thomas was full of farmers. I stopped at the Family Restaurant Cafe for breakfast. In the rack outside I read the headline of the *Grand Forks Herald*, which proclaimed in two inch letters, "Drenched: Foot of rain hits northern ND." Less had fallen here.

I went inside and asked an elderly farmer in an American Legion cap with an American flag pin who was pouring himself a cup of coffee how much he got. "Just right," he said, "an inch and a half." There's nothing like a farmer the morning after a just right rain in August. The little room was full of happy farmers, a few having breakfast, most only coffee, and a pair throwing dice. I helped myself to a cup of self-service, 50 cents for all you can drink brew, ordered two eggs, fried potatoes and toast for a buck and a half, and sat down to talk with Scott Stahl and his friend Bob.

What do folks do around here besides farm? I asked, meaning what other work. "Drink coffee," Scott said, as though there was nothing else worth doing. Then he added, of course on weekends the young guys go down to Grafton for curling. I imagined young farmers lined up in the beauty parlor waiting for a perm, but kept the thought to myself. "What exactly is curling?" I asked. I couldn't have revealed ignorance more painfully. Scott winced, but told me patiently about the sport, what size and kind of granite rock you use, how the handle is shaped, the techniques of hurling it down the ice lane toward its "house" – sort of like shuffle board, he said. Curling was brought to North Dakota from Canada, and to Canada by Scotch immigrants, of whom there are still many descendants in the region, including Scott.

I finished my breakfast, thanked Scott for the conversation, and headed on down the road toward the Mecca of curling, Grafton. On the way is the tiny town of Auburn, the cross on its one church tilting north at a precarious 45 degrees – just right for pigeons. I intended to stop at Jugville, a museum of antique machinery and junk that Scott told me about, put together by a farmer his neighbors call Uncle Sig Jagielski. But I missed the turn-off, and rolled into Grafton. On the north edge of Grafton, near the Park River, the Alchem Ltd. Company spewed nasty-looking smoke into the air, something I hadn't seen at the food-processing plants I'd passed. Alchem turns corn into ethanol to fuel cars.

Grafton is the county seat of Walsh County, and the biggest town so far in North Dakota, the place where snowy scenes of "Fargo" were filmed in 1995. In the front lawn of the WPA-built art deco courthouse rises a monument to eight local boys who lost their lives, mostly in the Philippines, during the Spanish-American War. What stake eight boys from Grafton, North Dakota had in aiding the transfer of Filipino power from Spanish rulers to tyrants of another sort I don't know, and I suspect they didn't know either, but the plaque says they died as "heroes in the struggle." They were a corporal, a wagoneer, and six privates of the North Dakota 1st Infantry. The inscription proclaims, "You can't stampede the 1st North Dakota." Apparently killing them was another matter. What sort of monuments might they have built with their own hands in Walsh County, I wondered, had they stayed at home and lived their lives.

Across the lawn, three dark-skinned children swung and called to each other in Spanish. North Dakota agriculture and food processing is labor-intensive, and I was encountering the advance guard of a wave of immigrant workers and their families who come from the south each summer to help with this work. In fact, according to James Paul Allen and Eugene James Turner's atlas of ethnic diversity, *We The People*, about 200 people of Mexican origin had taken up permanent residence in Walsh County.

On the west edge of Grafton is Heritage Village, an antique town consisting of several pioneer buildings and store fronts moved here as a centennial project in 1982 – the first of several restored pioneer towns I would encounter on my way south.

A few miles south of Grafton, at Minto, I took a five-mile detour off 81 to the Polish community of Warsaw, population 125. Besides its interest as a still strongly ethnic community, Warsaw is the home of the St. Stanislaus Church, whose elaborate stained-glass windows are dedicated to Polish saints. Across the street is the four-story St. Anthony's Academy; both buildings are listed on the National Historic Register. The church is a beautifully-maintained Gothic revival structure, built in 1900. St. Anthony's Academy had housed a convent and a Catholic school, and was now being restored to serve as headquarters of the Bethlehem Community, a group of 25 people who moved here from the west coast, bringing their communal lifestyle and their book-publishing business with them. The group, consisting of both nuclear families and single men and women, has been together since 1971. Just now they were scraping and painting windows. Two local women who were helping switched from Polish to English to tell me the St. Anthony story.

In Oregon the Bethlehem Community operated a Scandinavian bakery, according to Gabriel, a clean-cut young man from Portland who was hard at work torching old paint from windows. But soon they would be republishing "uplifting children's books," Gabriel said. Community members are committed to a life of "simplicity and sanity." They dress alike, the men and boys in dark pants, blue shirts and suspenders, the women and girls in long gray dresses with white trim and a Mennonite-style cap. They don't watch television, probably a good place to start in creating a sane community. The four-story building had been unused for two decades, but held great potential. They hoped to move in by winter, but the north wind was breathing down their necks.

Bethlehem is not the only religious community in Walsh County. West of the highway is a Hutterite colony, part of a string of communities of German Russians who migrated northward over the past 130 years, up U.S. 81 and the James and Red River valleys from the original Bon Homme Colony near Yankton, South Dakota. The Hutterites are German-speaking communal farmers with a deserved reputation for efficiency and order.

The next village, Ardoch, is a town of potatoes, Poles, and migrant Mexicans. On the north edge of town is the potato plant of J. R. Grzadzielewski and Sons. They do most everything that can be done with potatoes: potato chips, mashed potatoes, seed potatoes and more. The potatoes are Irish, but they originated in South America, among dark-skinned people such as the kids playing in the streets. Ardoch was a very poor town, consisting of fading framed houses, trailer houses, weedy lots, and decommissioned automobiles, the kind of place where immigrant farm workers might get a toehold and begin to dig in. All the businesses of Ardoch were closed, though a post office remained in somebody's living room.

Sunflowers had become more frequent, hundred-acre fields of yellow 10-inch blossoms, drooping in the sun. These are a hybrid variety, not the native that is the state flower of Kansas and common in roadside ditches across the plains. In *Huckleberry Finn*, when Huck was posing as a girl called Sarah Mary

Williams, the woman he was visiting concluded that he was really a boy, then tested his knowledge of farm life to see if his next lie could be true. If 15 cows are grazing in a pasture, she asked, how many will be facing the same way? Huck answered correctly, all of them. Sunflowers are like that, except that even the direction they face is predictable. Like devout Muslims, they ever incline to the east, bowing their heads to the rising sun.

The last surviving town before Grand Forks is Manvel. Just south of Manvel, the first white settler in North Dakota, Pierre Bottineau, homesteaded. As it had since Glasston, old 81 still follows what is now the Burlington Northern railroad on a route laid out by the St. Paul, Minneapolis and Manitoba Railroad in 1878, the year of the "Great Boom." The railroad soon became the Great Northern Railroad under "empire builder" James J. Hill. It was to connect the railroad towns, of course, that 81 originally veered northwest from Grand Forks. It was railroad builders, after all, who carved up this country, naming the towns it established at 10 to 12 mile intervals to fill its box cars with wheat and to supply its voracious appetite for water and wood. It was the railroad that determined which towns would prosper and which would die.

I pulled into Grand Forks, where U.S. 81 becomes Washington Street, got a room at the Lucky Inn, and stepped out for lunch. Within a two block walk up or down 81 were six fast food joints: Pizza Hut, McDonald's, Dairy Queen, Taco Bell, Burger King and Wendy's. Who says folks don't have choice on the Great Plains?

I drove to the university to meet Bob Lewis, a UND English professor who edits the *North Dakota Quarterly*. Bob came west from Pittsburgh after Army service during the Korean war, first to Nebraska, then to Illinois, then to Austin, Texas, and finally north up 81 to Grand Forks, arriving in the dead middle of winter.

"I was impressed with the bleakness and the cold," he said, "with block heaters and snow drifts. But I saw what I was getting into, stuck it out, and learned to love the place."

Bob was a bushy-mustached, sinewy and youthful man in his late sixties, who in every respect resembled a man in middle age, except for the slow deliberative wisdom of his words. The University of North Dakota where he teaches is the largest in the Dakotas and Montana, with 12,000 students, including 300 Native Americans, many involved in the Indians into Medicine program which prepares them to take health care back to reservation communities.

Bob said that the Garrison Keillor Norwegian stereotype is common here, but the area is actually more German, especially Russian-German, than anything else. In fact, census figures show that except for a couple of counties where Norwegian Americans are more numerous, I would find people of German ancestry predominant in most of the counties from North Dakota through Kansas, with Norwegians often second. Bob speculated that Germans may have assimilated into Anglo culture faster than Scandinavians. But he said Grand Forks had grown more diverse and sophisticated in the quarter century he'd been here, with greater variety of music and theater, and several good ethnic restaurants, not only Chinese, but even Pakistani and Mediterranean.

Bob said the Grand Forks Air Force Base has had a great impact on both the university and the community, not only financial, but also diversifying local culture. Without the air base the local population would probably be similar to that in Fargo, he said, 97 percent white. Though Grand Forks is regarded as among the Air Force's least desirable assignments, and though Bob had coordinated the inter-disciplinary Peace Studies program at the University, he said that on balance the facility's contribution to the city had been positive. He said many residents were concerned about the impact of decommissioning the nuclear missile wing.

I asked whether people were at least sleeping easier, with Grand Forks no longer a number-one target in the event of nuclear war. "Most people didn't think about the missiles much," he said. "Some adopted a fatalistic attitude. The majority never really countenanced the atomic threat." Later that evening I would drive west of town to the Air Force base. At the entrance is an outdoor museum of Air Force hardware, including a colossal camouflaged B-52. The military policeman at the entrance is called the "peace-keeper on duty."

Bob took me around town in his four-wheel-drive, four-on-the floor farm pickup, designed for getting into town (or out of it) in any kind of weather. We drove downtown to historic 3rd Street, where the old opera house had become a bar and bowling alley, the old train station the Chamber of Commerce. We went to the Urban Stampede for coffee, then next door to Sander's 1907 restaurant for a beer, served by a guy named Phil whose brother Richard is a friend of mine in Yankton. Both businesses were in tastefully restored downtown buildings. Both would soon be destroyed by the great flood of 1997.

Bob and I talked about Judge Ronald Davies, the 91-year-old Grand Forks justice who implemented Little Rock school desegregation in 1957, and about the UND "Fighting Sioux" mascot, which Bob said the Sioux in general, both elders and students, didn't mind, but which some of the region's Chippewa, Assiniboin, Cree, Mandan, Hidatsa and Arikara people didn't like very much. I asked about the winking happy faces on the Grand Forks water towers. Bob said the winks gave Grand Forks the edge over Fargo in the *Money* magazine ranking of best places to live.

Bob said the bio-region around Grand Forks is unique, a combination of unusually fertile soil and harsh climate, positioned on a major north-south flyway. Because the tall grass prairie had kept trees out, many pioneers thought nothing else would grow here. The sod was too tough to plow, so many kept going, and the area was settled late. Besides natural factors which have limited soil erosion, he said that once the tough sod was plowed, farmers discovered how rich the soil was and began planting trees to protect themselves and the soil from the wind.

I had begun to think that North Dakota is populated by billions of food plants, but only a few people, insects, animals and birds. I'd seen numerous western meadowlarks, the state bird not only of North Dakota, but also of Nebraska and Kansas, but since Winnipeg, not a single animal had dodged across my path, nor had I seen road kill. Sometimes in South Dakota I pass two or three decomposing creatures on my 12-mile drive to town. But Bob said those who look closely find a diversity of wild animals and birds here too, in farm groves and shelter belts, along rivers and coulees, even in fields and road-side ditches. "It takes a while to train your eye," he said, "but plant and animal life is very rich here." He delighted me with the list of species he'd seen while canoeing local rivers and hiking near his home on the Turtle River northwest of Grand Forks: cranes, geese and hawks, muskrats and mink, and many others. That I had seen no animals in daylight drives was probably not surprising. And North Dakota motorists are sparse, and perhaps more careful, possibly accounting for the absence of dead animals on the road.

Even more conspicuously infrequent in this farm country are farm animals. Great "bonanza farms" were established in the Red River valley beginning in 1878, mostly by railroad money. In the wake of the Panic of 1873, the railroad was facing bankruptcy. To raise cash and to insure future profitability, railroad executives and other investors established huge farms, managed like factories, an early version of modern corporate agriculture. The bonanza farms featured a vertically-integrated structure of production, transportation, and marketing of products. Single men came west looking for work, and some bonanza farms employed scores of workers. On the largest farms, Bob said, a man and a team could plow all day and make a single round!

By about 1920, low prices made the big farms less profitable, and a new wave of land seekers bought land and broke up the empires. The great draft horses which fueled the huge farms were replaced by tractors and steam engines. And of course winter is simply too cold here for animals to survive without shelter and feed, and too long for farmers to feed animals inside and still make money. By northern South Dakota, some diversified farms remain, where farmers feed what they grow to their cattle and sheep and hogs. But most North Dakota farmers now stick to feeding people, especially vegetarians. A difference on the landscape is that the great farm barns still common farther south, decaying or otherwise, are now rare here.

There is much more value added to farm products in North Dakota than in South Dakota or most other farm states. Potatoes and sugar are commonly processed locally, and a new corn-processing plant was to be built in Wahpeton, North Dakota, rather than in South Dakota, perhaps partly because South Dakota has high property taxes instead of an income tax, and partly because of North Dakota's solid tradition of processing farm products at home.

The American Crystal Sugar Company in East Grand Forks, for example, goes back to 1916 when the Non-Partisan League was founded to protect farmers against exploitative capitalist interests. The NPL actually took power in North

Dakota in the 1918 election, but was labeled "Bolshevik" by Theodore Roosevelt and others, and was soon bullied into oblivion. Previously, the railroad would load wheat in North Dakota as top-quality #1 wheat, Bob said, but it would come off the box car in Minneapolis labeled #4 wheat. But thanks to the power of organized farmers, North Dakota still has a state-run flour mill in Grand Forks and a state-owned bank in Bismarck.

The NPL also fought to control railroad rates in the state. Bob told a variation of a joke attributed to NPL founder Arthur C. Townley: "If you put a grain miller, a banker, and a railroad executive in a barrel and rolled them down the hill, there'd always be a son-of-a-bitch on top." Most of the millers were in Minneapolis, and another joke of the teens was that the capital of Minnesota was St. Paul, and the capital of North Dakota was Minneapolis. Even though North Dakota now often votes Republican, in 1995 the state's lone congressman and both senators were Democrats, and Bob said the populist philosophy is still strong.

Bob said human values remain strong in North Dakota too, even though North Dakotans tend to be wary of strangers. "You can live here for 10 years and you're still regarded as an outsider," he said. "But there's a sense of caring for your fellow citizen here that there isn't, say, in Texas, where they say to total strangers 'Y'all come back now,' but I don't think it's as genuine as here, where they won't say 'y'all come back' after you've gassed up. They'll just sort of grunt at you, but if your car breaks down they'll stop and help you out, another element of the geography." It is also worth noting that North Dakota had the lowest violent crime rate in the nation, and only a third as much of its population in prison as neighboring South Dakota.

I headed south from Grand Forks toward Fargo on old 81, which parallels I-29 a half mile away. Just beyond Generous Jerry's Locally Owned Fireworks Stand, I heard an apparent new complaint from my aging car. I was accustomed to slack in the front axle, and meticulously avoided unnecessary strain. But this alarming screech sounded like another wheel bearing screaming for grease.

I had needed a special car for this trip, old enough not to be valuable, but good enough to get me to Panamá, and maybe even back. It should be inconspicuous at border crossings, the kind of car nobody would remember seeing. It should be ugly enough to escape the notice of thieves, but not so unsightly as to provoke laughter or contempt. I'd settled on a 1980 Dodge Omni for $675. Not too much to lose.

I hadn't planned to buy an Omni. I didn't even know it had a Volkswagen engine, for which there might be parts in Central America. Maybe it was the name I couldn't resist. Omni: All. Far from omnipotent, it started, it stopped, and it ran. It was not omnivorous; in fact it consumed only gasolina sin pluma, unleaded, which I was assured I could buy in every country of the continent. It needn't be omnidirectional; we would visit omnifarious peoples, but only on the north-south axis. Perhaps its name somehow encompassed the wide-open scope of my quest. As my Japanese-American poet friend, Lawson Inada put it, mine would be an "Omni-scent journey."

When I bought the Omni, there was an ominous roar in the front end, which I gambled was a wheel bearing instead of the transmission or differential. My mechanic friend Charley Logue took a ride, and laughed out loud. "You're going to start for Panamá in that?" he asked incredulously. "I'd be afraid to drive it to Nebraska!" By the time I fixed everything wrong with the car, I was well over budget. I adjusted the carburetor and the brakes, replaced the starter and the rumbling wheel bearing, changed the plugs and the oil, fixed a door handle and some lights, checked everything, filled everything, lubed everything that moved, even built an armrest to lean on when the road got long. By the time I finished, the car was literally Jerry-rigged. I loaded my tools, both metric and ASE, threw in extra cans of oil and a water pump belt for the road. I ignored the little rattles and squeaks, hoping they weren't serious. I figured eight borders and 5,000 miles – one way – was too long to worry, so I told myself I'd make it, and hit the road.

Now I pulled off the road and killed the engine, expecting the worst. The shriek continued, and I exhaled my relief. It was only a ditch full of cicadas, lamenting the end of summer, drowning the other groans of my tired car. A red-tailed hawk swooped across a just-harvested wheat field, searching for a dispossessed mouse.

I passed the Saint Olaf Lutheran Church, a sure sign of Scandinavian country. Mine was the only car on the road; the others whined along the parallel interstate. I pulled off at Reynolds, which according to Mary Ann Barnes Williams' *Origins of North Dakota Place Names*, was founded by Dr. Henry A. Reynolds, a temperance apostle who homesteaded the land on which the town was built in 1880. Main Street now boasts the Beehive Lounge; apparently it is possible to buy a drink here, but the Beehive is balanced by several churches, so perhaps temperance prevails.

My odometer clicked off the miles, a gravel cross road coinciding with every revolution. Surveyors worked their way west from the 5th principal meridian through Dakota Territory after the Civil War, extending the pattern of the 1787 Northwest Ordinance by which newly-acquired land was carved into six mile square townships of 36 square miles each, beginning from the 1st meridian at the juncture of the Ohio River and the Mason-Dixon line. From here to Texas, the Great Plains are thus a patchwork quilt of almost-square 640-acre blocks, a crossroads every mile, row crops like potatoes and corn and beans in rows farmers scrupulously maintain on the east-west or north-south lines of the compass. The pattern is disturbed occasionally by irregularities of terrain, surveying errors, or the periodic correction lines necessitated by the curvature of the Earth.

At 50,000, Grand Forks is the state's second largest city. Fargo's 74,000 makes it number one. Midway between the two cities, considered a large town here, is Hillsboro, population 1,488. But the boro has no hill; it is named for James J. Hill, the Great Northern Railroad "empire builder." Hillsboro is home to another large sugar refinery, numerous agribusinesses, and four churches: Catholic, Methodist, and now two Lutheran. Hillsboro is a pleasant, shady town, an oasis amidst the farms. The Traill County Courthouse is an attractive older brick building, but unfortunately some misguided souls tacked on a new front of blue and gray steel.

State highway numbers in North Dakota are superimposed on an Indian chief in war bonnet. South of Hillsboro old U.S. 81 is labeled county 81. In the 35 miles to Fargo it passes through Kelso, Grandin, Gardner, Argusville and Harwood, small, gravel-streeted towns with a church and a business or two, a grain elevator and a bar. The gravel streets are logical. It is too costly to maintain concrete or asphalt streets in the north, where the formidable forces of frost each winter heave and crack pavement, requiring major annual repairs.

A steel grain elevator stands beside the train tracks in the center of most every small town here, the lifeline splitting them in half, main street parallel within a block. But rarely did either side of the tracks seem wrong or right.

Unlike scores of towns abandoned by railroad branch lines throughout the region, these towns remained alive in part because shipping grain still gave farmers a reason to come to town. As Frank Gohlke points out in his study of grain elevators in the American landscape, thousands of prairie towns created by railroads a century ago cling to life this way, while many of those abandoned by trains are in the throes of death.

Of the four towns, Grandin is perhaps the liveliest. It was named for brothers J.L. and W.J. Grandin, Pennsylvania bankers who bought 75,000 acres, 114 square miles of Northern Pacific Railroad land for bonanza farms. They even built the "Grandin" steamboat to haul their wheat up the Red to the railroad at Fargo. The largest Grandin farm was 50,000 acres, the biggest in the territory. In 1885, an elderly patron at the post office told me, the farm used 800 men at harvest time. The Grandins owned hundreds of plows and teams of horses; it took a dozen teams of horses and men a week to turn a square mile of wheat stubble.

The grain elevator in Grandin was now owned by Busch Agricultural Resources, Inc., presumably buying wheat or barley for beer. Just down the tracks, Agway Sunflower Products bagged seed for birds. If it hadn't been Sunday morning I might have stopped for a supply. Grandin had a small Presbyterian church, the first I'd seen, and a larger Lutheran, but for the first time since Winnipeg, no Catholic.

I was getting low on gas. The Grandin station was closed, and Gardner didn't have one, just the Happy Hour bar and liquor store, and the Hogfarm, a Harley cycle shop. I didn't see any churches in Gardner either, but you can buy a Harley and a six-pack to go.

I pushed on to Argusville, named for North Dakota's first newspaper, the *Fargo Argus*, and before that for the Greek mythological figure Argus, the watchman with a hundred eyes. I was keeping my eyes peeled for gas. A very long Burlington Northern train was headed my way from the south, but I beat it to the crossing. Unlike many of the smaller towns, Argusville had a school, and a nice baseball diamond called Bill's Field, dedicated to someone named Bill Erickson. I didn't find any gas, and if Argus was alive, all hundred eyes were closed. While a mile of coal cars passed I toured the entire village. As I waited for the last cars, I had time left to wonder if this beet country town was the Argus of North Dakota writer Louise Erdrich's novel, *The Beet Queen*. A long train and a small town.

The last town before Fargo, Harwood, was actually growing rather than dying. It was two towns really, the old and the new. Just 10 miles north of Fargo, Harwood is a convenient bedroom community, with two working class developments outside the older town. I didn't see Argus here either, but Harwood does have Neighborhood Watch eyes and paved streets, even in the old part of town. This all seemed somehow appropriate, since the place was named for A.J. Harwood, a real estate salesman and developer.

As I rolled into Fargo I passed a lumber mill, the first I'd seen on the route. The mill turns scarce cottonwood trees into shipping pallets. I passed farm implement dealers, an oil well service and the airport. I passed the FargoDome, a sports and entertainment center but not really a dome, and headed through the city center on 81, University Drive. The needle on the bottom of empty, I stopped for gas at last, supporting the local corn farmers by paying two cents extra per gallon for higher octane ethanol. In South Dakota ethanol was subsidized, taxed two cents less to encourage growth of the local industry.

I began my tour of Fargo with what is most important: the Roger Maris museum, located in the West Acres Mall. A 75-foot glass case displays commemorative bats, balls, uniforms, clippings, and photographs of Fargo native Maris with President Kennedy and most of the presidents since, as well as with fellow Yankee great and fellow cancer victim, Mickey Mantle. Though Maris' career was perhaps overshadowed by Mantle's, and his title would fall to Mark McGuire and Sammy Sosa in 1998, Maris is still celebrated here as the home run king, the slugger who broke Babe Ruth's record by slamming 61 in '61. The cancer center at the local hospital is named for him, as is the drive past the baseball fields at Lindenwood Park.

On the west edge of Fargo is Bonanzaville, the second of four pioneer villages on 81, this weekend celebrating the 25th annual Pioneer Days. Bonanzaville is a complete town as it might have appeared a century ago: homes, blacksmith shop, general store, hotel, print shop and church, all historic area buildings moved to the site. Old-timers play music and dance. Kids drink lemonade and eat German-style bratwurst. Steam tractors seethe and pop, engineers sweating in the sun as they feed the fireboxes with coal or wood.

Engineer Don Schroeder from Rollag, Minnesota, was running a seven-ton, eight-horsepower 1869 Case, which he said was a little heavier than a modern eight-horsepower snow blower, but also would do more work. "To operate a steam engine at Bonanzaville one must be a licensed engineer," Don said. "That requires putting up with a lot of hot air at steam school in Rollag and passing a test administered by the state boiler inspector."

I asked Don what happened to the giant farms which dominated the region in the early days. He said bonanza farms declined after steam came in, the first example of technology displacing farm workers. He said "bonanza" just meant "big big big." He said one historic bonanza farm, the Bagg farm, was being restored just down 81 near Wahpeton.

The late August heat had returned, so I escaped to shady Lindenwood Park on the Red River, the lowest point in the vast glacial basin that was once Lake Agassiz. The ancient lake was named for Swiss geologist Louis Agassiz, who developed the concept of the ice age in his native Swiss Alps before coming to the United States to live and study glaciation in 1846. Under a shady elm I visited with Mark Kolstad, a teacher at Agassiz Middle School just across the river in Moorhead, Minnesota. Mark told me about teaching in the state-funded summer program for children of migrant farm workers at Thomas Edison School.

Most of the Mexican American farm workers in the Red River valley are from South Texas, many from Crystal City and Carrizo Springs, Mark said. They migrate up U.S. 81 every year to hoe and thin beets in the Fargo-Moorhead area. Some of the migrants still live in shanties and small travel trailers on the farms where they work, but many families now live in apartment houses near Moorhead State University while students are away for the summer, an area some locals call "Mexican village." Mark said a number of migrants had established themselves here, that the permanent Latino population in Moorhead was about 800 and the school system about 6 percent Hispanic. He said there was some prejudice and discrimination against the migrants, both in housing and in employment, but that in general the communities got along.

Mark had published an essay about his experience in the *South Dakota Review*, focusing on a bright and creative boy he called Hector, a natural leader of his peers. Hector described "Mexican night" at the YMCA pool, when admission was just 50 cents, told how he and his friends got their clothes, at "rummitch sales," and shared his dreams of living in one of the fine mansions of Fargo. "I haven't heard from Hector lately," Mark said. "But in spite of his brilliance, odds are better than even that in a few years Hector and his wife will show up at school one morning to drop off their kids. They'll be on their way to the fields to continue the cycle of migrant labor."

When Mark went home, I took a walk along the Red. The river isn't really red; it is chocolate mocha, and looks as thick as a malt. It crawls northward, its progress marked by the occasional willow leaf or twig. When the namers arrived, I wondered, was its water clear, or already some opaque shade, carrying the earth in suspension above its fertile bed? I live by the last 60 miles of relatively wild Missouri, below Gavins Point Dam at Yankton, South Dakota, and above Sioux City, Iowa, from where the river is channeled and tamed for barge traffic all the way to New Orleans.

Whoever called the Missouri "Big Muddy" hadn't seen the Red. I wasn't tempted to dive in as I would in the Missouri on a muggy August day. I didn't even take off my shoes for an oozy wade. And yet, it was good to be here, sheltered by oaks and broad linden leaves and stately ash and a few remaining American elms, the North Dakota State Tree. And the Red is as full of history as it is of mud. It was the highway north long before I-29 or U.S. 81 or the railroad or the first aboriginal trail, home to 10,000 generations of muskrats, a highway old as the flight of geese.

Gray squirrels darted among the oaks, harvesting acorns. They too knew that winter was coming, and that, as always, it would be long. Nuthatches hopped down the trunk of a green ash; honey bees buzzed the pale pink flowers of the prairie rose, the state flower. I was at home by the river, at peace with the animals and birds. I felt the freedom that comes with traveling, or living, alone. One can eat when he is hungry, rest when he is tired, go to the last ounce of endurance, or do nothing at all. All at a whim and with no apology or explanation. But there is also loneliness. I would experience that too on the long road ahead.

I rolled out my 50-cent garage sale sleeping bag and lay down beside the river. The bag has known many a journey since Oklahoma City a quarter century back, a hitch-hiking trip through Canada and New England with my brother Paul in 1971, with sister Ruth to Oaxaca, Mexico in the seventies, to Nicaragua in 1985, rolled out twice beside Thoreau's chimney foundation stones at Walden Pond. Now it was my son's favorite bag. Twenty-five years for 50 cents. I'd got my money's worth and it still served me well. I closed my eyes on a million stars.

I got up before the sun, rolled up my bag, washed my face and headed south, down 81 toward Wahpeton, the historic Indian town on the Red by-passed by interstate builders. South of Fargo is a trailer park called "Selkirk Settlement," then upscale suburbs, the first since Winnipeg. Half an hour south of Fargo I jogged east with 81 to Abercrombie and old Fort Abercrombie, the Dakota settlement second in age only to Pembina. The fort and museum apparently attract enough tourists to pave a few of the streets. I was looking for breakfast, but the Aber café was long dead. Old-timers straggled into the community hall, and I figured there'd at least be coffee, so I followed.

Ed Herrick, the retired postmaster who was born on his grandfather's homestead on the river three miles north, invited me to join him and his friend Don for coffee and a cookie. Don is a Swedish-American who married an Italian woman in Italy during WWII. They ran the Aber café across the street until they retired. Ed said his grandfather homesteaded on the Red because during the Civil War an army officer who had fought Indians in Dakota Territory told him the soil was rich. And he wouldn't have to cut trees and grub stumps in order to farm. His grandfather bought a covered wagon and a pregnant cow in St. Paul and headed west.

Ed said his was a minority English-speaking family in the neighborhood when he was a boy. He swam in the Red with the French kids who lived on the other side, learning enough French to "swear and ask a girl for a date." Ed said in the early days five European languages were spoken here: Abercrombie was mostly Norwegian; a few miles north were Don's people, the Swedes; across the river in Minnesota were the French; and to the south were Germans. The Indians by then had mostly been pushed on, he said. Of the farm on which his family still lived, Ed said, "It's never been owned by anybody but us and the Indians, and they got a bad deal."

Ed said the town of Abercrombie dates from 1858, when the fort was constructed. Don answered my lingering Fargo question by recalling that when they were boys the Red was still clear enough to see the fish they were trying to catch on the bottom. Ed said it was when farmers started plowing the coulees, the draws where heavy rains drain from the fields, that the river lost its purity.

Fort Abercrombie is the oldest army fort in Dakota Territory, built four years before the 1862 Sioux uprising in Minnesota, which prompted construction of numerous other forts across the region. Rebuilt in the 1930s, the stockade walls surround perhaps 40 acres, fronting on the Red. The county highway to Minnesota cuts through the middle of the fort. This site was chosen because, though the Red begins a few miles farther south, Abercrombie was the head of navigation. From here one could go all the way to Europe by water.

During the 1862 uprising, in which scores of settlers and Dakota Indians alike were killed, Fort Abercrombie was under siege for two months until reinforcements arrived from Fort Snelling in Minnesota. The fort was abandoned in the 1870s after white settlers occupied the Red River valley.

Abercrombie, and Wahpeton, originally called Richville, are in Richland county, named not for the extraordinary soil, but for Morgan T. Rich, a rich man who arrived in 1864. The county was the province of rich men, including Jeremiah Wilbur Dwight, a New York businessman and investor in the Northern Pacific Railroad for whom the next town, Dwight, was named. In 1880 Dwight acquired 27,000 acres of choice Red River land and established New York Farm.

"Big Alex" McKenzie didn't arrive here rich. He began his career laying tracks for the Northern Pacific Railroad, but eventually became the railroad's representative to the Dakota Territorial Legislature in Yankton. McKenzie was instrumental in moving the Territorial capital to Bismarck, on the railroad's line, in 1883. With statehood in 1889, Bismarck became the capital of North Dakota .

Sorely exploited by the railroads and the "McKenzie machine," farmers organized, singing S. A. Fisher's poem, "The Farmers Must Rule North Dakota." John Miller, farmer, land speculator, and Dwight postmaster, opposed McKenzie and the railroads. With support of the Farmers' Alliance, Miller was elected first governor of the new state in 1889. Under his leadership, the first session of the North Dakota Legislature passed 14 laws regulating railroads and grain trade, forbidding price-fixing and other unfair treatment of farmers. Unfortunately, the laws were hastily written, proved contradictory, and failed to adequately protect farm interests.

*Fort Abercrombie, built in 1858, in Abercrombie (top), and
a North Dakota sunflower field*

Wahpeton is the largest town in southeastern North Dakota, a regional agricultural center, the headquarters of hog confinement tycoon Rich Bell. "Wahpeton" is a Dakota word variously translated "edge of the woods" or "dwellers among leaves." Here, as it frequently would on my way south, Highway 81 marks the transition from woods to the east, and prairie to the west — the eastern edge of the Great Plains. Except for the Wahpeton Indian School, which educates American Indian children from many tribes, Wahpeton no longer appears an Indian town. The Chamber of Commerce brochure didn't even mention the 125-year-old school. It was still closed for the summer, so I headed on south, continuing up the Red to its source on the South Dakota border, Lake Traverse.

Just north of Fairmont, the last town in North Dakota, I passed a farm with a whole fence made of wood-spoked wagon wheels, scores of them. A monarch butterfly flitted across, heading south. Maybe we'd meet again in Mexico or Costa Rica. Lake Traverse came into view, and I crossed the state line, from the "Flickertail" and "Peace Garden State," to the "Sunshine State," renamed the "Rushmore State" by the tourism-conscious South Dakota Legislature. Ahead was the almost imperceptible curve in the Earth between Lakes Traverse and Big Stone, the continental divide from which waters flow north or south. I had completed my upstream navigation; for the next 1,400 miles I would go with the flow, downstream toward the Gulf of Mexico.

# SOUTH DAKOTA

*"Give me the strength to walk the soft
earth, a relative to all that is."*

*~ Black Elk, Oglala Sioux holy man*

I crossed the line into South Dakota and the home of the Sisseton Sioux.
Most recent maps don't indicate a reservation; in 1975 the United States
Supreme Court ruled that the reservation, created by treaty in 1867, was termi-
nated 20 years later by the Dawes Act. The Act allotted 160 acre plots to eligible
tribal members, opening the "surplus" land to white settlement. The Sisseton
Reservation was the first in the nation opened to whites, in 1892. But despite the
checkerboard of land ownership, this is Indian country, home of the Sisseton and
Wahpeton Yanktonai Sioux, now a minority in the land guaranteed them in 1867
forever.

At the state line, I pulled off to read the historical marker, which reminds
travelers of the South Dakota motto: "Under God the people rule." A profound
sentiment, but of course the question arises, which people? I had just regained
my speed when a flickertail, the 13-striped ground squirrel mascot of the state I
had just left darted into my path. I swerved and hit my brakes, but a barely per-
ceptible bump said my tires had crushed the little body. Suddenly the crisp
morning seemed old, and the hills ahead less luring.

At the edge of South Dakota the terrain begins to change. The infinite flatness yields to rolling hills, and the Red River, I found, does head in a real valley.
Small glacial lakes appeared. South Dakota's state animal is the coyote, and this
was good coyote country. Crops became more diverse too, alfalfa and soybeans
competing with the ten-foot corn which sometimes blocked my view on both
sides. Off to the east a marshland breathed vapor into the air. A half dozen cranes
floated across the valley, looking for a new fishing hole.

Old 81 curves west, the Coteau des Prairies, as the French explorers called
them, rising before me, the first time on this road that anything not made by man
had loomed on the horizon. I rolled into the first hilly town of the route,
Rosholt. A teen-aged girl met me, roller blading down the middle of Main.
Rosholt is a pretty, shady, and three-dimensional town, and a recent one, founded in 1913 and named for Julius Rosholt, who helped build the Soo Line railroad
to town. Its agricultural main street is still thriving in spite of the town being jilted by the interstate.

The next town, Victor, seems in jeopardy of parodying its name. Named for Victor Renville, son of Sisseton Sioux chief Gabriel Renville, and grandson of Victor Renville, who lived as a trader among the Sioux before white settlement began, Victor now consists of a dozen houses and a couple of businesses. The Victor Supper Club, like most restaurants and bars in this part of the world, is announced to the public by a Grain Belt beer sign.

West of Victor, the old highway crosses I-29 on its way to New Effington and Sisseton. Just east of New Effington, I encountered the first pair of "X Marks the Spot" signs, black and white steel signs erected by the Department of Transportation all across South Dakota to mark the site of fatal traffic accidents. In Mexico and Central America, friends and family put up wooden or cement crosses at the place of tragedy, a memorial to the lost loved one, committing their soul to God. In South Dakota the state does the job, with an X rather than a cross, marking the spot where the victim has been Xed out, accompanied by the question, "Why die?" and the injunction to the living to "Think!" lest they be next.

New Effington, population 217, was the smallest town on U.S. 81 listed in the population table of the Rand McNally Atlas. On the edge of town is the big Faith Lutheran Church, seemingly out of proportion to the town, but testimony to the strength of Scandinavians and Lutherans in this part of the world. New Effington native Clarence Pederson said the church was built in the late sixties to consolidate several smaller churches in the area, including Zion, Bethany, and Nidaros, the congregation of which his Norwegian immigrant grandparents were founders. Clarence's grandfather, Ole Pederson, left Norway for South Dakota alone at age 16.

For half an hour I drove dirt roads, skirting glacial ponds and lakes, search-ing for the big square two story house where Clarence grew up, but found only ducks and geese and cormorants, and one lonely pelican sailing a wide expanse of prairie pond. I didn't find my friend's now abandoned farm home, but I did see how he acquired his love for hills and woods and birds. He became a man amidst a slew of sloughs.

I headed for Sisseton, hoping to find Lorraine Rousseau, a former colleague at the University of South Dakota. Our paths parted when Lorraine returned to her home reservation and became a tribal judge, and later, the first tribal chair-woman of the Sisseton Sioux.

Sisseton lies in a long glacier-gouged valley, a different world from the limit-less plain a few miles north. Lorraine lives west of Sisseton on the Prairie Coteau, high hills of glacial moraine – soil, gravel, boulders and rock, debris churned into ridges and mounds by the drift of gigantic chunks of ice 10 millennia ago. For the next hundred miles south, rolling hills are dotted with sky blue glacial lakes and ponds. After that, the highway settles into the sometimes monotonous rou-tine of the eastern Great Plains, occasional ripples and swells and river valleys punctuating a flatness at times comparable to the Red River Valley I'd left behind. Not until the highway skirts the Balcones Escarpment from Waco to San Antonio, Texas, would I again find such hills. And not until a hundred miles into Mexico does one find an end to the plains.

I actually downshifted to climb into Sisseton. I called Lorraine from the Tekakwitha Art Center, then strolled through the ten galleries of Native art, including the works of Calvin Frenier and former artist-in-residence, Paul War Cloud Grant.

I met Lorraine and her friends Rose and Florence for lunch at the Country Kitchen. Florence was an animated Chippewa grandmother, pushing ninety, Lorraine said, who married a Sioux man and learned to speak the Dakota language like a native. Whenever an Indian passed the window she rapped loudly on the glass and waved a greeting.

After lunch Lorraine showed me the reservation, the Indian Health Service Hospital where she was born, and Agency Village south of town, home of tribal headquarters and offices, the new Head Start Center planned by her administration, and the tribally-owned bag factory. We visited the Sisseton Wahpeton Community College, and the Nicollet Tower, built by Harold Torness and his friends on a ridge west of town. The 75-foot tower is named for Joseph Nicolas Nicollet, the Frenchman who first mapped the region in 1839, identifying places by native names. From the top I surveyed a wide expanse of both Dakotas and Minnesota.

Lorraine took me to the casino by the interstate, the second the tribe had built. Machines shelled out quarters to truck drivers and elderly ladies, who immediately recycled them. The gamblers were mostly white, the employees mostly Indian. Lorraine was happy for the revenue and jobs the casinos have brought, but doubtful of the wisdom of building the economy on gambling. She joked that reservation gambling might be a fitting Indian revenge, a way to redistribute wealth to those from whom it was taken. But Indians and whites alike are susceptible to the trap of gambling, and she feared the social cost for both communities would be high.

Two weeks before my visit, Lorraine had failed in a bid to return as tribal chair. Like her successor, her first term ended in ouster by the Tribal Council after she exposed a surplus property sales scheme and other instances of alleged mismanagement under her predecessor's leadership. Lorraine was planning a book on tribal politics and her struggle to eliminate corruption.

Lorraine was a big woman in her late fifties, bursting with robust laughter, a judge at the Turtle Mountain Chippewa Reservation in North Dakota. She epitomizes her people's encounter and assimilation with European culture. Her father was a full-blooded Sioux, her mother the daughter of Pennsylvania Dutch pioneers who made the land rush on April 15, 1892. Her maternal grandparents claimed a quarter section of "surplus land" exactly four days before my own great-grandparents on both sides acquired Cheyenne-Arapaho land the same way in Oklahoma territory. Lorraine's mother was among the first white women here to marry an Indian man; Lorraine remembered that as a child, when her family visited her maternal grandparents, her grandfather would stay in the barn to avoid seeing his son-in-law. But "grandma eventually forgave dad for being an Indian," she said.

Lorraine said relations between whites and Indians have improved a great deal over her lifetime. Though half white, she was raised Indian, and as a teenager didn't consider dating white boys. And most white boys, she said, "wouldn't have dared date an Indian girl." But now, she said, inter-racial dating and marriage have become more accepted. She said that some whites resent the revenue Indians acquire from gambling ventures. But most white business people have begun to appreciate Indian buying power, even hiring native people as clerks in their stores. "You never used to see any Indians working in a gas station," Lorraine said, "but now all the stations have one or two."

Lorraine headed me into the point of the arrowhead-shaped reservation, toward Watertown, and said good-bye. I crossed the 45th parallel on Indian land in Codington County, half way from the North Pole to the Equator. It was still 37 degrees to Panamá, and a long way east.

In these glacial hills, I was in cattle country at last. The land is too steep and rocky to farm, but it grows good grass, and water is abundant. The land is not so valuable as in the Red River valley, producing far less food. But visually, the landscape was a lavish feast, compared to a fourth bowl of oatmeal.

Just below the reservation lies lake-surrounded Watertown. A few weeks earlier, the Immigration and Naturalization Service had rounded up 59 workers without legal documents at the Oak Valley Farms turkey processing plant and shipped them back to Mexico. Plant manager and former Watertown mayor, the late Herb Jenson said he didn't know the workers were illegal, and Mexican workers with papers remained a substantial part of Oak Valley's work force. Having encountered migrant Mexican and Mexican American workers all along the route, I decided it was time for a closer look.

I stopped first to visit Jeanne Koster, director of the South Dakota Peace and Justice Center in downtown Watertown. The 700-member, state-wide grass-roots organization has been around since 1980, educating citizens and raising consciousness on issues of peace, justice, environmental protection, and inter-ethnic reconciliation. Jeanne was closing for the day, but invited me to her house for dinner, and even offered me a bed for the night.

We walked in the pear grove north of her house, home to the heaviest concentration of turtle doves I've ever seen. She talked about the long-term projects of the Center, especially about the campaign for white-Indian reconciliation, which began as a proposal from Center member Harold Iron Shield. Statewide discussion led to a public proclamation of a Year of Reconciliation by the late Gov. George S. Mickleson, and continued to prompt efforts of people around the state to confront a history of racial prejudice, as well as the illegal 1877 Congressional expropriation of the Black Hills region from the Sioux two years after Col. George Armstrong Custer learned there was gold in the Hills. A few years ago, the state Legislature even changed Columbus Day (Pioneer Day in South Dakota) to Native American Day.

I asked Jeanne about the INS raid, and about the local immigrant community. She said the non-European immigration to Watertown began with the Vietnamese, who arrived in 1977 to work at the turkey plant. Jenson later sent buses to south Texas to bring up Mexican workers, including some of the 59 who had been arrested and deported. Jeanne said the presence of illegal aliens willing to work for the minimum wage in Watertown indicated the failure of the North American Free Trade Agreement to protect workers' rights and to establish living minimum wages in Mexico. She said the raid was part of a nation-wide crackdown, precipitated by the anti-immigrant climate in Washington. She suggested I talk the next morning with Del Schryver of the Midwest Farm Worker and Employment Program.

Del's cozy office in the old hospital building on U.S. 81 was decorated with carved wooden figures from Costa Rica and El Salvador, clay figures from Nicaragua where Del once lived, and a photo of his half Nicaraguan teen-aged son. A sign on his desk proclaimed: "Please do not inquire as to the apparent inefficiency of my work. The nature of it requires such a high degree of secrecy that I am not permitted to know what I am doing." Del was a thin and balding man of middle age, of Flemish extraction. He smoked cigarettes and drank coffee steadily as we talked.

Del came to his job through labor organizing and social work. His program was contracted with the Department of Labor, and his clientele were mostly Mexicans with legal social security and resident alien cards. He helped workers find jobs, temporary housing, food, gas for transportation to work, and where possible, education. He told his clients to call him any time, day or night, if they needed help.

Del said there was discrimination in Watertown, and that even legal workers were sometimes treated as "wetbacks." To "inoculate" and prepare them, Del said he told his clients that Watertown has a population of 16,000 – 15,000 great people and a thousand idiots. When someone discriminates against them they can say "by golly, Del was right; I just met one of the idiots."

Del introduced me to two clients, Salvador, an educated Mexican man who spoke no English and was sending his money back to his family in Texas, and Juan, who was born in Texas and spoke fluent English. Both were employed making computer parts, though they were originally brought to Watertown by a headhunter to work at the turkey plant. Juan was a certified fork-lift operator, but at Oak Valley he was put on the kill-line, the lowest-status and lowest-paying job in the place. They were told accommodations would be provided, but in a complaint he filed with the labor department, Juan said some beds lacked mattresses and blankets, and pay and working conditions were misrepresented.

Following the INS raid, the turkey plant was short-handed, so more of the workers were now local people, including numerous Vietnamese and Indians from the Sisseton reservation. But even after the raid, Del said, Latinos remained the largest contingent at the plant.

I drove out to Oak Valley Farms on the edge of Watertown to talk with the manager, former mayor Herb Jenson. Herb was a big, gruff man of retirement age, still going strong. His office was decorated with prints of birds, mostly colorful mallards and pheasants, and one turkey. Herb was a busy man, but he agreed to give me some time. Our talk was interrupted by several calls from associates concerning the city election that day on a new sewage system to replace one the Environmental Protection Agency deemed inadequate. Herb wasn't telling people how to vote, but he was clearly opposed because of the expense. Another call was from a construction foreman, busy digging a private sewage lagoon for the turkey plant, from which the effluent would be diverted to the Big Sioux River. "Ask anything you want," Herb said, "as long as you're not from the government."

Oak Valley Farms has operated in Watertown since the 1930s, but was bought by a New Jersey corporation in 1970. The plant buys tens of thousands of turkeys each year, mostly from local Hutterite colonies. Oak Valley markets processed turkey meat under its own name, and sells a third of its products to school lunch programs in 37 states.

A truck pulled into the kill room, and the process began. The turkeys are grabbed from their cages and suspended by the neck from a conveyor belt, which inches them toward a blade which slits their throats. The belt bears the birds through scalding water; then they are plucked and gutted and transported to processing. Enough to turn you against Thanksgiving.

Herb said he knows Oak Valley isn't "the greatest payer in the world," but he said his difficulty in keeping local workers isn't because of the wages. He said people have changed in his lifetime, and that now most people don't want to work. He said he could double the wage and still have trouble keeping employees. Normally I would have suggested he try it, but I remembered I was there to ask questions.

Mr. Jenson insisted he knew nothing of the Mexican workers' illegal status, and praised them as good workers. His wrath was reserved for the various arms of the federal government – the Immigration and Naturalization Service, the Occupational Safety and Health Administration, and the Environmental Protection Agency – which he saw as interfering with his business. Incidentally, the citizens of Watertown voted overwhelmingly that day to build a new sewage system. A year later the state of South Dakota would sue Oak Valley Farms when its new private lagoon overflowed and polluted the Big Sioux River.

Before leaving Watertown I visited the home of Arthur C. Mellette, the last governor of Dakota Territory, who in 1889 was appointed first governor of the new state of South Dakota. The Mellette house was built in 1883, old by South Dakota standards, a red brick Italianate mansion with a three-story tower and a spiral oak staircase. Ornate and extravagant, the house even had an indoor bathroom, a big advantage in Dakota winters.

Mellette was born and raised in Indiana, practiced law, and moved to Dakota Territory in 1878 to run the land office. Influential in bringing South Dakota to statehood, Mellette is remembered for his honesty. When his friend and State Treasurer W. W. Taylor defaulted on repayment of state loans, Mellette turned over his real estate and other assets, including his home, to repay the people's debt, an act probably inconceivable to most modern politicians.

At Watertown U.S. 81 and I-29 touch once more and again part ways. The old Pan American Highway merges with the interstate system again just north of Salina, Kansas, I-35. But for the next 462 miles on 81, the viability of the towns and cities still depends on this historic artery.

South of Watertown I passed Corson Emminger's 1910 round dairy barn, a flock of pelicans sailing regally across Clear Lake, and a big red International tractor disking wheat stubble, an American flag fluttering in the dust above its cab. I stopped at Kones Korner Kountry Store at the Castlewood turn-off, an odd marriage of an old-fashioned country gas station with one of the region's biggest gun stores. Vic Carter showed me an 1898 Colt .45 he said was carried up San Juan Hill by Col. Stover from Watertown. To my west was Bryant, home of the International Amateur Baseball Hall of Fame. Sparkling glacial lakes dot the hills, Lake Poinsett, Lake Albert, Badger Lake, and scores of ponds.

Whereas I hadn't seen or smelled a single dead animal on the highway through Manitoba and North Dakota, now the odor of August-ripened road-kill was frequent. The lake region, with its water, fields of corn, and wooded cover, obviously is great habitat, not only for pelicans, herons, ducks, geese, cormorants and other fowl, but also for raccoons, skunks, opossums, muskrats and other fur-bearing animals, some of which fail to make it across the road. Several wet years had raised waters to historic levels, and duck and goose production was high. It looked as if I'd have lots of company on my migration south.

Just north of Arlington I passed dozens of bee hives, reminding me that South Dakota is a leading producer of honey. Besides sweetening our lives, the official state insect also helps farmers by pollinating their crops.

The noon whistle blew as I rolled into Arlington, a lively town distinguished by having simultaneously borne three names. According to local lore, in 1880 the post office of this Norwegian town was named Nordland by the Dakota Central Railroad. But the Western Town Lot Company thought the cold-sounding name might discourage other settlers, so in 1884 the county commissioners named it Denver. The Post Office Department refused that name and arbitrarily called the place Arlington for Arlington, Virginia. In 1885 the post office was still Nordland, the railroad station was Denver, and the town was officially Arlington.

On the wall of the bowling alley, a 1989 centennial mural depicts South Dakota life and history, from buffalo to farm scenes to town life, cleverly displayed within the letters of the town's name. The "O" contains the South Dakota seal with the motto about the people ruling. I recalled that when Populists dominated the South Dakota Legislature in 1899, the notion of citizen rule inspired invention of the initiative and referendum, two great democratic institutions which have since spread to other states.

Arlington is on the Brookings County line, named for Wilmont Brookings, a Sioux Falls pioneer and railroad builder who, one evening in February 1858, fell from his horse into Split Rock Creek. The temperature was 30 below zero. He ran several miles to Sioux Falls by morning, badly frozen, and had both legs amputated with a butcher knife. Brookings was elected president of the Territorial Council, which met in his cabin in Sioux Falls in 1859. He later became a justice in the state's Supreme Court.

Just north of Madison is the site of an 1880 Swiss settlement called Badus. The town didn't last, but Swiss names in Lake County remain. Madison is the county seat of Lake County and the home of South Dakota's longest-serving Congressman, Karl Mundt, who served nine terms in Washington. It is also the home of Dakota State University, where Mundt taught speech before winning his first election in 1938. As a Congressman, Mundt chaired the House Un-American Activities Committee (HUAC). He resigned his fourth House term to run for the Senate in 1948, the year he co-sponsored the anti-communist Mundt-Nixon bill, which defined the Communist Party as a foreign agent and required American communists to register with the Justice Department. Failure to do so would be punishable by a $10,000 fine and loss of citizenship. As a U.S. Senator (1949-72), Mundt sat on Joseph McCarthy's Subcommittee on Investigations, continuing the great American witch-hunt.

Perhaps the most interesting feature of Madison, besides its location between a nice pair of lakes, is Prairie Village. Prairie Village is the largest and most elaborate of the four restored pioneer towns on 81: Heritage Village at Grafton, Bonanzaville at Fargo, the restored Bagg Bonanza farm near Wahpeton, and now Prairie Village, the granddaddy of restored prairie towns.

The immigrant peoples of the Dakotas have now lived on these plains long enough to develop a sense of their South Dakota history, in addition to the histories with which they came. The first century here, they concentrated on the present and the future, but as they entered their second century, they at last began to realize their new past, to delight in it, to savor and preserve it. Ironically this recognition coincided with the already apparent decline in population, the withering of small towns and prairie institutions, and the rapid aging of remaining population.

Perhaps it was the recognition of impending loss, nostalgia for an already fading age, that reawakened people to their past. Perhaps after a hundred years of struggle to "tame" the land, as many put it, they at last had leisure to contemplate from whence they had come, and the wildness they had subdued and lost. Add to that the now universal recognition and pursuit of the tourist dollar, and the awareness that modern America yearns for a simpler and more romantic past which a walk through "Prairie Village" might satisfy. Capitalizing on history simultaneously teaches, inspires, helps to preserve, and brings in needed revenue.

Prairie Village is built on Lake Herman, across the lake from the log cabin of the pioneer for whom it was named. The village consists of eight city blocks — hotel, church, land office, general store, and all the businesses needed to support pioneer life. Homes range from a sod shanty to several log cabins to early frame houses. Most of the buildings are more than a century old, moved here from around Lake County. Prairie Village even has a steam train to carry passengers around the lake and town. During the Steam Threshing Jamboree in August, visitors relive pioneer farm operations — steam threshing of oats, lugging competition between antique tractors, and all the other tasks and crafts involved in the maintenance of life and commerce on the plains.

Before heading south again, 81 jogs 12 miles west through the tiny town of Junius to Winfred, a town of about 70 that the mistress of the half-day post office told me had recently unincorporated. A funeral was in progress as I pulled off the highway; at the moment the cemetery was the liveliest place in town.

As if to accent the decline of these little towns and the great sagging barns of surrounding farmsteads, the road kill escalated. The stench of flattened animals, especially skunks, permeated the air. This was the flip side of the celebrated past at Prairie Village. But decay also generates life, including a sleek mink which streaked across the road before me.

In Salem, an 1880 town named by postmaster O. S. Pender for his bewitched home town of Salem, Massachusetts, I stopped for a burger at the Heritage Delight Cafe. It was well after noon, and I was the only diner. The cook and server, a young woman whose family operated the period-decorated cafe, said this was one of the few Main Street buildings to survive the catastrophic fire of 1910. In its life, the Heritage Delight building had served Salem as a drug store, a jewelry store, and a bar before becoming a soda fountain and cafe.

I crossed Interstate 90 south of Salem and headed for Freeman, probably the most Mennonite town in South Dakota. This stretch of 81 had been under reconstruction for a couple of years, and sure enough, about 10 miles down I reached its temporary end. "Road Closed." Period. The contractor had provided no instructions for a detour around the next 15 miles of closed highway, so I had to find my own. I took to the gravel, first west, then south to a dead end, back east across 81 and south again, back across to the west, and finally, after 20 miles of meandering, my unofficial detour ended at a sign proclaiming "Freeman: The Right Place."

According to local legend, Freeman got its name in a unique way. It was supposed to be called Menno to honor the founder of the Mennonite faith, Anabaptist leader Menno Simons. But apparently when railroad employees were nailing up the signs, they accidentally switched two. Thus Menno is a town eight miles west of 81, surrounded by Hutterite colonies, and Freeman is named for an early settler in Menno.

What seems odd is how quickly such history as the origin of names can be lost. The town's centennial committee searched in vain a few years ago for documentation of the name switch, but oral history is apparently all that remains. I had begun to realize that most people have little idea how their town was named, including some elderly people whose grandparents were founders.

I stopped to visit with Tim Waltner, editor of the *Freeman Courier*. He was out for a few minutes, so I browsed in the Et Cetera Shoppe next door, a volunteer-run import and recycled clothing store operated as a self-help project by the Mennonite Central Committee. Marge Graber told me that such stores are common in Mennonite country. They provide low-cost clothing and other consumer goods, as well as a marketing outlet for artisans and crafts people in third-world countries where the Mennonite Central Committee works. In this small town shop I found goods from India, Bangladesh, Laos, Central America, Peru, Chile, and several countries in Africa.

Marge said the Mennonite Central Committee was established just after the Russian Revolution, when Mennonites sent wheat to Russia, from whence most had immigrated. The Committee is still involved in relief work, but also now in third-world self-sufficiency projects. Shopper Steve Herman told me about another project of the Central Committee. A mobile meat-packing truck tours Mennonite country, slaughtering and packing donated beef for export to needy people in Africa and other third-world regions. The aid is provided, he said, because Jesus said to feed the hungry, not in order to proselytize for their particular faith.

Back at the *Courier*, I found Tim at his desk. He talked about the uniqueness of his community, and about Mennonite traditions. He described U.S. 81 as the "Mennonite Highway," directly connecting the Freeman community with the large concentration of Mennonites at Newton, Kansas, just north of Wichita, where many young people from Freeman attend Bethany College. I resolved to check out those connections down the road.

Tim estimated that Freeman is about half Mennonite, but a higher percentage German Russian. He said he still hears German spoken among old-timers in the post office, and the town's annual celebration is Scmeckfest, where visitors from near and far gorge themselves on German sausage, sauerbraten and desserts.

I asked Tim whether there was a downside to such a strongly homogeneous community, whether it was possible for a newcomer to ever be fully integrated. He said the town has a "global sensitivity, which leavens the attitudes of its people." He pointed out that Freeman is better educated than most small towns. The Freeman Academy, a Mennonite elementary school, is still strong, and until recently the town even had a church-operated junior college. Also, many of the residents have traveled internationally, including to many third-world countries, doing mission and Central Committee work. Yet, he added, a key to integration into the community is involvement with the churches, the backbone of the town, not just various Mennonite congregations, but Lutheran, Christian Reformed, and Missionary Alliance.

Tim said there are several Mennonite "strains," because over the years they have "split hairs over a multitude of issues. All believe in adult baptism, for instance, but should you be immersed or sprinkled, and if you're immersed should you go down frontwards or backwards?"

This small town has strong churches, a diverse economy, and a healthy professional sector. Though Freeman College is now closed, Tim attributed much of the community's vitality to its lingering contributions to intellectual life. In the final analysis, he said, what Freeman has going for it is a real sense of community, based partly on shared history and values. "Of the 1,300 people who live here, I figure I know about two-thirds on a first-name basis," he said.

Amidst family pictures on his wall is a color print of Tim and his wife with Bill and Hillary Clinton, taken at the White House during a visit by journalists. Tim had visited the president three times, and though he hadn't agreed with all of Clinton's actions, he still believed that Clinton is "genuine and sincere, a real person." Strangely enough, he said, Mennonites often vote Republican because of their "prairie populism" and fiscal conservatism, though they tend to be liberal on social issues, environmentally sensitive, and opposed to war and foreign intervention.

Tim suggested I visit a local couple who probably don't vote Republican, and who on the surface don't appear to fit this community, but who he said embody Mennonite social values, Michael Sprong and Beth Preheim. I left Tim's office and headed down Turkey Creek to Rose Hill Farm to talk with Mike and Beth. A pair of ring-necked pheasants, the Chinese-import state bird, cackled up from a thicket beside their drive-way.

Beth was a county health nurse, the daughter of Marion and Vern Preheim; Vern was general secretary of the General Conference of Mennonites, a man I wanted to meet down the highway in Newton, Kansas. Beth and Mike's home on the bank of Turkey Creek is Beth's old family homestead, also the site of the 1974 Mennonite centennial meeting. Rose Hill is a long way from New York, and an unlikely place for a book publishing business, but that's what I found.

Both in their thirties, Mike and Beth are well-known peace activists. In 1987 they worked with Sam Day, former editor of the *Progressive* magazine, mapping and naming the 150 ICBM nuclear missiles in South Dakota, which were removed in the nineties by the Strategic Arms Reduction Treaty.

The couple's publishing venture has two arms; they publish regional peace-oriented poetry and prose under Rose Hill Books, and in 1994 they acquired the Fortkamp Publishing Co. of Baltimore, Maryland, and its 28 titles, including books by Sam Day, Barbara Ehrenreich, Daniel and Philip Berrigan, Elizabeth McAllister, and other nationally-known peace activists. The Fortkamp Press publishes works on peace, justice, and non-violent resistance. It is supported by the Franz Jaegerstaetter Memorial Fund, which honors a German citizen who refused conscription and was executed by the Third Reich. Rose Hill Books were printed in Freeman by the 95-year-old Pine Hill Press. The current printer is Joe Mierau, a conscientious objector during the Vietnam War who is sympathetic to their work.

In March 1994, Michael and Fr. Frank Cordaro, a parish priest from Iowa who served two terms at the federal prison in Yankton for war resistance, went to El Salvador as election observers. While they were there they delivered a van load of crutches and artificial limbs to repatriated refugees and former guerrilla soldiers at Nuevo Gualcho, a settlement near the Pan American Highway, built on land purchased for them by the European Community.

Back on the highway, I crossed the James River, the roadside still littered with flotsam from spring flooding that had closed the highway for several days. I passed the last two "X marks the Spot" signs, remembering the two bodies I saw sprawled on the pavement one fine spring day in 1994, killed on the curve in a head-on crash. Now on familiar turf, I climbed the next hill and pulled off at the former Red Rooster.

The Red Rooster was built about 1930 as the Farmers' Union Hall. Farmers had no money during the Depression, and the place went broke, but it reopened in the late thirties as a dance hall. According to legend, it is one of several local places where Lawrence Welk played. In fact legend has him playing everywhere in these parts, every barn, every bar. He must have played 10 times a day.

In the late fifties the hall became the Red Rooster, and acquired what former Yankton police chief Leon Cantin called a "lively reputation," the out-of-town place the chief and his college friends frequented around 1960. The Rooster was gutted by fire, but rebuilt as a home in the seventies. Alan Ferris, who lives there now, said the garden yields fragments of broken bottles every spring.

The last town in the Dakotas, built on a Missouri River bluff, is Yankton. U.S. 81 through town honors NBC News anchor Tom Brokaw, who grew up here. But that is only a recent claim to fame. Yankton is a historic city, the "Mother City of the Dakotas." As they poled their way up the Missouri, Lewis and Clark ordered the prairie set afire on August 25, 1804, and again on August 27, to summon the Yankton Sioux to a conference. Both ill, perhaps from too much Elk the night before, on August 29 the explorers held council with Dakota chiefs at Calumet Bluffs across the river.

Yankton was a major steamboat and trading town in the 1850s and 60s, and for two decades, immigrants got off the boat in Yankton and headed overland. Yankton became the Territorial Capital in 1861, a territory which in the early sixties included most of Montana and Wyoming, as well as North and South Dakota. In 1873 the Dakota Southern Railroad arrived, and river traffic declined. But every August the town celebrates River Boat Days amongst the towering cottonwoods at Riverside Park, beside the replica of the territorial capitol building.

Many fine mansions from the 1870s still grace the ash and hackberry-lined streets of the historic district, Capital, Pine, Mulberry and Douglas Streets. A marker on the courthouse lawn at Third and Broadway indicates the site of Fort

Yankton, a stockade hastily constructed after the 1862 Sioux uprising in Minnesota. The territory's oldest newspaper, The Yankton *Press and Dakotan*, was established in 1861, and still publishes beside the post office on Walnut Street. In 1877, Jack McCall, who killed Wild Bill Hickok in Deadwood, was tried, hanged and buried in Yankton.

Yankton College, Dakota Territory's first institution of higher learning, opened here in 1881, eight years before statehood. Its founder, Joseph Ward, wrote the South Dakota motto, "Under God, the People Rule." Today the campus houses a minimum security federal prison in the middle of town.

At Eighth and Burleigh, on the banks of Marne Creek (Rhineland Creek until its German name was changed during World War I), Col. Custer and his Seventh Cavalry camped April 13, 1873, on their way from Indian Territory in what is now Oklahoma, up the Missouri River to Fort Abraham Lincoln at Bismarck. Three years later, Custer's band would be annihilated at Little Big Horn in Montana Territory, the place where, as a bumper sticker popular in Indian country puts it, "Custer Got Siouxed." Peter Binder, a stable boy with Custer's band, got drunk in Yankton and didn't make muster when the troops embarked, which is why Mount Marty French professor Sr. Cynthia Binder, his great-grand-daughter, is here today.

Hutterites arrived in Yankton in the 1860s, founding the Bon Homme Colony just up the river. Since then, dozens of colonies have spread up the James River valley and as far as Manitoba, Canada, where many of them, pacifist and German-speaking, fled to escape persecution during World War I. On the river bluff west of town, Swiss missionary to Dakota Indians Martin Marty founded his bishopry, and in 1887, the Sacred Heart Convent and Sacred Heart Hospital. The complex now includes Mount Marty College, converted from a girls' boarding school to a liberal arts college in 1936.

In 1885, a former slave named Lewis built Allen Chapel, the African Methodist Episcopal Church, at 508 Cedar, the oldest black church in the Dakotas. The church is a small but sturdy brick structure. The piano belonged to Lewis' daughter. Allen Chapel is named for Richard Allen, the Methodist minister in Philadelphia who in 1776 began holding services in a blacksmith shop for a racially integrated congregation. Even today the symbol of the A.M.E. church is an anvil superimposed upon the cross.

I attended Sunday worship with Nate Blakey, a spiritual experience I won't soon forget. The sweet songs of this 80-year-old truck gardener and refuse collector haunted the little church with a spirit of genuine peace. "What A Friend We Have in Jesus" was never more believable than when Nate sang it, spontaneously, a cappella, alone. Except for military service, Nate has lived his entire eight decades here, one of 12 children of parents who eloped from the south to Yankton in 1905 to join a tiny African American community. Nate and wife Josephine raised seven children here.

Yankton also has historic international and interstate connections. In the first decade of the 20th century, portland cement quarried just west of town was shipped to Panamá to help build the Panamá Canal, the farthest south crossroads bisected by the Pan American Highway. WNAX, the powerful regional radio station, whose call letters stand for W North American Experiment, began here in 1922. In 1927 it was bought by Chan Gurney and moved to Gurney Seed and Nursery, a name known to gardeners across the nation. In that year a five-state audience first heard Lawrence Welk and his Honolulu Fruit Gum Band, live from Yankton.

The Gurney nursery moved to Yankton from Nebraska in 1893, operating as a family business for a century before selling to an international corporation, which gradually replaced many local workers with immigrants willing to work for low wages. Now it has been sold again, and is leaving town for Michigan.

I talked with a dozen men from Mexico who shared a Gurney-owned house on the east edge of town. Most send every penny they can to their families in Mexico. On the living room wall hung the picture found in more Mexican homes than any other, the Virgin of Guadeloupe, who miraculously appeared to Aztec Indian Juan Diego near Mexico City in 1531, directing him to build a church there. The church, the most important shrine in Mexico, still stands beside the Pan American Highway, 2,000 miles south.

The Missouri is the biggest river crossed by the Pan American Highway, and including headwaters and the portion named "Mississippi" below St. Louis, the longest river on Earth, 4,240 miles, though it was shortened by over 100 miles by channelization between Sioux City and St. Louis. The river bed was gouged by melting ice; the leading edge of the vast Laurentide Ice Sheet shouldered up its final ridge of debris, ceased its drift, and began to thaw, its waters seeking their course to the Gulf.

When planners met in Salina, Kansas, in 1911 to map the route of U.S. 81, they called it the Meridian Road, for the 6th principal meridian which it closely parallels, and from which Nebraska and Kansas were surveyed. Here the 6th meridian met the Missouri, and here the planners found the greatest challenge to completion of their project. The Meridian Bridge was completed in 1924, the last link in the Canada to Mexico chain. The locally-financed toll bridge, built where the 1858 Frost Trading Post stood, is unique, a double-decker with a lift span, designed to carry trains on the lower level and wagons and Model Ts on top. But the trains never came, so now traffic flows south below and north above. By the 1950s the bridge was paid off, and the Army Corps of Engineers dammed the Missouri, rendering the lift section obsolete. Now a new bridge is being planned, and whether and how to save the historic bridge is hotly debated in Yankton.

Before five mammoth dams were constructed on the upper Missouri in South and North Dakota, the river flooded regularly. But THE flood came in 1881. Most of the steamboats on the river were wrecked or sunk, and the town of Vermillion, 25 miles downstream, simply washed away, later to revive on the north bluff. Yankton survived, and thrives at the upper end of the last relatively wild stretch of North America's longest and purest big river. The Meridian Bridge remains the only way to cross in over 100 miles between Running Water and Sioux City, Iowa, except by boat, or on ice in the dead of winter.

But the wildness of the river is mostly illusion. For half a century the water flow has been controlled to float an ever-declining number of barges from Sioux City to St. Louis, hauling little grain and producing less than one percent of the revenue generated by the river. American Rivers has rated the Missouri the second most-endangered river in the U.S. Because most of the river is channeled or dammed, its natural rises are controlled, and its bed is scoured ever deeper, cleaned of organic material. The upper ends of the reservoirs are clogged with the silt that should be feeding the river. Twenty percent of the Missouri species are on watch or endangered lists. Tourism is the big industry on the Missouri today, an industry dependent on a healthy river with abundant wildlife and fish. Thus, a major struggle ensues between the navigation industry and those who would improve the river's health.

The Missouri is still home to prehistoric paddle-fish and pallid sturgeon, featured in the film "Ancient Survivors of the Missouri" by local filmmakers Doug and Judi Sharples. I had worked with Doug and Judi on this film, as well as in New York and Mexico City on a Jack Kerouac film called "Go Moan for Man." Doug would meet me in San Antonio and ride to Mexico City, filming the Mexican portion of Kerouac's classic, *On the Road*.

The Missouri is not only awe-inspiring; it is treacherous. Almost every summer another swimmer is swept away by its current, which normally runs six to seven miles per hour. But this year the river was the highest and wildest in recent memory, as the Corps dumped excess water from the reservoirs, including Lewis and Clark Lake above Yankton. From August through early fall, operator Michael Cappel told me, the Corps was releasing 54,000 cubic feet of water every second, enough to fill a municipal swimming pool. Water was raging through the turbines, spinning them at maximum speed, and the excess 20,000 cubic feet per second was roaring over the spillway gates, creating a misty atmosphere not unlike that experienced at Niagara Falls. My home east of Yankton overlooks this mighty river.

Before continuing south I had things to do. I stopped across from the *Press and Dakotan* for a haircut from Don Dickes, the only man who had cut my hair for 14 years. I was bummed to find a note taped to the locked door, saying Don had retired a month ago, just after my last visit. I felt jilted, or maybe as if I'd read the obituary of a friend. I got back in the car, reeling. What would I do now? I didn't know any other barbers. But after awhile I realized that Don had, after all, barbered for 42 years, so he was due a rest. And the more I thought about it, I had to admire his clean get-away, no sloppy good-byes or explanations about what he'd do without a pair of clippers in his hand. On the other hand, I now faced a choice: resume my former life as a hippie, or take my chances elsewhere. I decided to put off the decision for another day.

*A round dairy barn, built south of Watertown in 1910 by Corson Emminger (top), and the last link in the Pan American Highway, the Meridian Bridge, built across the Missouri River at Yankton in 1924.*

Before hitting the road again, I would spend a few days at home on Turkey Ridge east of Yankton with Norma and our two children, Walter and Laura. With fall approaching I had to cut firewood, clean the chimney, help bring in the garden, put the snow scoop on the tractor, and see to the other chores of a rural Dakotan preparing for winter.

At home I walked in the native grasses I had planted, a mixture of big and little bluestem, Indiangrass, switchgrass, sideoats grama, western wheatgrass and sand lovegrass. This season, at least, the Indiangrass seemed predominant. Perhaps that was as it should be. Long before I came to this prairie, the land on which I stood was home to the Yankton Sioux, who relinquished it to the United States in 1859. The oldest oaks in my woods were here when the last Yankton camp-fires were extinguished.

Monarch butterflies fluttered by my house on their way to Mexico and Central America for the winter. But their flight is nonchalant, and soon I would overtake them. When angles of geese honked their way south, I would be with them.

# NEBRASKA

*"That is happiness; to be dissolved into
something complete and great."*

~ Willa Cather, tombstone epitaph, from My Antonia

I resumed my journey before daylight, and by the end of the driveway I realized a headlight was out. I crossed the writhing dark water of the Missouri and entered Nebraska in a grove of towering cottonwoods, the state tree here as well as in Kansas. I was welcomed to "the good life," in the state where the official motto is "Equality before the Law." I pondered the ambiguity of the word "before" as the lights of Yankton faded in my rearview mirror, the Meridian Bridge and the Mount Marty chapel accents against a purple morning sky. Then the road rises from the valley to the scenic overlook near Calumet Bluff, where Lewis and Clark met the Sioux.

Nebraska became a state in 1867. A decade later, the Poncas and Omahas who lived here were forcibly removed to Indian Territory in what is now Oklahoma. Ponca Chief Standing Bear's defiant return, and his lawsuit against Gen. Crook, yielded the landmark 1879 decision which determined that Native Americans are people, "entitled to the same Constitutional protection as a white man." In his testimony, Standing Bear proclaimed, "I wish to die in this land. I wish to be an old man here." In an uncommon gesture, the government allowed Standing Bear and his people to remain.

At the turn-off to Niobrara, I remembered a man who traveled the Pan American Highway before me. Danny Liska was a Niobrara farmer who, in the midst of a 1960s mid-life crisis, got on his BMW motorcycle and rode to Alaska, then turned around and went the other way down the American artery, all the way to the end of South America. He told the story in *Two Wheels to Adventure*. Danny had recently died of leukemia, in spite of treatment by the wife he met in Colombia, psychic Regina 11. A Colombian senator, Regina was later kidnapped by narco-terrorists. I hoped my journey would be slightly less hair-raising than Danny's.

Fog shrouded the rolling hills and valleys, but by first light I found alfalfa competing with corn and beans. I pulled into Jerry's Hilltop Cafe, some 30 miles south of Yankton. I'd passed the place many times in annual migrations to Oklahoma and always wanted to stop, mostly to meet my namesake. Besides, it was time for breakfast. Jerry was frying eggs for a dozen farmers and travelers gathered at this early hour. Located on a prominent rise half way between Yankton and Norfolk, the Hilltop Cafe has been open for 45 years, the only place to eat in a 60 mile stretch of townless highway. Besides feeding people, Jerry and his wife Toots sell gas for cars and Golden Sun Feeds for cows.

The waitress that morning was Darlene, a retired truck driver. Darlene was past middle-age, short wavy hair, lacy blouse and tight western jeans. She'd driven many a mile up and down 81, hauling everything, she said, but mostly feed. She said when she started driving she was one of three women in the business. "I always had trouble backing the big rigs," she said, "until one night I did it perfectly in my dreams. From then on I never had a problem." Darlene brought me the special — eggs, sausage and toast for $1.85, a real Nebraska breakfast.

Darlene is from Magnet, a tiny town two miles west of 81. She said during the recent centennial the community pulled together, raising several thousand dollars to spruce up the town. Besides wanting to see where Darlene lived, I was drawn by the name. A town called Magnet would have to be attractive, though perhaps polarized between positive and negative forces. I decided to pull off and put Magnet to the acid test, to see what kind of charge folks get from living there. My first encounter with Magnet was positive. A sign said litter is collected by the Magnet Socialite's Club. Beside the first house in the town of 45 residents, another hand-painted sign proclaims: "Magnet, the town too tough to die." Abandoned by railroad and highway, Magnet still has a grip on life.

A few miles north of Norfolk is Ronspies Implement, a hillside and valley cluttered with rows of aging farm implements, tractors, and combines, some sort of museum I presumed. And so it is. But it's also a business, run by Wilfred and Dennis Ronspies. Dennis, in his mid-fifties, was enjoying the morning air in his front yard when I stopped. He said his older brother Wilfred started the business about 1950. In the late forties Wilfred went to Texas every year to follow the wheat harvest. When he finished the season he would sell his combines at a profit and haul back grain binders, which were in high demand in Nebraska. When he sold the binders he had to take something old in trade, and the business "just sort of mushroomed," Dennis said.

Finally Wilfred quit his annual migration and started dealing closer to home, buying old machinery and parking it, waiting for a chance to turn a profit. Some of the machines have now waited half a century, and are of no use to modern farmers. But the Ronspies still sell parts, as well as the occasional whole implement to a hobby farmer or collector, and every year they recycle tons of iron. Dennis and Wilfred have lived their whole lives on Highway 81. The semis roaring by were an irritant to me, but Dennis ignored them as we talked, just another element, like the wind.

Near Norfolk, farms became more diversified. Some still host a range of stock, not just cattle, but hogs, chickens, sheep, and one place even goats. All consume hay and silage and grain raised on the farm, all produce food for the family and for sale, as well as manure to fertilize next year's crops. Such a farm is a balanced eco-system; everything has a place, and nothing goes to waste. Diversified farms were the norm not many years ago, but they are labor intensive compared to raising just corn and beans. As farmers have aged, families grown smaller, and kids gone to college and the cities, this older model is almost as rare as a Ronspie binder.

At least as significant as shifting demographics is the rise of behemoth industrial farms such as Murphy Farms of North Carolina and Bell Farms of North Dakota, which have spread their tentacles across the Great Plains. Millions of hogs live in cramped confinement, pushed to slaughter weight on high-protein diets and hormones, their waste collected in huge tanks or earthen "lagoons." The per animal profit is sliced to the bone by these vertically-integrated factory farms, so a real farmer can no longer make a living with a few dozen cows and hogs. Nebraska farmers have some protection against corporate control of land and livestock through Amendment 300, the Family Farm Act passed by the state's Unicameral during the farm crisis of the early eighties. In 1998 South Dakota voters approved similar restrictions on corporate ownership. But no state law can raise the prices of cattle and hogs and corn, and increasingly, only the big survive.

In the road ditch were patches of another "crop" that grows profusely here, as well as in South Dakota – cannabis, hemp, marijuana. During the second world war the government contracted with Midwestern farmers to grow hemp for rope. The plant proved tenacious, went wild, and inhabits road ditches and abandoned farmyards throughout the region. Now the same government spends millions every year trying to eradicate the plant, with little success. Known locally as "ditch weed," the stuff has a low THC content. It often attains a bushy Christmas tree height of eight feet, and looks just like what people pay big money for. Every summer a new crop of teenagers and tourists have to give it a try, but so far nobody's gotten much more than a headache for their efforts.

Norfolk is on the north fork of the Elkhorn River, and early pioneers logically called the place North Fork. But apparently somebody in the Post Office Department couldn't read, so the town was officially christened Norfolk. Norfolk is the largest town on 81 in Nebraska, and the biggest since Fargo. On the north edge of town is the Prospect Hill cemetery, where wild west showman "Diamond Dick" reposes. After a successful career, first with Buffalo Bill and then solo, Diamond Dick became Dr. R. J. Tanner and practiced medicine in Norfolk until he died in 1943.

I stopped to visit old friends Bob and Barbara Schmitz, who live with their son Eli about as close to the Pan American Highway as you can be and not get run over. In fact, when the highway was widened some years ago, it took part of their front lawn. In return they got a tall stockade fence, which provides privacy, but does little to mute the rumble of semis downshifting for the stop light on "Johnny Carson Boulevard," next to Johnny's boyhood home.

Barbara and Bob both teach at Northeast Community College. At first glance they are an odd couple, she tall and slender, he short and stocky, with the long bushy hair of a man who has not forsaken the sixties. But as they talk it is clear that their lives, and even their thoughts, are marvelously in sync. Rarely does one complete a sentence without a word or phrase appropriately supplied by the other, a team telling a story that is richer and more verdant than if told by either alone.

They've lived here since 1972, long since integrating the drone of traffic into their morning meditation on the front porch, just another kind of mantra, rhythm for the poetry Barbara writes here. A few years ago she wrote a poem called "Highway 81" which begins with a reference to me as a child of 81, and ends, "When the traffic comes we pretend/ it's a river flowing from Canada/ on down to South America."

Bob said he can "feel the connection to South America on this highway." He said it's natural that people have explored and migrated up 81. His German ethnicity puts him squarely in the mainstream of the Great Plains, and especially northern Nebraska, but in recent years significant migration has been from the south. Hundreds of Mexican and Mexican-American workers have come to Norfolk, mostly to work at meat packing plants here and in nearby Madison, Bob's home town. The Beef America plant in Norfolk closed amidst a labor strike in 1998, leaving 1,000 workers jobless, but later reopened under IBP.

As a high schooler Bob carried groceries across the Pan American Highway from the Madison IGA to cars on the other side of Main. He didn't think of 81 as a highway then, let alone as the major artery of the continent. Bob said it was "unbelievable that Madison would have become so multi-cultural, because it was then a staunch German Catholic and Lutheran town, very provincial, and suddenly it became half people of color, and people there were in a state of shock." Bob heard that just north of the Río Grande bridge in Laredo, a billboard in Spanish invites Mexicans to Norfolk for jobs. Barbara said the INS had conducted a raid in Norfolk too, deporting the men, but strangely leaving women and children. Bob said that crime had increased, but that before the Mexicans arrived, Norfolk had a reputation as a cross-roads drug-trafficking town.

Barbara and Bob had classes to teach, so we said good-bye, and I drove to Johnson Park to meet Jean Dederman, beside her great-great-grandfather's log cabin, which he built on the bank of the Elkhorn River. This is the oldest house in town, built in 1868 from willow trees John Frederick Dederman cut from the river bank. Dederman was born in Germany, and came to Nebraska from Wisconsin with the first wagon train. Except for college, Jean has lived her whole life here. Her daughter Sara, the sixth generation Dederman in Norfolk, was married beside the cabin. "Dedermans owned most of Norfolk," Jean said with a laugh, "and here we are broke." Across the river is the Old Mill shopping center, which replaced the 19th century flour mill Jean remembers from her teenage years in the sixties.

Once Barbara and Bob took my family and me to the Uptown Eating

Establishment on Norfolk Avenue. It's in the historic five-story Madison Hotel, the tallest building in town, now the Kensington Hotel. I stopped to see the ballroom upstairs where Bob said Johnny Carson's first radio broadcast originated, and where Wendell Wilke conceded defeat to Franklin Roosevelt in 1940.

A half block west is the Carlisle shoe store, in back of which is the Carlisle Museum of Fireworks and Rocketry. Proprietor Jim Carlisle gave me a tour of the cramped dusty back room where his father's treasures are kept. In the early days of space travel, Orville Carlisle, who ran the family shoe store but whose hobby was collecting fireworks dating back to the civil war, began building miniature rockets and missiles, including a parachute recovery system, and putting on demonstrations for school groups. One of Carlisle's rockets went to the Smithsonian in Washington. Jim said his father was born on July 6th, "a firecracker with a slow fuse." He died in 1988, having been featured in many national magazines, and even having helped the FBI solve an Omaha bombing without leaving the shoe store.

On the south edge of Norfolk, on the Elkhorn River, is the sprawling and historic Riverside Ballroom, one end of which had become the Mexican Restaurante del Río. I stopped for a taco and a look at the 100-foot dance floor where, according to posters on the wall, Jimmy Dorsey and the German polka had given way to a Mexican band from Texas, Puro Corazón, Pure Heart, and a troupe of bikini dancers from Colorado.

Ten miles south I passed the De Groot apple orchard, the first commercial fruit operation I'd seen on the highway. The land flattens, and corn is again dominant, justifying Nebraska's nickname, the "Corn Husker State." The highway skirts Bob Schmitz' hometown of Madison, where Mexican immigrants, now numbering 60,000 statewide, celebrate Mexico's 1862 defeat of French rulers on Cinco de Mayo in May. In June the more long-standing "Days of Swine and Roses" features hog-calling, husband-calling, and a smelly boot contest.

Highway 81 also bypasses Humphrey, Tarnov and Platte Center. Every German Catholic town has its steeple, but the Saint Francis Church in Humphrey has the proportionately tallest steeple I've seen. The ostentatious spike reigns over town, church, and water tower, certainly over humble Saint Francis. But the people of Humphrey I found down to earth.

A few miles north of Columbus is the Loup Canal, a 1930s WPA project which diverts water from the Loup River to two hydro-electric generating facilities northeast of town. Then the highway plunges into a deep and broad valley where the Loup and Platte rivers converge below Columbus.

Just outside town seven men were replacing railroad ties by hand. I stopped to talk with what turned out to be an all-Mexican six-man section crew, led by foreman Pedro (Pete) Rese. Pete was a small, middle-aged man with a ready smile, his face blackened by work in the sun. His crew consisted of three sons, two nephews and a friend, all from Crystal City, Texas, just west of the Highway 81 town of Dilley, and the home of many Mexican-Americans living in Fargo.

Pete and his crew had worked 60 miles of track from the west, replacing up to 250 ties each 10-hour day. In four days they would finish the job to Columbus, then head down 81 to their families. "These are all my people," Pete said. "We work together." Their teamwork was beautiful to see. Spanish was their language, but little talk was necessary; they moved together like a tightly wound clock, one loosening spikes, another levering them out, a third prying up rails, two sliding old ties out and new ones in, the last man replacing the spikes.

In Columbus I stopped at Wal-mart for a headlight bulb, figuring I'd save time. Wal-mart represents everything I was trying to avoid – homogeneity, corporate values, chain restaurants and motels. And yet, I grudgingly admit old Sam was pretty smart. I stopped at his store not because I believe the myth that the price would be the best in town, but because I would know exactly where to find a headlight. I probably could have found it blind-folded. Once inside the front doors I flashed back to Yankton. Or was it Fargo, or Wichita? You've seen one, you've seen them all.

Alan Ferris of the Yankton Red Rooster grew up in Columbus. He said that Columbus, like Belleville, Kansas, El Reno, Oklahoma, and many other towns where two U. S. highways intersect, claims to be the "crossroads of America." Probably the people of Cahokie, the pre-Columbian city near the confluence of the Missouri and Mississippi rivers, felt the same way. And surely the residents of Teotihuacán in Mexico and Tikal in Guatemala assumed that the universe radiated from their cities.

Columbus does have a historic claim. U.S. 30, which connects Atlantic City, New Jersey to Astoria, Oregon, intersects 81 here. But eight decades before the first highways, two historic pioneer trails crossed the plains to Oregon and California at Columbus. The Mormon branch of the Oregon/California Trail, later called the Council Bluffs Road, followed the Loup River. And though the Platte was too broad and shallow for navigation, "a mile wide and an inch deep," Alan said, the Platte River guided travelers on the Oxbow Trail, later the Old Fort Kearny Road. Probably for every pioneer who homesteaded near Columbus, dozens saw this valley on their way farther west.

In the 1860s the first trans-continental railroad, the Union Pacific, pushed through Columbus on its way to an 1869 rendezvous with California's Central Pacific near Ogden, Utah. Alan said the main railroad shipments of his youth were California fruit and vegetables, but the Union Pacific now moves thousands of cars of Wyoming coal through Columbus every day, plus container cars with oriental imports from the west coast.

Columbus was a lively town, still mostly white, though with a growing number of Latin Americans. Alan knew only one non-white family in this mostly German town when he was a boy, a family from Bangladesh whose father worked at the power plant.

Columbus was named for Columbus, Ohio, and ultimately, for Christopher himself. Alan said the town used to celebrate its heritage with a big parade on

Columbus Day, but now angles for summer tourists. For the 1992 quincentennial of Columbus' arrival, architecture student Craig Dunham designed a phalanx of towers beside 81 to display 10 historic area bells donated by Columbus resident Leonard Fleischer.

Ironically the Columbus monument stands in Pawnee Park. Central Nebraska was once the domain of the Pawnees, who gradually ceded their land to the government, except for a 10 by 30 mile reservation along the Loup. Five years after statehood the Pawnees were squeezed off this small tract too, and moved south to a reservation in Indian Territory.

A historical marker in Pawnee Park says a Spanish military expedition led by Pedro de Villasur arrived here from Santa Fe in 1720, reconnoitering the valley of the Platte, which they called the Río de Jesús María, the deepest penetration of the Spanish into the Great Plains until almost a century later. The marker says they were attacked by Pawnees and Otoes, and 46 men, including the commander, a priest, and 11 Pueblo Indians accompanying them, were killed, the greatest number of Europeans ever killed by Indians in what is now Nebraska. There is no mention of how many Indians were killed by Europeans in Nebraska, then or later.

I stopped for lunch at Glur's Tavern on 11th Street. Founded beside the railroad tracks in 1876, Glur's claims to be the oldest continuously-operated tavern west of the Missouri River. The little tavern occupies a small two-story frame house with a wrap-around porch. Legend has it that Buffalo Bill Cody once slapped a hundred dollar bill on the bar. I had a real hamburger with fried onions and a beer, served by Carolyn, a middle-aged woman in a t-shirt her son-in-law gave her which proclaims "I've got an attitude." She'd served burgers and beer in Glur's for 18 years, "the oldest barmaid in town," she claimed.

"You must like it," I said.

"Too dumb to do anything else," she laughed.

Two long coal trains barreled by while I talked with four old-timers who had frequented Glur's for 60 years. Arnold worked at a shoe factory across the street as a young man, and had cheeseburgers and root beer here for lunch. During Prohibition, gin rummy players kept the place open, he said. When spirits returned in the thirties, tap beer was a nickel.

Heading south across the Platte River valley, I found no historical marker where my map shows the Oxbow Trail intersecting 81 at the present junction with Nebraska 64. But I did find lots of oxen, or rather heifers and steers, in the biggest feed lot I'd found on the highway. I pulled off at the Witt Feed Yard.

Four men were loading a double-decker semi with cattle bound for slaughter. Burnell Witt was in charge, a powerfully-built man of 68 in Big Mack overalls and a Platte River cap with a steer on front. Helping were his son, a hired man, and the truck driver. The Witts were in the pen, pushing the cattle along, while the driver, who'd temporarily changed from cowboy boots to rubber knee boots, yelled encouragement and applied an occasional electric prod from outside. A

*Glur's Tavern in Columbus, the oldest tavern west of the Missouri River (top), and Ronspie's Implement, beside Highway 81 north of Norfolk.*

blue healer dog nipped at the hooves of stragglers.

When the truck was full and the driver pulled away, I joined the other three men for their break in the office, a room in the corner of the barn, maybe 10 feet square. The floor was covered with tracked in dirt and manure. From the depth around the walls I guessed it hadn't been swept for decades. The men ignored the constant buzzing of flies as they ate cookies with unwashed hands. On the wall behind Burnell's desk a rifle rack held two cattle prods and a BB gun.

At first Burnell was reluctant to talk. He said he'd been interviewed before and misquoted. But when he learned I'd grown up on an Oklahoma farm, and that my brother was in the cattle business, he relaxed a bit. He said he'd been feeding cattle here for 30 years, buying 800 pound steers and heifers from South Dakota to Kansas, putting another 400 pounds on them in four months with ground alfalfa, corn and distiller's grain, a byproduct of ethanol, and selling them for slaughter. He fed about 12,000 head each year in pens which criss-cross the hundred-acre yard.

A hormone implant salesman in shiny boots and rodeo belt buckle stopped by to deliver a couple of implant guns, used to inject a growth-enhancing hormone capsule behind the ear of each animal when it arrives. Though Burnell doesn't believe the stories that products like "Steeroid" are dangerous to human consumers, he said he'd rather not use growth hormones. But he has to, he said, to compete with the big boys of agribusiness, such as Monfort, owned by meatpacking giant Con-Agra which runs its own 100,000 head feedlot in Colorado. He'd rather go organic, but didn't see enough market for naturally-fattened cattle.

I asked Burnell if he was making any money. "Not for so damn long I can't remember," he said. With cattle going for 64 cents a pound on the hoof, he said there was no profit to be made, and that year his feed prices were up. He hoped for a short-term upturn in the market, but saw the future as bleak. "We're not very friendly to this operation anymore," he said. "I should have quit long ago when I was ahead, and laid back on Social Security." At age 68 he was still working 12 hours a day, seven days a week, but he said he couldn't quit because he was too far in the hole. Burnell admitted he didn't understand all the forces at work, but he knew the increasing control of every stage of the process by giant agribusiness corporations was a factor. Burnell got a phone call from a buyer, and his tone shifted from wistful to swearing defiance. He wasn't ready to throw the towel in yet.

While we talked, Burnell and the other men each had a soda, Burnell munching crackers and the younger men their cookies. The blue healer sat patiently in the middle of the circle, his bushy tail sweeping an arc of dirt from the center of the room, waiting for the last bite of cracker or cookie he knew he'd get from each man. I asked Burnell what he thought about having a feedlot on the Oxbow Trail. "I've lived here all my life and I don't know a thing about it," he said. "I've been too busy making a living." I thanked Burnell for his time, and he went out to saddle his "lot pony" for a ride around the herds, "looking for anything that's not right."

A few miles south of the Witt Feed Yard the highway rises from the Platte valley back to high flat plains. The brilliant red heads of milo now competed with corn and cattle and beans. This is rich and prosperous land, the farms large and houses infrequent. Fertile, productive, and for most strangers, probably boring. At times the highway was a tunnel through 10-foot corn. Rebounding from its eastward dip to Columbus, 81 jogs 13 miles west through Shelby and Osceola before heading south again, the longest offset to the southward traveler anywhere on the Pan American Highway.

Osceola seemed a strange name for a small Nebraska town. A historical marker says the town was named for the Florida Seminole chief in 1871. Osceola led a fierce war of resistance to U.S. forces in the Everglades, but eventually was captured, and died a prisoner of war. I was fascinated by how and why a Nebraska town chose Osceola's name, so I set out to ask. In the senior citizens' center, an elderly chap at the pool table said there are two stories: one is that the town is named for some bad Indian, and the other is that an early Swedish settler looked over the hill and said "Oh, see Ole!"

Not satisfied with either explanation, I visited the register of deeds and the county superintendent offices in the courthouse, but got no answers. At the town library, Sara Beck showed me Mildred Flodman's book, *Early Days in Polk County*. Flodman says the town was named "in 1870, through the influence of V. P. Davis, who had come from Osceola, Iowa, who thought it would be fun to say that he had moved to Nebraska, but was still in Osceola. As Osceola was also an Indian name, the commissioners went along with the idea." Now if I knew why a small town in Iowa would name itself for a Florida Seminole chief, why, according to Flodman, the county commissioners seemed set on an Indian name, and most of all, why nobody really has answers to such questions. Another reminder of our vanishing history on the plains.

Unlike some of its neighbors, Osceola looks healthy. I saw no empty houses, for example, even though the population had declined from over 1,200 in 1920 to 879. Presumably that means the number of persons per house has declined, as families have grown smaller and the median age rises. Unsatisfied with my grasp of Osceola's history, I drove across town to the Land of the Lakes Husker Coop, the CENEX-related grain elevator, for a fix on the town's present reality.

In size and function, the Osceola elevator is not unlike the dozens of others I'd passed on my journey. The one obvious change is that by central Nebraska the steel construction common from Manitoba to South Dakota had given way to concrete, which I would find almost universal from here south. The shift is related to the availability of concrete, the era in which the elevator was built, and to some extent, the frost factor of the north, the ability of deep winter freezes to heave, crack and shift foundations, endangering what sits upon them. Steel contracts, expands and twists, thus withstanding much more stress than concrete.

While both steel and concrete replaced the wooden elevators still standing gauntly beside weedy railroad branch lines across the Midwest, the concrete elevator became common here after about 1900, when the "slip form" construction method was implemented. When the concrete of one level has dried, the steel form is raised and the next level of the cylindrical silo is poured atop the previous stage.

I talked with elevator manger Dave Coffin, a friendly, heavy-set and bearded young man who looked as if he belonged there. Dave said with the heavy rains and blight in Kansas and Oklahoma, wheat prices were over $4 per bushel, and everybody wished they'd planted wheat. But in seasons of average rainfall, eastern Nebraska grows good corn and soy beans, so winter wheat has been largely relegated to the more arid south and west. The Osceola elevator, probably the biggest business in town, employs four people full-time plus temporary help during the corn and bean harvests. While the elevator ships much of its grain out by rail and truck, Dave said about half the corn is ground and mixed with supplements, returning as feed for cattle and hogs to the farms from which it came.

The next town is Stromsburg, the "Swedish Capital of Nebraska," declares a sign painted on the grain elevator, an official proclamation by the governor in 1966. The town was founded on this hill in 1870 by Swedish immigrants led here from Galva, Illinois by Lewis Headstrom. Hence the name, "Strom" for the leader, and "burg," Swedish for a village on a hill. A banner beside 81 read Volkomen (welcome). The housing project for the elderly is Swede Haven; the main restaurant in town is Bit of Sweden. The third week of June each year a traditional Swedish Festival celebrates the summer solstice. The town has five Protestant churches and no Catholic, probably the first all-Protestant town since somewhere in North Dakota.

The downtown hints of the old world. Brick streets had replaced the gravel of Manitoba and North Dakota and the asphalt and concrete of South Dakota. I visited the staff at the *Stromsburg Headlight and Polk County News*, who collectively estimated the town to be three-quarters Swedish, of which they were quite proud. Though Stromsburg's homogeneity is uncommon, census statistics bear out the shift from Norwegians as the second most numerous ethnic group across the Dakotas, to Swedish, English, and Czech peoples in Nebraska.

On Prairie Creek, a tributary of the Big Blue River on the south edge of town, Stromsburg provides a pleasant shady park with water, rest rooms, even electricity for those who want it, and invites anyone who wishes to camp for free. I accepted their hospitality. After supper at the Wagon Wheel cafe, I pitched my tent in darkness on a grassy knoll far from the highway rumble. Recalling having been run out of towns in several states in my hitch-hiking days for the crime of sleeping in parks, I fell asleep, secure in the trust of a friendly town.

In Stromsburg I sensed the presence of something that is sadly disappearing in the U.S., even in rural America – not just friendliness, but sincere and open trust of strangers. Perhaps this is related to the town's own immigrant heritage, and specifically to its homogeneous Swedish character. Though ethnic diversity enriches a community, it sometimes also produces conflict, discouraging the collective work and mutual respect necessary to build and maintain a community in which all take pride. Shared values and goals encourage community building, and mutual respect can be extended, even to strangers. Like it or not, homogeneity is disappearing along the 81 corridor across the plains.

At dawn I awakened to the garrulous quarrel of a pair of blue jays, probably over the fruit of the mulberry tree under which I lay. I brushed off the berries and rolled up my gear and went to the Bit of Sweden for coffee – and for pancakes so big they were served on a platter. Over breakfast I visited with Mrs. Rystrom, whom I'd met at the newspaper office, and her husband Ron, a retired civil engineer who'd spent his professional life building bridges up and down Highway 81. His great-great-grandparents and their five children came from Sweden in 1870 and homesteaded just south of town. When I took my bill to the counter, I found by the cash register a big bowl of money, not just coins, but dollar bills, from which patrons made their own change.

The next town is York. On the middle fork of the Blue River, York is the third largest Nebraska town on 81, founded in 1870 by settlers from York, Pennsylvania. There are 20 churches, one Catholic and 19 Protestant. Sr. Eileen Neville, a professor in Yankton, grew up among the Catholic minority here, daughter of a rural school teacher. Eileen said that Elijah Levitt, a Ukrainian Jewish banker, was among the most respected old-timers in York. The massive limestone German American Bank building still stands on 81, now occupied by Nebraska Public Power.

But Sr. Eileen also remembered the Friday night when the American Protective Association, an anti-Catholic organization akin to the KKK, burned a cross on her family's lawn. William Cowper Brann, publisher of the *Iconoclast* in Waco, Texas, called the APA the "Aggregation of Pusillanimous Asses." The APA was long gone, and I found York a mellow town. I headed on south, across the Nebraska City Cutoff of the Oregon Trail which put York on the east-west map, and its successor Interstate 80, which keeps it there.

South of McCool Junction, I entered the high plains "Divide" country of Willa Cather, a territory so tenuous that in the early days most of the towns changed their names, usually to court or show gratitude to a railroad. Geneva and Hebron, the largest towns before Kansas, have kept their names. But Hesperia, Belle Prairie, Prairie Star, and Elm Grove traded their lovely home-spun names for Fairmont, Strang, Bruning and Belvidere. Belle Prairie, which I'm sure it was when tall grass waved as far as the eye could see, was briefly called Media and then Bixby before windmill dealer A.L. Strang gave the town a windmill in 1886 in return for eternal local fame. Pat Hennessey, the namesake of my hometown of Hennessey, Oklahoma, had to be strapped to a wagon wheel and burned to get a town named after him. What price glory? Anyway, I drove down the one block gravel main street of Strang, and sure enough, right in the middle of Main, in front of the Strang Tavern, stands a historic windmill.

Other towns lost their home-grown names for a less noble reason, to fit the alphabet soup of the railroad lines, the executives of which apparently couldn't find their way down the tracks if the towns weren't alphabetized. Fairmont fits between Crete, Dorchester and Exeter to the east, and Grafton, Harvard and Inland to the west, while Belvidere is a bead in the string of Alexandria, Belvidere, Carleton, and Davenport, names which have nothing to do with the places, the people who had come, or the people who lived there before, but often were chosen to stroke the ego of a railroad man. For a slightly better reason, Prairie Star surrendered its elegant name to the glory of resident Frank Bruning. According to Eilert Wilhelms, Frank's great nephew, a railroad boss stayed with his uncle Frank, one of five Bruning brothers to homestead in the area, so the town was renamed in his honor.

Three miles south of Fairmont I stopped to read a historical marker at the Fairmont Army Air Field, World War II home of the 451st Heavy Bombardment Squadron, a kind of finishing school for war-bound bomber crews. Don West, who runs a hardware and construction business in Fairmont, told me that Lt. Col. Paul Tibbets recruited pilots from Fairmont Field in 1944. Tibbets headed the top secret atomic bomb training mission and piloted the "Enola Gay," the plane named for his mother, which dropped the first atomic bomb on Japan. West organized a reunion of Fairmont pilots in June 1996. A historical marker, four cavernous Quonset huts and two dust-drifted runways mark the dubious place in history of this blood-red field of milo.

Of the southern Nebraska towns, Geneva is perhaps most attractive. Like most larger towns here, the downtown streets are brick. In the square of this county seat is the elegant gothic-looking 1893 Fillmore County Courthouse, named for that memorable last Whig president, Millard Fillmore. A monument on the courthouse lawn honors the "pioneers who broke the sod that men to come might live."

But what intrigued me most was a farm a few miles southwest of town, the home of communal life for most of a century. High school history teacher Doug Rung said that in the 1920s and 30s it was the county poor farm for indigent people. Then it was a group home for foster children, and then a nursing home. Now it was the Holy Protection Gnostic Orthodox Monastery. The monks, whose name sounded as if they took themselves quite seriously, carved wooden religious icons. I drove out, hoping to visit with Brother Simeon, the chief iconographer, or perhaps with Father Seraphim, named for the six-winged angel who appeared to the prophet Isaiah. With two wings he covered his feet, with two his face, and with two he did fly. The gnostics were an early Christian sect that valued inquiry into spiritual truth, even above faith, and I was curious to ask the gnostics, "Whadaya know?" But it was past visiting hours, and they wouldn't open the door of the rambling ranch house, not even a crack. Soon after my visit the monks left the state, and the monastery became a home for troubled youth, its fifth incarnation as a home for non-nuclear families.

Just north of Hebron I crossed the main branch of the Oregon Trail, the route of half a million adventurers, pioneers and gold seekers who, beginning in 1842, traveled by wagon from Independence, Kansas, as far west as Oregon and California. This was also the route of the Pony Express before completion of the transcontinental railroad. Hebron is a pleasant town in the valley of the Little Blue River. It is the home of Kim Johnson, newspaper publisher and president of the Pan American Highway Association.

Hebron was currently in the international news, or at least its namesake was. According to Lilian Fitzpatrick's *Nebraska Place-Names*, Hebron was named for the Palestinian city of Hebron by Disciples of Christ pioneers who arrived here in 1869. Abraham, patriarch of both Arabs and Jews, chose Hebron as his home in the "promised land," avoiding the sinful cities of Sodom and Gomorrah. As I drove into Hebron, National Public Radio reported progress toward a long-sought agreement between Israel and the Palestine Liberation Organization, which would return parts of the West Bank of the Jordan to the Palestinians. The sticking point was Hebron, where 400 hard-core Jewish settlers feared control by the PLO, but refused to move. Hebron, Nebraska was much more peaceful that evening. Her twin Biblical town of Gilead lies to the east. Ten miles south is Chester, Nebraska, and then Kansas.

# KANSAS

*"Where seldom is heard a discouraging word,*
*and the skies are not cloudy all day."*

~ Brewster Higley, "Home on the Range," Kansas State Song

Just before the twister whisked Dorothy off the Kansas plains to Oz, she stood in Aunt Em's doorway, seeing "nothing but the great gray prairie on every side." When I arrived in Kansas the wheat fields were bare and brown. A great dry emptiness yawned below a dome of blue.

I reached Belleville, the first town in northern Kansas, in time for the 85th annual meeting of the Pan American Highway Association. I was greeted at the bar by 82 year old Merle Miller, former Association president. He is the son of A. Q. Miller, Association founder and tireless promoter of Highway 81, the Belleville journalist for whom the journalism school at Kansas State University is named. I spent a delightful evening with Merle, current Association President Kim Johnson, and other highway buffs and promoters.

Before dinner we toured the new Belleville and Kansas Information Center and the Republic County Museum. The Information Center hopes to be self-sustaining from the sale of Kansas products and crafts. The museum features the largest collection of hand tools I've ever seen, most donated by Bertil Olson of Courtland, Kansas; a display of Meridian/U.S. 81 memorabilia provided by Merle Miller; and reminders of the ethnicity of Republic County, the only county on the highway where the number one country of origin is Czechoslovakia.

At 82 most folks have long since kicked back in the recliner for a deserved rest. But not Merle. The long-time publisher of the *Belleville Telescope* was still hard at work, whether at his life-long task of promoting the highway, or advancing his political views and encouraging citizen involvement. Merle was first to leave after dinner. He had to get back to the office to tabulate results of his annual reader poll. He makes up 20 questions (some of them loaded, according to Belleville Mayor Ron Sankey) and asks *Telescope* readers to respond. He then distributes the results to members of Congress, "so they will know what people in the heartland really think."

Merle said he used to try to balance his paper's political coverage, but he gave that up because "the Democratic Party has lost its leadership." Now he unabashedly promotes Republican views. I wondered whether, in all their years of promoting highways and regional development, Merle or his father had ever been troubled by conflict between journalist and promoter roles. "No," he answered. "We were always too busy trying to make a living."

When the road association began its work 89 years ago, the idea of a highway across Kansas — let alone across the United States or the North American continent — was a pipe dream. When Alexander Quintella Miller read in 1910 that 181,000 cars were on the road in the United States, he envisioned a future when people could get in a private car in Belleville and actually drive in minutes to Concordia, 17 miles south. The elder Miller and his associates reached out to interested parties in adjacent states to north and south, beginning the decades-long work of selling an idea, designating a route along the 6th principal meridian, and turning muddy trails into a connected and marked gravel road. The group's first meeting was convened in Salina, Kansas in 1911 as the Meridian Road Association. In the absence of a road, delegates traveled to the meeting by train, the alternative to horse-drawn travel which had come to Belleville in 1884.

Merle said that in 1916, May 1 was designated "Sign-Posting Day," but bad weather canceled travel north of Kansas. In 1919, with World War I behind them, the International Meridian Road Association changed the name of the route to the Meridian Highway. By 1920 all the streams on the road were bridged except the Missouri River at Yankton and the Canadian at Minco, Oklahoma. In the 1920s, Merle said, his father spent $500 from his own pocket every summer to send men north and south to tack the black and white Meridian Highway signs to telephone posts along the way.

On a trip to calculate distances between points for a AAA Blue Book, A.Q. was accompanied by Kansas Gov. Hodges, Merle said. The governor observed that the mileage readings would be inaccurate because the rear wheels were spinning in the mud. A.Q. explained that the odometer was driven by the front wheels.

The Meridian Bridge at Yankton completed the route in 1924, and the federal government officially designated the road as U.S. 81 in 1927. In a 1932 *C.S.M. Magazine* article, Association president Miller bragged it was "the only highway entirely completed north and south across the United States as an all-weather road and the only highway reaching from Canada to the Mexican border, carrying one federal marker." By then the highway was well-established; train passenger service ended in Belleville in 1935, a casualty of increased automobile travel. Did those foresighted planners see that in another generation an improved road and a faster car would whisk their sons and daughters off the Great Plains to Omaha or Kansas City, taking their toll on the small town itself?

Also in 1924, delegates from most countries of Central and South America met in Washington, DC, to form the Pan American Union and to map a highway to link the capitals south of the Río Grande. Capitalizing on the direct connection of the highway to the evolving international road, the Meridian Highway Association became the Pan American Highway Association in 1936.

By about 1950, Merle said, the entire U.S portion of the highway was paved, as was most of the road through Mexico and Central America. In 1967, long-time Association president Merle Miller lead a caravan of 23 automobiles and 63 people on a three-month journey from Winnipeg to Panamá, by ship around the Darién Gap to Colombia, and on to Buenos Aires, Argentina. Merle drove the flag car, a new Buick Roadmaster. The expedition must have been a marvel in the mountains of Mexico and the jungles of Panamá.

Current Association president Kim Johnson said the average daily traffic count on the highway in Belleville is 4,000 vehicles, a third of them trucks. He lamented that the 462 miles of highway from Watertown, South Dakota, to Minneapolis, Kansas, which I'd just traversed, were primarily still two-lane. Where heavy traffic bottle-necks onto the narrow, aging road, conditions range from rugged to unsafe. In fact, according to the Nebraska Department of Motor Vehicles, the stretch of U.S. 81 I'd just driven from Fairmont to Strang, Nebraska, was the deadliest piece of road in the state; 19 people had died on the 20 miles in the previous 11 years. But the Association's goal of closing that gap with a four-lane highway is being realized, several miles each year.

The next morning the formal Association meeting was to be held in the historic Main Street Station, a garage and gas station restored as a restaurant. I had been asked to address the assembly about my project. But first I drove around the brick streets of Belleville, named for the first postmaster's wife, Arabelle. I stopped to visit Bud Hanzlick, reportedly the world's only maker of bois-d'arc furniture. His house and shop are across from the Belleville park, where my family and I had picnicked on a couple of Oklahoma trips. At first glance the rambling blue house is distinguished from its neighbors only by the six-foot bois-d'arc stockade fence which surrounds it. But inside is a unique world.

About ten years ago, Bud's wife, Pat, asked him to make her some lawn furniture that would not blow away with the famous Kansas wind, which not only whirled Dorothy away to Oz, but which routinely tumbles plastic and aluminum furniture to the neighbors' yards. Bud looked around. His eye fell on a pile of aging fence posts, and the Bekan Rustic Furniture Company was born.

I introduced myself to Bud and told him I was interested in his bois-d'arc furniture. "Are you from Texas, or Oklahoma?" he asked. He had me pegged. Bud explained that only along the Red River, the Oklahoma-Texas boundary where the tree is indigenous, is it called "bois-d'arc." Farther north it is the Osage orange, horse apple, or yellow wood, he said, and in Kansas, the scrubby tree is commonly known as hedge. The Osage Indians, who now live in northern Oklahoma, gave the tree one of its names, but the French called it bois-d'arc because it was prized among Indians across the plains for making bows. Bud said bois-d'arc bows were an important trading item, having been found among tribes as far away as Montana.

As a farm boy in Oklahoma, I was familiar with the thick hedge rows which formed inviolable livestock boundaries, and I also have experience with bois-d'arc posts. I know that to get a staple into one you need three things: a short staple, a big hammer, and lots of luck. Bud explained that in early pioneer days, when farmers couldn't afford barbed wire, the state of Kansas actually paid farmers to plant hedge rows as living fences. The trees spread by roots, quickly forming impenetrable barriers. But soon farmers were harvesting sprouts for posts too, and the furniture Bud makes is recycled posts from fences built half a century ago.

How can that be? Bud said bois-d'arc is not only the second densest wood in North America, second only to black iron wood from Mexico and Honduras, but also among the most durable, practically impervious to water, insects, and rot. He said that a century ago, the State Bank of Commerce, Texas, would loan money for a new house only if the foundation was made of bois-d'arc. He said the streets of Dallas were once paved with bois-d'arc bricks.

The wood is a unique orangish-yellow, requiring no stain, oil, or varnish for beauty or preservation. All of Bud's tools are carbide-tipped; steel is quickly dulled and ruined by this hard and resiny wood. The legs, arms and structure of the tables and chairs are made from aged wood, but the table tops and bench slats are from green bois-d'arc, because, Bud said, "there isn't a man alive that can rip cured hedge. And they don't make such a saw." Because it is also virtually impossible to drive a nail or put a screw in bois-d'arc, Bud and his two assistants construct all their furniture with an exposed tenon system; each piece has a saw-lathed dowel end which fits a hole in the next piece, so no material whatsoever is used in the furniture except bois-d'arc wood; even the glue which holds the joints together is mixed with bois-d'arc saw dust. A single-person chair weighs 70 pounds, and a two-person love seat over a hundred.

Bud is a tall and powerful man. He speaks in a slow drawl, which seems to have absorbed the Oklahoma Red River accent along with the bois-d'arc dust he's breathed. But he's native to Belleville, having grown up on a nearby farm. He showed me around his shop, in a garage he built onto the house he and Pat moved in from the country 40 years ago, soon after their marriage. He took me up the limestone steps he'd salvaged from his grandparents' basement, into his museum-like house, and showed me the unique creations with which the home is furnished. I leafed through a pile of national magazines in which he's featured, *Wood Magazine*, *Log Home Living*, *Midwest Living*, and Robert Redford's catalogue, *Sundance*.

Bud uses nearly every scrap for something, and what's of no other use he burns for winter heat. He said bois-d'arc burns almost as hot as coal, and that one major wood stove's label warns users not to burn coal or Osage orange. "You wouldn't dare burn the wood in an open fireplace," he said. "It explodes, flinging sparks clear across a room." Besides tables and chairs, Bud showed me bowls, trenchers, clocks, flower stands, walking sticks, cutting boards, and custom-designed items he's made from this unique amber wood. "Your imagination is your only limitation," he said. He gave me a pen and letter-holder made from an end bit of post before we said good-bye.

The next town on the map is Concordia. But between Belleville and Concordia lie a couple of ghost towns. Actually the towns have all but disappeared, but in the second, the "ghosts" persist. The first, just past the Republic-Cloud county line, was Minersville. I searched in vain for remnants of the town where 500 coal miners lived in 1882. Some of the low-grade coal they dug remains, and somewhere, I was told, are the foundations of the no doubt makeshift houses in which they lived.

I did find the other town, a place to which the spirits had just returned. Three miles north of Concordia, on what was then U.S. 81, are the remains of Camp Concordia, a German prisoner of war camp. Camp Concordia was not the only POW camp on 81, but it was among the largest. A small group of Germans was held just north of Yankton, South Dakota; in fact, they drove pilings in the Missouri River to stop it from eating the Meridian bridge. There were large camps at Fort Reno, Oklahoma, and at Bowie, Fort Hood, and San Antonio, Texas, a few of some 140 major POW camps which housed at their peak in June 1945, over 425,000 prisoners of war, mostly Germans, but including a few Italians and Japanese. Between 1942 and 1945, over 4,000 men were imprisoned at Camp Concordia.

The 160-acre camp consisted of over 300 buildings, including a hospital, theater, library, gymnasium and newspaper. Now the camp was a mirror image of the heavy bomber field back in Nebraska, another sea of burnished red milo, its perimeters marked by the water tower on the north and a restored guard tower on the south, beside old 81.

In Concordia I visited the Cloud County Museum, where I talked with Beryl Ward, who more than 50 years ago helped build and run the camp, and with World War II veteran Wayne Switzer. "My family came from Germany," Switzer said, "and here I was in Germany fighting Nazis. I was shocked to find out when I came home that the farm work I'd left behind had been done by my enemies." Germans had replaced local farm boys, working in crews of one guard and three prisoners on area farms. The POWs were paid a minimum of 10 cents per hour. Switzer said he eventually came to realize that the Germans were not necessarily bad men, but like himself, victims of the Nazi regime.

The museum houses much memorabilia from the camp, including numerous art works produced by prisoners. Local residents have maintained contact with some of the Germans, one of whom became a famous architect. On October 21, 1995, a dozen former POWs, now in their seventies, returned from Germany to participate in the 50th anniversary commemoration of the end of Camp Concordia. Apparently, both in war and in peace, Concordia lives up to its name, though north of town a citizen's sign reading "Please drive safely; Unmarked nuclear warheads travel these roads" had been vandalized with orange paint.

Concordia is also home to two impressive historic structures, the Nazareth Convent of the Sisters of St. Joseph, founded in 1884, and the Brown Grand Theatre, built in 1906 by Col. Napoleon Bonaparte Brown. The 650-seat audito-

*One of Bud Hanzlick's bois-d'arc love seats, in Botanica Gardens in Wichita (top), and a restored guard tower at the World War II German prisoner of war camp at Concordia.*

rium operated as a legitimate theatre from 1907 to 1925, when it became a silent movie theatre. The convent, the theatre and the St. Joseph Hospital are testimony to the historic presence of French Canadians in Concordia. In fact, Cloud County remains the most significant French Canadian community on the highway south of Manitoba.

Between Concordia and Minneapolis, I stopped to examine a monument that has intrigued me for years, a tall stone arch on the Pipe Creek bluff east of the highway. A closer look at the arch piqued my curiosity, so I dropped in at the Ottawa County Historical Museum down the road in Minneapolis to ask who built the thing, and why. I talked with Mr. Condray, whose farmer father Warren achieved local fame by discovering a previously unclassified dinosaur in Ottawa County. Mr. Condray showed me pictures of the *Sylvisaurus condrayi*. He also dug out a yellowed newspaper clipping from the *Minneapolis Messenger*, which said the arch was built about 20 years ago by Ron Parks, just for the heck of it.

"I had no special reason for building the arch," said Parks, a local boy turned English teacher. "I like to work with stone and I like arches," he said. "It's not a monument to anything." What a disappointment. All those years I'd imagined it built by prehistoric Indians, or at least by some prairie-crazed pioneer. But on the other hand, it's nice to know there are still people around who go to all that trouble just for fun.

Actually I'd like to meet Mr. Parks; he reminds me a bit of myself. A couple of years earlier I'd bought my 14-year-old son Walter's idea to build a tower on our hill overlooking the Missouri valley. But our monument is at least slightly functional, a hexagonal structure with three floors, the first glassed in for winter, the second with open walls, the third exposed to the sky. I never know what to say when neighbors ask what it's for.

A mile south of the Solomon River, a lone windmill still whirred and pumped up water for a pasture full of cows, its tail riding the north wind, pointing me south. Not many years ago travelers across the Plains could monitor changes in the wind by these weather vanes as they drove. But now few windmills remain.

I stopped to visit the Land Institute, established in 1976 by Wes Jackson on the banks of the Smoky Hill River, southeast of Salina. I had talked with Jackson a few years ago about his work to replace extractive industrial agriculture with sustainable agricultural practices, and I wanted to see what progress had been made.

Wes was at a conference in Tennessee, so I talked with Jon Piper, director of research in natural systems agriculture. A sturdy, bearded man in his late thirties, Jon had been with the Institute for more than half its history. Originally from New Hampshire, he tried the West Coast for awhile too, before settling in the geographic dead-center of the country. Now he spoke in the thoughtful tone of a man of the plains.

Jon said he and his colleagues were working to design a sustainable agriculture which functions in fundamental ways like a native prairie eco-system. The goal is to develop perennial plants which will bear grains for human and/or live-stock consumption and to grow them in diverse systems, rather than as mono-cultures, the common goal of most current agriculture. Researchers are focusing on several species of native grasses, nitrogen-fixing legumes, and several family members of the state flower, the sunflower, which appear to hold potential for this kind of agriculture.

The Institute operates on the assumption that natural diversity is good. In addition to various research projects, they have restored plots to native prairie vegetation. The Land Institute also owns 100 acres of virgin prairie, in which, Jon said, they have identified 230 species of prairie plants.

For the past 15 years they have pursued answers to four research questions: Can a perennial grain yield well? Can a perennial polyculture produce its own nitrogen fertility? Can such a culture over-yield (can you get more seed from such a polyculture than from the respective monocultures)? And finally, can a peren-nial polyculture effectively manage weeds, insects and plant diseases? Jon said they had evidence to support progress toward all those goals.

Though Jackson and his colleagues never ruled out the possibility of genetic engineering, they have relied on more traditional and natural methods. For exam-ple, they have cross-pollinated sorghum and milo, common crops on the arid Kansas plains, with a hardy wild relative, Johnson grass, to develop a hybrid which is low growing and perennial but has good grain qualities such as large seeds in large compact heads. Such an approach, Jon said, "takes advantage of thousands of years of human domestication of these grains, and then seeks with a few steps to create a hybrid perennial intermediate." He compared their work to that of German researchers who have produced a hybrid of rye and a peren-nial relative. But mostly, Jon said, the Institute relies on natural "open pollina-tion," and selection of the top 25 percent of each season's crop to develop new strains.

I told Jon about my own efforts to control the South Dakota scourge, leafy spurge, a non-native noxious weed which proliferates by both seeds and a deep root system. The seven native grasses I planted several years ago on a particular-ly infested four-acre hill top so far appeared quite effective in controlling the leafy spurge. I am also experimenting with Eastern European flea beetles in a spurge-infested tree grove, where chemical use is a particularly bad option. In both their larval and adult stages, these beetles allegedly eat only leafy spurge, though how effectively, remained to be seen. Jon said the Land Institute is not involved in biological control research as such, but is concentrating rather on providing a polycultural environment which will allow natural enemies (predato-ry insects such as lady bugs, lace wings, and assassin bugs) to thrive and to con-trol damaging insects.

Jon described the group's "community assembly" experiment, which involved planting a large diversity of seeds, then letting nature take her course. Recognizing that nature's planting methods can't be fully duplicated, they wanted to learn more about the relationship between plants in a larger community, and to see what sort of diverse but stable polyculture would emerge from an initial planting of 16 prairie species.

Researchers attempt to reproduce the natural effects of periodic prairie fires by controlled burns on individual test plots in March every three to five years. They are careful not to burn large areas in a single season, Jon said, because some animal species are "fire-positive" and others "fire-negative." They want to avoid selecting and de-selecting particular species of birds, mammals, and reptiles by ensuring that they always have the refuge they need to survive.

Another project is the Sunshine Farm, an experiment to see whether a farm raising conventional crops and livestock can provide its own nitrogen fertility and its own energy, or in other words, be self-sustaining without the introduction of petrochemicals and energy. Grains, oil-producing plants such as sunflowers, and nitrogen-fixing crops such as alfalfa are grown in rotation. This project is focused on sustainable answers for the here and now, whereas the perennial polyculture research may not produce widespread application for the present generation of farmers. Both have the same ultimate goal: a sustainable agriculture.

Jon said local farmers have grown less skeptical of the Institute's work. During the farm crisis of the eighties, many began to question their own assumptions about the stability of industrialized agriculture, and about the wisdom of over-production as a primary goal. He said that even agricultural universities and the U.S. Department of Agriculture are now "respectfully interested" in their work. Recalling the silted muddy rivers and eroded hillsides I'd passed, the work of the Land Institute seemed to me not only important, but urgent. In much of the Great Plains, more than half the top soil has eroded away in just a century of conventional agriculture, and the land now produces only with massive annual infusions of water-polluting petrochemicals and fertilizer.

I took the self-guided tour of the grounds, through the big blue stem and native flowers, past the green house, the vegetable garden, the orchard, and the classroom. I found Wes Jackson's earth-sheltered home on the bank of the Smoky Hill River, now brown with its burden of top-soil, goading Wes on in his work.

Back on Highway 81, I headed south through more plowed wheat fields toward Newton, where I planned to visit Vern and Marion Preheim and to camp for the night. The road took me through Lindsborg, near the terminal point of Coronado's 1540 trek into the heartland in his gold-crazed search for the legendary "Seven Cities of Cíbola." Instead he found what he called Quivira, the grass-thatched lodges of the Wichitas on Cow Creek, a few miles west. Lindsborg is today the Swedish Capital of Kansas, the Kansas equivalent of Stromsburg, Nebraska, though this burg is a borg. According to John Rydjord's *Kansas Place-Names*, Lindsborg was named in 1869 for five local Swedish families whose names began with "Lind." Lindsborg also celebrates summer solstice at Midsummer Fest.

At McPherson, the oil country of U.S. 81 begins. The city is home to a large refinery and the Jay Hawk Pipeline Company; the odor of crude oil permeates the air. The city is named for Gen. James Birdseye McPherson, the highest-ranking Union general to die in the Civil War. Though the town's Scottish population is less than one percent, the McPherson Scottish Arts Society capitalizes on the town's name with the Scottish Festival and Highland Games each September. I crossed the 1822-72 Santa Fe Trail just south of McPherson, the path of thousands headed from Independence, Missouri to Santa Fe, New Mexico.

When I got to Newton, Vern was at choir practice, so I drove south of town to Camp Hawk, a county park on Sand Creek, and set up my tent. There were no other humans around, but I was greeted by a deafening roar of locusts, celebrating the sunset of the end of summer evening, or perhaps lamenting the coming frost that would soon end their lives. Before that time, there was so much left to do. Each must find a sturdy branch in an elm or cedar or Osage orange, dig his claws into the bark, climb out of his skin, and in the case of females, find a place to lay her eggs to ensure the next generation. I walked toward Sand Creek, feeling "home on the range." No buffalo were roaming, nor antelope playing, but I did find deer tracks in the mud.

Back in historic Newton, I cruised the shady downtown streets, lined with well-preserved Victorian houses. They were the homes of cattle and railroad barons of the past century, as well as Mennonite patriarchs such as Bernhard Warkentin, the German Russian who arrived in 1874, bringing Turkey Red hard winter wheat to the plains, and his dream of establishing a Mennonite homeland on the Kansas prairie. He succeeded in both. Kansas became the wheat state, and the Newton area has among the highest concentrations of Mennonites in the nation. Several towns in the vicinity, Goessel, Moundridge, and others, bear the Mennonite imprint, and Bethel College, founded in 1887, has educated half a dozen generations of their young.

But Newton had a history before Warkentin arrived. From 1871 to 1873, Newton was the wild west, the terminal of the great Chisholm Trail, the most famous of several trails over which cattle were driven from Texas, across Indian Territory, to railheads in Kansas. Over a million cattle lumbered up the Chisholm Trail to meet the advancing railroad, first in Abilene, then in Newton, and still later in Wichita and then Caldwell. In the early 1870s Newton was a town full of thirsty cowboys, gun-slingers, gamblers, and ladies of the night, or "soiled doves," as the local newspaper called them. In 1872 alone, Newton documented a dozen murders, though an unknown number went unrecorded. By 1873 the railroad was extended south, and Wichita became the new cowtown, leaving Newton more peaceful for arriving Mennonites and other pioneer farmers.

I set out in search of the historical markers for the Chisholm Trail, of which my Newton map showed three. There had to be one near the railroad station, so I stopped at the post office across from the tracks to inquire. Nobody who worked there could tell me where the marker was, though I would eventually find it just one block west. Similarly, I asked a couple of local folks about the contents of the historical museum in the beautiful old Carnegie library. They embarrass-edly admitted they'd never been. I had begun to realize that most people go to museums only in other places, usually ignoring the wealth of history and art in their own back yards.

Modern Newton has become a multi-ethnic town. For two generations it has been a haven for Latinos, who began working their way north on the railroad in the 1930s. Now, according to Vern Preheim, the population of Newton is perhaps 10 percent Mexican-American, and the town boasts several good Mexican restau-rants. I stopped at the family-run Acapulco on 81 for a platter of south-of-the-border enchiladas. The cooks and waiters all spoke Spanish among themselves, but switched readily to good English with English-speaking diners.

I drove to the Preheim house to meet Vern and Marion after choir practice. Vern's mother was born at Rose Hill Farm, which I had visited in South Dakota. Vern came down 81 as a youth, the "Mennonite highway" Tim Waltner had called it, to attend Bethel College. He returned years later as general secretary of the General Conference of Mennonites. In this position Vern had worked for 15 years to unify his group of Mennonites with the larger Mennonite Conference.

Though the Mennonites who began arriving in the Great Plains about 1874 were mostly of Dutch and Low German extraction, most had sought religious freedom in Russia under Catherine the Great. And though they shared funda-mental doctrine and values, the denomination had splintered along liberal-con-servative lines on both policy and theological issues, not just whether one should be baptized backwards or face-first, but on questions such as resistance to World War I.

The reunification of Mennonites had actually been in process for three-quar-ters of a century. The 1920 cooperation among major Mennonite groups to sup-ply relief in post-revolutionary Russia provided impetus for the merger. By the 1960s, when formal discussion toward unifying the congregations began, the work of the Mennonite Central Committee was focused on third-world develop-ment projects and social justice issues. In 1983 Vern suggested that the two major congregations join in updating their hundred-year-old profession of faith, and for six years an integration exploration committee of the Mennonite Church and the General Conference of Mennonites had worked to bring about unification of the two groups' 160,000 members. In the summer of 1995, delegates to a Wichita conference agreed to merge.

I returned to my camp on Sand Creek and merged with the natural noctur-nal world. The sky was cloudless, and the stars close and friendly. The locusts had yielded to the more sedate crickets, who serenaded me to peaceful sleep.

At 4:00 a.m. I awakened to the distant wail of a train, screeching to a halt in Newton. Probably it was the Amtrak, pausing briefly for west-bound passengers. Somewhere a pair of coyotes answered the whistle with their own cacophonous yaps. Three great horned owls joined the conversation from their respective trees on Sand Creek, their differing ages and status in the owl community clear in the pitches of their lonesome who-who-whos. I crawled outside to relieve myself, and some night creature, startled by my presence, scuttled for safety behind a cedar. I stood naked, marveling at the brilliance of the pre-dawn sky, now lighted by the just risen waning moon. I returned to my tent and lay fully awake, dreaming sweet dreams of the past and the future, unfathomably happy to be alive in the present on U.S. 81.

I recalled the night before, sleeping in the Best Western motel in Belleville, courtesy of the Pan American Highway Association. I was awakened at 4:00 a.m. there too, but by the bustle of a pair of disgruntled travelers next door, who probably had 800 miles of interstate America to roar across, and couldn't wait for daylight to begin. They cursed their alarm clock, flushed their toilet, showered forever, slammed every door, started their big engine and let it run for a quarter hour, burning more energy than a third world family uses in a week, stowed their collection of suitcases, gathered their yapping dog Oscar, hurled a parting curse as they slammed the door, and hit the road for somewhere they probably didn't even want to be, over a road they would not see or remember, rushing hundreds of miles this day to perhaps another motel beside another highway in another town the name of which they would not remember either, and when they got where they were going they would tell their friends how boring Kansas and Nebraska, or wherever they were going, was. Getting there was only an inconvenience and a waste of time, not a chance to experience the diversity of the American continent. Modern motels and fast-food restaurants are designed to hurry them on their way, ensuring they don't see the towns of America, or taste the local cuisine.

When they were gone at last I lay in my comfortable motel bed, inhaling the stale odor of cigarettes and Lysol and resentment, unable to sleep, dreading the hours until dawn. How much better this rise to consciousness, not a rude wrenching from sleep, but a true awakening here on God's Earth at Sand Creek.

At first light I emerged and rolled up my bag and tent. Night creatures had surrendered to robins and quail and crows. A meadowlark, the black and yellow-throated state bird of Kansas as well as North Dakota and Nebraska, sang his seven-note song from a fence post. By sunrise I was heading south again, down old 81 toward Wichita. From here to San Antonio, Texas, I would follow the trail established by Cherokee-Scotch freighter Jesse Chisholm in 1863, who in turn followed the route marked in 1861 by Delaware scout Black Beaver.

A few miles north of Wichita I became aware of a dirty gray cloud on the horizon. Air pollution. Not like Mexico City yet, thank God, but the first chemical dome of the Pan American Highway, centered over the aircraft plants and industrial sector of southeast Wichita. After all, this was the first city of over 75,000 in more than 800 miles since Winnipeg.

Population thickened with the sky, and I was among people of color, blacks, Latinos, Asians and others. Mexican restaurants and businesses grew numerous. Like Mexico City, Wichita is an urban magnet, drawing rural folks and minorities to its factories. Some of my black Oklahoma high school mates came up 81 to Wichita in the sixties, and I hadn't seen them since.

I turned west on 13th street and headed downtown. Wichita has recognized the aesthetic value of the Arkansas River, which snakes its way through the city. The river is lined with parks, and chain saw artists had turned dead American elms along the parkway into dozens of marvelous sculptures, mostly of people. The city's museums are here too: Botanica, the museum of natural and floral beauty; the Art Museum; the Indian Center; and Old Cowtown. I visited the beauty of Botanica in the crisp morning air. Everywhere I turned I found folks relaxing on Bud Hanzlick's bois-d' arc love-seats. Then I went to see the cowboys and the Indians.

The Indian Center is inter-tribal, displaying the flags, artifacts, art and history of most of the Indian nations of the plains, including the Wichitas, who grew corn, squash, beans, pumpkins, and tobacco by the Arkansas River to supplement their hunting. A major commodity of international trade was local flint, ideal for arrowheads and tools.

Kansas became a Territory in 1854, and "Bloody Kansas," a pawn in the pre-Civil War struggle over slavery, was admitted as a free state in 1861. In preparation for the creation of Kansas and Nebraska Territories, Congress in 1853 authorized negotiations with Kansas and Nebraska tribes, the aim of which was to move them out. The Wichita Agency was established in 1859 at Fort Cobb in Indian Territory, and the Kansas Wichitas joined indigenous cousins on the Washita River. South of Wichita were the Osage. Pushed west when Missouri became a state in 1821, they had settled on a large reservation in their former hunting range in what is now southern Kansas. But under pressure from settlers, the Osage were in the way once more. This time, they too were moved south to Indian Territory, in 1870.

Rivaling Prairie Village at Madison, South Dakota, Cowtown is perhaps the most elaborate of the city's museums, a reconstructed town of several square blocks built on the north bank of the Arkansas. Many of the buildings are restored homes and businesses of the early 1870s, moved to Cowtown from nearby Wichita sites. The city was incorporated in 1871 by 123 men and one woman – the mother of Billy the Kid. By 1873 the railroad had been extended, and Wichita replaced Newton as cowtown; a quarter million head of cattle were loaded here by the mid-seventies, when the railroad pushed farther south to Caldwell on the border with Indian Territory.

From Wichita I continued south on 81, the Chisholm Trail. I was in ever more familiar territory, nearing my native Oklahoma. Old 81 south of Wichita is an alley of dejection, deposed by parallel I-35. Lined with remnants of better days, it is the home of those who would escape the city, but can't afford the real suburbs. It appears to have evolved without planning, trailer parks and random ranchettes, sometimes with a little corral and a horse or two in the back yard. Such a place is Uncle Harold and Aunt Velma's former home on SE 79th Street east of 81, just a block from I-35. When the big road came, Uncle Harold put the best face on things. Never mind that a stinking chicken farm had sprung up across the street, or that the whine of traffic on the new highway never ceased. Harold would nod his head to the overpass which carried the airborne traffic by and proclaim the little frame house he had built his "mansion over the hilltop." He and Velma lived here until they died.

My first trip out of Oklahoma as an adolescent was to this house. Actually to the garage, which Harold built first, and where the family lived while he built the house in evenings and weekends after work at Boeing Aircraft. I spent a few days here with my favorite cousin, Glen, and got lost for the first time in a big city, peddling our home-made pot holders door to door in Wichita. The house still looks about the same, except there's a horse in the back yard, and the trees Harold planted in the fifties are now gracefully mature. I peered in the picture window as I crept past, maybe looking for somebody I knew. But there was no sign of life, so I headed on down 81 to Wellington, past the trailer houses and junk cars and defunct Chisholm Trail Bar, past where cousin Glen and his wife once operated a goat dairy on the Ninnescah River.

At Wellington I visited the Chisholm Trail Museum, which occupies the old three-story hospital. I was graciously shown the attractions of the place by Margaret Lammy, a 44-year veteran of elementary school teaching, the first 13 in a one-room country school. Margaret spoke in the drawl I knew so well; it began with Bud Hanzlick, and by southern Oklahoma people would be saying "y'all." Margaret also shared a couple of books on the Trail, one of which included the most complete map I had seen, showing where the Trail began southeast of San Antonio, at the King Ranch near Corpus Christi. I thanked her for the tour, and jogged west to Caldwell, the final terminus of the Chisholm Trail. The border town with cowboy-infiltrated Indian Territory, Caldwell was the wildest of cow-towns.

At Caldwell, which has the admirable nerve to call itself the "Border Queen City," not to mention the governor-declared "Ornate Box Turtle Capital of the World," I saw where the Red Light Saloon welcomed dusty-throated cowboys at the corner of Chisholm Street and Avenue A. That was before somebody shot George Woods in a fight over one of the girls upstairs, and wife Mag burned the place down and fled for Wichita. George is buried in the cemetery north of town; Mag's whereabouts are unknown.

But George wasn't the only man murdered on the wild streets of Caldwell; Main Street is virtually littered with historical markers showing where Marshall George Flatt was flattened, where two cowboys killed each other in a duel, only to lie eternally together in the same box in the local "boot hill," where ex-mayor Mike Meagher killed George Spears of the Talbot Gang, just before another gang member plugged Mike, and where Marshall Henry Brown shot down Spotted Horse for being an "offensive Indian." From all the markers and hoopla, one gets the impression that town promoters only wish there had been more.

Two miles south of town on the Oklahoma border, I found beside Highway 81 the wagon ruts of the old cattle trail. Local artists have installed "Ghost Riders of the Chisholm Trail," a sculpted steel silhouette of horses and riders and cows on the horizon. Travelers on 81 can look to the east and imagine it's 1870. The cows, after a month-long journey across Texas and Indian Territory, are about to board a train. And the cowboys are so close to town they can almost taste the illegal liquor George and Mag have waiting for them.

# OKLAHOMA

*"Prettiest clouds that ever did blow, prettiest girls that
ever did grow: makes my toes all itch to go — down in Oklayhoma."*

~ *Woody Guthrie, "Down in Oklayhoma"*

It's known as the "Sooner State," a reference to those who slipped in illegally to grab Indian land. But the welcome sign, like the vehicle license plate, calls this "Native America." The "O" of Oklahoma is the Indian shield from the state flag, olive branch and peace pipe superimposed. Oklahoma is Choctaw for "red people."

Once northern Oklahoma was the hunting grounds of the Osage, and later of the Cherokee. Now it is wheat country; the fall fields were greening with winter wheat. I headed south through the Cherokee Strip on a narrow and marginally maintained 81; parallel I-35 to the east is draining its life-blood.

I was now so near to "home" that I didn't need a map, a great relief. For a thousand miles I'd been reading the map upside down, and I had 4,000 miles to go. Medieval European maps typically were oriented east, with Jerusalem at the center. But after the Chinese invented the magnetic needle in the 12th century, maps rotated with the compass, into alignment with the north pole. Map-wise, my journey would have been easier from south to north, the way modern map-makers view the world.

I cruised through Renfrow, where the 20-foot wheat heads painted on the elevator are beginning to peal and fade, but I stopped in Medford to meet some friends of my folks. Eleuterio (Luke) Munoz and his family came up the Pan American Highway from Hidalgo, Mexico years ago, and Luke got a job at the natural gas refinery in town. While Luke talked about northern Mexico, the chili aroma of his wife's tamales drifted from the kitchen, increasing my eagerness to be south of the border. But in the meantime, I wanted to be in Hennessey by dark for a bowl of Mama's stew.

The road was flanked by red earth and oil wells, mostly shallow "strippers" by modern standards, but still pumping. I passed Pond Creek and the road to Kremlin, named by Russian settlers for the Kremlin in Moscow. I sailed through Enid, the little city where I spent many a Saturday night as a teenager; I would return tomorrow.

Like most of the towns in the old Cherokee Outlet, Enid was a product of the last rush of settlers into Indian Territory, September 16, 1893. While the nation celebrated four centuries of post-Columbian progress at the Chicago Worlds' Fair, the last free Indian land fell into white hands.

The Cherokee Outlet, 60 miles wide and two-thirds the length of Oklahoma from the Panhandle east, was set aside in 1828 as hunting land for the Cherokee, driven west on the Trail of Tears from the Smoky Mountains. A surveying error left a two and a half mile strip of undesignated land on the Kansas line – the Cherokee Strip – a name later applied to the entire Cherokee Outlet.

In 1868 the Cherokee agreed to allow other "friendly" Indians to settle in the Strip; by 1872 it was populated by the Osage, Kaw, Tonkawa, Ponca, Pawnee, Missouri and Otoe peoples. Hundreds of thousands of cattle were driven through the heart of the Strip to Kansas on the Chisholm Trail in the 1870s. In 1883 the mostly unoccupied western part was leased to the Cherokee Strip Livestock Association; huge herds of cattle grazed the open prairie. Before long ranchers began fencing off tracts, which put an end to the cattle drives and intensified territorial conflict. In 1890 President Benjamin Harrison ordered the cattlemen out, and the federal government took possession of the Strip, paying the Cherokee $8.5 million, about $1.40 per acre for the land. Three years later, the Strip was opened to whites.

With a population of over 45,000, Enid is the largest city and the unofficial capital of the Cherokee Strip. Most sources say the city was named for Enid, the wife of Geraint in Tennyson's 1859 epic, *Idylls of the King*, popular not only in Victorian England, but also in late 19th century America. I prefer the other story, that it was named for a flipped over "DINE" sign on a cook tent at Government Springs, a major watering hole for cows and people on the Chisholm Trail. Whatever the truth, Government Springs was the center of the new town.

I pushed on to Hennessey for the night, but the next afternoon I came back to Government Springs with my family. My earliest memory of the springs was a rare family trip to Enid in the mid-fifties. We visited the bears and monkeys in the little zoo, and at a picnic table on the shady hill above the springs, consumed a whole half gallon of ice cream from Gold Spot, where we sent our cows' milk. Now we meandered through a meticulously groomed park, looking for landmarks. The monkey pit was gone, replaced by a formal garden. At center stands a big bronze sculpture by Harold Holden called "Holding the Claim."

The major attraction of the park, though, is the Museum of the Cherokee Strip. The museum contains memorabilia from cowboy and pioneer days, the history of the Strip and the Indian nations which were moved here, and a photograph of the all-black "Buffalo Soldiers" infantry from Fort Reno evicting a group of David Payne's "boomers," settlers who illegally occupied Indian land, then lobbied officials to make their claims legal. There was the by now familiar commemoration of the Chisholm Trail, and of course, photographs and artifacts from the land run, including an actual red claim flag with instructions for staking a claim. The land runs brought people from across the states, but mostly Yankees and people of English origin from the middle eastern states. In Garfield County, for the first time on my route, the predominant reported ethnicity was "American," with English second.

Enid was the home of "Little Doc" Roberts, who peddled patent medicines in Enid with his 1930s medicine show. His son, Oral, built on his father's skills, not only becoming a well-known TV preacher, but founding his own university in Tulsa, where a few years ago he holed up in his prayer tower and threatened to die if people didn't send him a million dollars before a deadline he claimed God had set.

I've already noted that while people will drive across the state or even the nation to see other people's scenery, historic sites, and museums, they tend to overlook those in their own back yards. I'm guilty too. Right in the middle of Enid, at the intersection of U.S. 81 and U.S. 60, is one of the most remarkable houses I've ever seen. As a kid I used to marvel at the place, but dared not go near such an extravaganza. After all those years, my family and I went for a closer look at the Midgley house, now a museum run by the Masonic Lodge. We found a carefully crafted structure of more than 30 varieties of exotic rocks, fossils, crystal, agate, sandstone and massive chunks of petrified wood, which the Midgleys, wealthy local farmers, had gathered in their extensive travels, a monument to unbridled human passion.

Like all cities, Enid has changed in the last 40 years, some ways for the worse, some for the better. The Chisholm Trail drive-in theater on the south edge of town — my favorite place for teenage dates — was long since closed, a peeling monolith in a patch of weeds. But gone too are the separate rest rooms and drinking fountains for white and "colored" at the county courthouse which I well remember from the 1950s, and the segregated bathing area for blacks at the east end of Government Springs Park. Now nobody can swim at the springs, but each August, a Hispanic Festival at the park celebrates the cultures of Enid's Spanish-speaking community, now numbering in the hundreds. Beside the highway a Mexican-style wooden cross marks the site of a fatal crash. And now all races, black, white, and brown, may enjoy the skating rink, the bowling alley and the theaters. As late as 1960 my black teenaged friends were denied admission to all these hang-outs when we went to town on Saturday nights. That didn't leave much to do besides drag main, in this case Van Buren, or U.S. 81.

Some things haven't changed. The Sonic still stands at the south end of the Van Buren loop, and you can still order a burger over the intercom and a teenaged car-hop brings it to the car.

It was getting late, and we had to get back to Hennessey to work on my Omni's carburetor, trying to curb her omnivorous appetite for a too rich mixture of fuel, so we didn't get to visit George's Antique Auto Museum, where I'd hoped to see one of the few remaining Geronimos, a car built in Enid from 1916-1920, one of the first products to exploit the Apache leader's name. Geronimo died in 1909, released from jail, but his wild spirit confined to the Apache Reservation near Fort Sill, Oklahoma.

On the south edge of Enid we passed Vance Air Force Base, where pilots learn to fly fighter planes. The base is named for Enid native, Maj. Robert Vance, posthumously awarded the Congressional Medal of Honor for heroism in World

*Harold Holden's sculpture, "Holding the Claim," at Government Springs Park in Enid (top), and the Pat Hennessey grave and memorial in Hennessey.*

War II. The last towns in the Cherokee Strip are Waukomis and Bison, the latter taking its name from Buffalo Springs, the Chisholm Trail watering hole just north of town. Pat Hennessey is thought to have spent his last night alive camped at the springs before his death at Hennessey next day, the Fourth of July. Bison is a Catholic Bohemian town, home of the Our Lady of Fatima shrine.

Half way between Bison and Hennessey I entered Kingfisher County, where the 1996 block-buster movie "Twister" was set. Decades ago, people with Garfield County licenses were married in shady road-side ceremonies under the "marrying tree," a maimed old cottonwood that still stands on the county line. I left the Cherokee Outlet and entered the "Unassigned Land" of old Indian Territory.

From 1830 to 1866, the Creek Nation extended from this line south to the Canadian River. The Indians of Indian Territory were virtually abandoned by the Union during the Civil War, and the Confederacy persuaded parts of each tribe to join. Some members of each of the "Five Civilized Tribes," as we learned to call them in school, had slaves. (Was that what distinguished them from the "uncivilized" tribes?) Thus, like the Cherokee, Chickasaw, Choctaw and Seminole, the Creek were forced into their own civil war. More than 3,000 Creeks fought, about half on each side, and nearly a quarter of the population died in warfare or as displaced refugees. Their participation in the white man's war also produced great internal strife and disintegration. In 1866, their service was rewarded by the confiscation of the western half of their territory for 30 cents an acre. This land would become the heart of Oklahoma, including Oklahoma City, the original state capital of Guthrie, and some of the richest farm land and oil reserves in Oklahoma.

The two million acres of "unassigned" land was the first chunk of Indian Territory opened to white settlement by land run, on April 22, 1889. By nightfall an estimated 10,000 people had raced into the district by horse, buggy, bicycle, or foot, and staked their claims. My great grandfather, George Seneker, made the run from Kansas and staked a claim near the Cimarron River. He was driven off next morning by a claim-jumper with a shotgun.

Across the Cimarron to the west lies Cheyenne Arapaho land, the four million acre Indian Territory reservation established by the Treaty of Medicine Lodge in 1867. The reservation was split into 160 acre plots by the 1887 Dawes Act, and 3,320 Indians were assigned individual allotments. The remaining 88 percent was declared "surplus," up for grabs in the second great land run on April 19, 1892. For this 3.5 million acres, each adult tribal member could come to the agency and claim 75 silver dollars. Grandpa Seneker tried his luck again, this time claiming and holding a quarter section of Cheyenne Arapaho land on the west river bank. Another great grandfather, William Bedwell, was his new neighbor. I was born on Cheyenne Arapaho land half a century later.

I made a side trip to visit my grandmother, Grace Bedwell White, in Okeene. A century old, she was among the first white children born on Cheyenne Arapaho land, a decade before statehood. In her memoir she described the last

Arapaho pow wow held on Spring Creek near her father's claim in 1908, how the Indians caught fish and turtles and rabbits and roasted them on a big open fire, the all night dancing and the beat of drums, the calm after sunrise as they slept under shawls and blankets in the sun.

Like other towns in the region, Hennessey was born April 22, 1889, the day of the first run, 15 years after the July 4, 1874, murder of Irish Chisholm Trail wagoneer Pat Hennessey and three of his drivers. Hennessey was tied to a wagon wheel and burned; his grave and a little memorial tower mark the site on the west edge of town. The "massacre" was attributed on the historical marker at the monument to unknown Indians (perhaps Cheyenne Dog Soldiers) though a second marker at the adjacent Pat Hennessey Park says the murderers may have been white outlaws masquerading as Indians. While I mused at the memorial, Lee Enix saw my out-of-state plates and stopped to visit.

Enix was born just a mile up the Chisholm Trail, which ran between his family's house and barn. At 75, he was the youngest of six children, the one who stayed on the farm.

"When I plowed as a teenager, I had to downshift the tractor to cross the old Chisholm Trail," he said. "That tight red dirt was packed hard by millions of hooves." He said that after a century of farming, when the land is bare the trail is still visible as a long depression across the field. Lee said a Yukon insurance man was putting up cement markers at every section line where the trail crosses Oklahoma.

When I was a teen-ager there were three distinct communities around Hennessey. East and north of town were the Catholic Bohemians, who talked funny, and according to my Bohemian friends, danced and partied at church. On small farms in the sandy blackjack oak land east of the Cimarron River was a community of black people. I grew up on the edge of the black community, part of the third group, non-Bohemian whites, the froth of the American melting pot, descendants of poor farmers from just about everywhere who had here staked their claims to a piece of the American Dream.

It was in this blackjack country that I first observed nature's perennial effort to maintain balance, and a corresponding perennial problem, man's interference. One year the rabbit population would soar. The next season coyotes were abundant and rabbits virtually disappeared. Nature's plan was not allowed to work. Men with dogs and traps and guns, masking their ancient blood lust as civic responsibility, launched campaigns to exterminate the coyote, setting the stage for the next explosion of rabbit and rodent populations. I've since watched the same phenomenon in South Dakota, where a local sheep man and state agents trapped, shot and poisoned 30 coyotes in a single winter, and where men gather at a rural bar each spring to map their crusade to eradicate the state animal.

My first job beyond the family farm was haying on farms around Hennessey. In fact, bucking bales provided my introduction to the capitalist system of production. One teen-aged summer I worked for Matt Choate, a local entrepreneur whose assets included two aging Chevrolet trucks, a field bale loader and a barn elevator, the equipment necessary to bring hay from field to barn. Matt's total investment amounted to less than $5,000, so he wasn't exactly a tycoon. But his ownership of the means of production allowed him to sit in the driver's seat and collect 15 cents per bale, while Shorty, Albert and I did all the work for a penny a bale each. I handled 100,000 bales that summer, and earned $1,000.

In the early sixties things began to change. The blacks of my generation mostly left for the cities – Oklahoma City, Dallas, or Wichita – so that by now most of the black people remaining in the neighborhood are elderly. Then came the oil boom. A few people got rich, at least by local standards, almost over night. Others could finally pay off the mortgage. Of course the big money left the county. Oil brought a whole new culture, the "oilies," some people called them, from other communities which preceded Hennessey's cycle of boom and bust. I myself was briefly an oilie, working for Chris Well Service on U.S. 81. For the biggest wage I'd ever drawn, $3.50 an hour, I helped pull up mile and a half deep oil pumps, hot oil dripping down my back all day. Ten years later the boom went bust, and Oklahoma oil is in a two-decade slide; junk and rust and blackened earth remained.

Though farming and occasional blips in the oil economy have kept most people alive, a new industry arrived in 1992. Jack Choate, Matt's millionaire brother, sold a square mile of farm land to the Pig Improvement Company of Franklin, Kentucky. PIC soon had acquired over 2,000 acres, encircling the family farm where my brother and his wife still live with large-scale hog confinement facilities. The industry has created needed jobs and has helped to repopulate the old neighborhood. In fact, before it became the office of an oil well service company, Chisholm Trail Resources, a PIC employee and his family lived in the house where I grew up.

According to Dwayne Bankson of the PIC corporate office, the hog confinements were "multiplier farms," the top of a pyramid which sold breeding stock to other hog confinement operations across the U.S. and to 26 foreign countries. PIC had 8,500 sows in the neighborhood, each producing a score or more of pigs each year. The waste from tens of thousands of pigs who never see the light of day is piped to cesspools which they call "lagoons," then spread on the surrounding farm land by irrigation in what PIC calls its "nutrient management plan." PIC chose my old neighborhood, Bankson said, for its cheap land, available agricultural labor, plentiful shallow water, and sandy soil. Unfortunately the sandy soil means that the "nutrients" soak in fast, and in time will undoubtedly pollute the shallow water, already contaminated with nitrates from fertilizer. And by 1998, corporate mass-production had driven hog prices to a 44-year low of 10 cents a pound, forcing thousands of diversified hog farmers across the plains out of business.

About 1980, the relatively good oil patch wages began attracting Mexicans, and soon there were hundreds of Mexican people in town, some legal and some not. From the beginning, my parents, Wesley and Mary, befriended this latest wave of immigrants, developing friendships with Mexican people on both sides of the Río Grande. On Sunday we went to the Mexican church in Ringwood and sang old Baptist hymns in Spanish.

Among the early arrivals from Mexico were Santiago (Jimmy) Vasquez from the rural ejido of La Piragua near Ciudad Victoria, and his wife Elvira, from Ciéniga, just north of Monterrey, both on the Pan American Highway. Santiago and Elvira came illegally at first, he working construction jobs as he had done in Mexico until they gained legal status. Eventually they bought what I knew as a teenager as LaPorte's Drive-in on the north edge of town and turned it into Los Vasquez Mexican Restaurant. On Sunday evening my parents took me to meet the Vasquez family. Santiago and Elvira told me how to find their families in Mexico, and asked me to visit them.

Early Monday morning I crawled out of my parents' wedding bed, I presume the bed where I was conceived back in 1944, fired up the Omni, hoping we'd fixed the carburetor, and headed south. It was just getting light when I hit Dover, formerly Red Fork Station, another stop on the Chisholm Trail. Dover is on the Cimarron River, a name derived from the Spanish Rio de los Carneros Cimarrón, or river of wild sheep. Two historical notes about Dover: On May 15, 1957, the great Cimarron flood, the 14-inch deluge which took the lives of my aged pioneering great grandparents, George and Edith Seneker, almost washed Dover away. And in 1980, the INS conducted its first local raid on illegal Mexican immigrants at the Dover Baptist Church. I crossed the Cimarron where the locomotive from a deadly 1906 train wreck still lies in the quicksand.

The county seat of Kingfisher County is Kingfisher, where my parents were married in 1939 by a justice of the peace at the courthouse, and where I got my driver's license and first hit the road in a '54 Mercury I bought in a lot beside 81. King Fisher ran the stagecoach station here, but Kingfisher's best-known son is Sam Walton, who by 1985 was the richest person in America. The automobile may have begun the erosion of the small town, but Walton's Wal-mart empire drained main streets in countless towns across America, and now has moved into Mexico. But Kingfisher was also the home of Molly Shepherd, the crusading Cheyenne journalist whose syndicated column of Indian news was written for the Kingfisher Free Press.

The next town, Okarche, is heavily German and Catholic; Okarche basketball players regularly unnerved my teammates and me with the sign of the cross at the free-throw line. The town name, as George Shirk notes in *Oklahoma Place Names*, is formed from the first letters of Oklahoma, Arapaho and Cheyenne. On the outskirts of town I saw the first dead armadillo on the road, the armored creature which was never seen in central Oklahoma when I was a kid. Once the rivers were bridged, he gradually migrated north up this and other highways.

On a high ridge overlooking the north branch of the Canadian River is Concho, site of the Cheyenne Arapaho Agency and headquarters, and a former

Indian school. The school is closed now, replaced by a bingo hall and a tax-free cigarette shop. The agency village was Darlington. Both school and agency were named for white Indian agents. At Darlington the first Oklahoma Territory newspaper, The *Cheyenne Transporter*, was published. Now Darlington is a state game bird hatchery, producing pheasants, quail and other birds for hunters.

A few miles south is El Reno, originally Fort Reno, named for Gen. Jesse L. Reno who was killed in a Civil War battle near Harper's Ferry, West Virginia. Fort Reno was established in 1875 on Cheyenne Arapaho land to put down a Cheyenne uprising prompted by the wholesale slaughter of buffalo and the destruction of their sacred burial grounds by a Kansas wood contractor. For five years the Cheyenne and Arapaho had battled the U.S. Army, and for another five years they had been confined to the reservation, but neither had produced peace.

The Cheyenne were formidable warriors; like their allies, the Sioux, they resisted domination to the end. According to Angie Debo's *History of the Indians of the United States*, in 1867 Cheyenne warriors captured the horses of a party of buffalo hunters and stole 40 horses and mules from a wagon train. Infamous Indian fighter and division commander, Gen. William T. Sherman, sent Maj. Gen. Winfield Scott Hancock to teach the Indians a lesson. Sherman told Hancock, "Our troops must get among them, and kill enough of them to inspire fear."

Hancock assaulted a Cheyenne village, sending Col. Custer after those who escaped. Sherman appointed Col. William B. Hazen as agent to deal with the survivors, a "residue" he hoped would be small. Then he dispatched Gen. Philip Sheridan to attack the Indians in their winter camps.

In the "Battle of the Washita" on November 27, 1868, what the Cheyenne call the "Black Kettle massacre," Custer and his Seventh Cavalry attacked the peaceful village of Chief Black Kettle at dawn, killing the chief and his wife and an estimated 200 men, women and children, burning their village. Two months later, when Gen. Sheridan was presented with Comanche Chief Toch-a-way (Turtle Dove) at nearby Fort Cobb, Sheridan said, "the only good Indians I ever saw were dead." Soon Gen. Grant was president and Sheridan commander of the Plains Division, and the war against the Cheyenne intensified.

Defeated at last in 1869, the Cheyenne joined the Arapahos on the reservation. In just 23 years their land would be opened to white settlement.

Besides fighting the Cheyenne, the cavalry stationed at Fort Reno also tried to keep the "boomers," illegal squatters, out of Indian Territory. They also fired the starting shots at high noon to set off the land runs of '89 and '92. During World War II, Fort Reno was another German P.O.W. camp, with 1,350 prisoners. The Fort Reno cemetery has three sections: for cavalrymen, for Indian scouts and warriors, and for German prisoners of war.

After World War II, Fort Reno was divided between a U.S. Department of Agriculture experimental farm and a federal prison. In 1995 the best-known prisoners were numbers 12076-064 and 08157-031, Timothy McVeigh and Terry

Nichols, charged with the deadliest terrorist attack on U.S. soil, the April 19, 1995 bombing of the Federal Building in Oklahoma City which killed 168 people. The bombing marked the second anniversary of the assault on the Branch Davidian compound at Waco, Texas, and ironically, the 103rd anniversary of the Cheyenne loss of the land on which the prison stands. McVeigh and Nichols were held in isolation from 1,100 other federal prisoners. I drove to the prison entrance, where I was addressed via intercom by a heavily armed guard in the control tower. I told him I wanted a look at the place where America's most notorious suspects were held. "You can't take no pictures," he said, "and that's as close as you're going to get."

On the west edge of El Reno, a dozen mangy buffalo and longhorns grazed weeds in their own prison on Country Club Drive. At the football stadium of the El Reno INDIANS, the "A" is formed by a teepee. Downtown I found the county museum at the old Rock Island Depot. Besides the depot itself, the museum complex includes Gen. Sheridan's headquarters cabin, the 1869 jail where rebellious Cheyenne warriors were confined, and the hundred-year-old El Reno Hotel, closed in 1974 when I-40 drained the blood from Route 66 as the main east-west highway.

Along with Columbus, Nebraska, El Reno has a legitimate claim to the title, "crossroads of America." Here the north-south transcontinental highway, U.S. 81, intersects the east-west transcontinental highway, U.S. 66, the "mother road" of Steinbeck's Joads and thousands of other "Okies," escapees from the misery of depression and dust in Arkansas and Oklahoma who found the misery of homelessness and abuse in California. Unable to leave Oklahoma, Grandpa Joad was buried beside Route 66 a few miles east of town. The intersection is remarkably unremarkable — a snack shop, a beer joint, and a Goodyear tire store.

Looking for some perspective on historic El Reno, I talked with Cheyenne poet Lance Henson, who grew up with his grandparents at an old Cheyenne campsite on the North Canadian River near Calumet, northwest of El Reno. Lance said "Calumet" is Choctaw for pipe, or peace pipe. Lance's grandfather, Bob Cook, helped charter the Native American Church in 1917.

Lance said that following the 1874 uprising, conditions for the Cheyenne continued to worsen. By 1877 their numbers had been reduced a third by disease and hunger. In 1878, 370 people, led by War Chief Little Wolf and Peace Chief Dull Knife, fought their way back north to their old hunting grounds on the Yellowstone River, a heroic struggle dramatized by Mari Sandoz's 1953 historical novel, *Cheyenne Autumn*. Lance said the 1868 Fort Laramie Treaty provided for the establishment of Army forts on Indian land, but according to the treaty, if forts were abandoned, the land was to revert to the tribes; the Southern Cheyenne were trying to get the several thousand acres of Fort Reno back.

I told Lance about my great grandfathers making the run of '92 to take Cheyenne-Arapaho land. I'd heard the story from the pioneer perspective, but I wondered what stories he'd heard as a boy about the land transfer. "My grandparents didn't talk much about the great losses their people had suffered," he said. "But I have seen decaying army blankets and cavalry saddles in many a home. They were trophies of war, proudly displayed, painful reminders of a valorous struggle." Lance's poem "The Ageless" captures the loss, but also the determination of the Cheyenne to endure: Where the road ends there/ is no weeping the drying/ river full of death echoes/ in the songs of children/ as above the fading/ mountains/ the/ pale sun/ floats."

The last tiny town in the old Creek Nation before the South Canadian River is Union City, known before 1891 as Sherman, for the Indian-fighting general. I stopped and questioned residents, including the postmaster, but no one seemed to know who duly dishonored Sherman by wiping his name from the town.

Two miles south of Union City I began to see mistletoe, the state flower of Oklahoma, the European parasite which grows on trees south and east of here, but not north and west, and beneath which it was, at least before the days of political correctness, permissible to kiss otherwise unkissable people. Perhaps it is no accident that the famous KOMA radio "kissing tone," heard and responded to by teenagers from North Dakota to Texas, originated in Oklahoma City, right in the corner of mistletoe country.

I crossed the South Canadian, entering what was left of Indian Territory after 1889, roughly the southeastern half of what is now Oklahoma. In pre-European times this had been Wichita country all the way to the Red River. For most of the 19th century, all of what is now Oklahoma was Indian Territory, this part the Chickasaw Nation. But in 1890 Congress set up a separate government for "Oklahoma Territory," the northwest half of the present state, and in 1900 the two territories were combined under the Oklahoma name.

Residents of the former Indian Territory, including both whites and members of the "Five Civilized Tribes," tried in vain in 1905 to establish the state of Sequoyah, the name honoring the chief who created the Cherokee alphabet. The proposal passed by a 6:1 vote in November 1905, but the U.S. House tabled the bill to recognize the state of Sequoyah. Congress uncivilly abolished the governments of the civilized tribes in 1906, preparing to admit the single state of Oklahoma in 1907.

I cruised through Minco, where the Chisholm Trail intersected the northern California Road over which gold seekers traveled west from Fort Smith, Arkansas to the gold fields in the 1850s. A few miles east, on Lost Creek, Washington Irving killed a buffalo in 1832, a feat he sadly recalled in *A Tour on the Prairies*. Cotton fields, hardwood trees and little barbecue joints now became common.

The main street of Pocasset was littered with junk. A 1970 Chevrolet still reposed on its top 10 feet from Main, as it had a year earlier. Here Al Jennings -- lawyer, evangelist, candidate for governor, and outlaw -- robbed a train, blowing up the railroad car containing the safe, but leaving the safe and its contents intact.

The largest town in the Washita valley is Chickasha, the proper spelling of the Chickasaw Nation. There are at least a thousand Indian people around Chickasha, but the only mention of Indians in a big color brochure from the Chamber of Commerce was the statement that "members of the Chickasaw Nation played an important part in the development of early Chickasha, allowing white men to become landowners, ranchers and citizens of the Chickasaw Nation by virtue of marriage to an Indian citizen." Hmm. I thought of George Orwell's famous essay "Marrakech," in which he describes his recognition of the invisibility of people of color.

From Chickasha to the Texas line, I drove through sandy rolling hills and fertile valleys, cattle ranches and small farms, even an emu ranch. Woods are common, cottonwood and willow, oak and pecan, and the state tree, the red bud. The area produces cotton, wheat, peanuts, alfalfa and watermelons, the latter long synonymous with the little town of Rush Springs, which holds a watermelon festival every summer. Two bars on the north edge of Rush Springs were surrounded by cars at 10:30 on a Monday morning. A big banner on Main Street said "Help the Rush Springs economy. Buy Something, Anything!"

A historical marker beside the road tells the story of the "Battle of Wichita Village." In 1858 a band of Comanches returning from a peace council at Fort Arbuckle were attacked by four companies of soldiers commanded by Captain Earl Van Dorn. Seventy of the Indians were killed. The word "massacre" is not used to report the incident, as it generally is where whites were killed by Indians.

The next big town is Marlow, named for Dr. Williamson Marlow. Marlow and his sons, Boone, Alfred, Epp, George and Charles, established the sprawling Marlow Brothers' Ranch near the Chisholm Trail in the 1880s. The official story is that the Marlow boys were unjustly accused by a U.S. Marshal of stealing horses. In his *Oklahoma Travel Handbook*, Kent Ruth says they were run out of the area for rustling cattle on the Chisholm Trail; in a phrase of the time, they were "GTT" – gone to Texas. Marlow is apparently a religious town today. The phone book lists 31 churches for its 4,416 residents, one for each 142 people. One church is Catholic and the rest Protestant, including 11 Baptist.

The biggest town in south central Oklahoma, population 21,732, is Duncan, the seat of Stephens County, the western part of which was in the Kiowa, Comanche and Apache Reservation of Oklahoma Territory. Stephens County is the home of former UN Ambassador Jeane Kirkpatrick, as well as lots of pleasant people, which most Oklahomans are. Named in 1884 for William Duncan, who had married a Chickasaw woman, Duncan calls itself "the Buckle on the Oil Belt." That belt is now a bit frayed, and the buckle in need of lubrication, but one of the giants of the oil industry, Halliburton Services, still calls Duncan home. And the city still provides unlimited free watermelon to all comers every summer during Melon Jubilee. The Indian Base Line, from which most of Oklahoma north was surveyed, is marked in Duncan.

Another half-dozen small towns are strung along Highway 81, the old Chisholm Trail, before it crosses the Red River to Texas: Comanche, Addington,

Waurika, Sugden, Ryan and Terral. Comanche folks are proud of their famous rodeo stars: world champion calf ropers Clyde Burk and Junior Garrison, and world champion barrel racers Joyce Burk and Connie Combs. I was in ranch country now; Hereford cattle drank from opaque ponds that matched their reddish-orange hides.

North of Waurika I pulled off to see Monument Hill, three miles east of the highway. The hill itself is monumental, but from miles away I'd seen atop its summit some sort of structure thrusting into the Oklahoma sky. Rising as it does from the lower plains and valleys of Cow and Beaver Creeks, Monument Hill was a landmark on the Chisholm Trail. But someone long ago built a 30-foot cement obelisk on the brow of the hill, and more recently, the state has implanted the usual granite plaques in its four sides, explaining the history of both the Chisholm Trail and Monument Hill. When I reached the summit I could see at least 50 miles to the south and west, all the way to Texas. But I would have missed most of what I found there if not for the chance encounter with Snake.

Snake, who declined to give any other name, had parked on Monument Hill to watch for his fishing buddy Jack, with whom he hoped to repeat his recent feat of pulling over a hundred crappie from a local pond. He was a rugged-looking character of about 60. His rusted yellow Courier pickup was full of junk, both front and back: oil cans, beer cans, spare tires, baling wire, fishing gear, clothes, cigarette butts. The truck was older than my Omni, and I'd bet so was the collection of debris. Only an artist could produce such an artifact in less time.

"Hell, I've been by this sombitch a thousand times," Snake said, "but I never took the time to drive up here." I asked Snake who put the monument on Monument Hill. "I don't know," he said. "Beats the snot outa me." He said the whole country to the south was the Price Ranch, but about 20 square miles had just been sold for "three something million." But Price wasn't exactly homeless, Snake said. He still had several square miles.

Talking about Price reminded Snake of a story he'd heard, that "Nigger Tom" was buried someplace up here. We went in search of the marker, finally finding it in a patch of weeds 50 yards southeast. The marker reads "Trail driver Tom Latimore, Died 1944." The stone didn't give Tom's birth date or his age, but in 1944 the Chisholm Trail had been history for 60 years. "The true story," Snake said, "is that Price runned over him, backed over him with a truck." Snake fired up the battered Courier, took a long pull that emptied his Budweiser, threw the can in the back and bounced off down the hill.

I stopped in Waurika to see one more Chisholm Trail museum, but also because the town of 2,000 people has a certain prominence as county seat of Jefferson County. Waurika is an Indian word for "clear water"; the town is built at the confluence of Cow and Beaver Creeks, which Snake told me are no longer clear, and are usually dry. Copying my birth town of Okeene, Waurika has a rattlesnake hunt every April; Molly, who works at the town library, said hundreds of pounds of snake are eaten here each spring, their hides tanned, and some of their venom collected to treat snakebites. A few years ago the Oklahoma Legislature also proclaimed Waurika the "Parakeet Capital of the World," she said. Almost a million of the colorful little birds were produced here in the peak year. But as with all such fads, the market soon was saturated; Molly said only one family still raised parakeets for sale.

The next day was Halloween, and Molly and three volunteers were busy hanging black plastic bats and bagging popcorn, getting ready for the annual party which lures kids into the library. But she cheerfully took time from her work to show me around the fine library and museum in the beautifully restored 1912 Rock Island Depot. Beside the main lobby was a separate "Colored Waiting Room," not much larger than a broom closet. In this cramped space, a black man was hanging plastic spider webs.

Though passenger service ended in the 1950s, and Rock Island went broke in the seventies, several Union Pacific freight trains still rumble by the depot every day, Molly said, hauling wheat south and oil north. But these days the trains don't stop. It's a long way from Chicago to Mexico City, and the railroad can't be bothered anymore by little towns like Waurika. Molly said that during the Gulf War thousands of military trucks and tanks rolled by on their way to Houston and the Middle East. Most everything about the trains has changed, but they haven't strayed from the Chisholm Trail where the Rock Island Line laid its tracks over a century ago.

South of Waurika both sides of the highway were grass and cattle country. Some stands of native grasses, especially big blue stem, were still healthy and strong; other pastures were overgrazed, sprouting mesquite and weeds. Pecan groves dotted the prairie, and "pecans bought" signs were frequent. A flock of wild turkeys scratched for nuts beside the road.

Just north of Ryan I encountered the giant orange tracks of some unknown creature on the highway. I followed to where they turned off at the 4-H grounds and football stadium. I couldn't figure what made the tracks until I saw the sign proclaiming the Ryan Cowboys "Number One." It was, of course, Big Foot the Cowboy, in three-foot orange boots. I hoped I wouldn't meet him on the road.

I came to the Red River just south of Terral, the second Red River on the Pan American Highway. This Red was the United States boundary with New Spain from 1803 to 1821, with Mexico from 1821 to 1836, and with the Republic of Texas from 1836 to 1845. The river here is wide, shallow and murky, its origin in the red soil of the Texas Panhandle and western Oklahoma. Below the cottonwood bluffs, water birds darted and fed on twisting sandbars.

It had been fun revisiting my home state, sad recalling the deplorable treatment of Native peoples here, and a pleasure making some new acquaintances. Now I was leaving Oklahoma, and I still hadn't seen the state bird, the scissor-tailed flycatcher. Apparently they had preceded me in southern migration. Just across the river lay the sprawling empire of Texas, the place many Texans, as well as some Oklahomans, consider another country.

# Texas

*"I saw miles and miles of Texas. I'm gonna live there til I die"*

*~ Asleep at the Wheel, "Miles and Miles of Texas"*

The Lone Star State, the only state in the U.S. that was once an independent nation. The state where six flags have flown, and in the south at Laredo, seven. In 1541 Coronado heard there were Indians called Teyas on the western plains, but not until 1689, when natives welcomed a Spanish expedition with "Techas" (friends), did Europeans realize this was the greeting of the Caddos and Wichitas, not their name. Today the Texas state motto is "friendship." But Texas is also the only state on the Pan American Highway which joined the Confederacy during the Civil War, the only state where slavery was a way of life.

In the 1990s Texas became the prison and death penalty capital of America. Besides the state's own exploding inmate population, by mid-decade private prisons in Texas warehoused over 23,000 felons from other states for profit. More than a third of the executions carried out in the U.S. since the resumption of capital punishment in 1976 were in Texas. In fact, up to the mid-nineties, over 10 percent of the legal executions in North America took place in Houston's Harris County alone, this one county having sent more people to death than any other whole state in the union. Over 400 inmates awaited their turn on death row; as governor, George Bush, Jr. stepped up executions. Boy did I feel safe to be in Texas.

Instead of the usual welcome sign at the border, I was greeted by three admonitions: "DWI: You can't afford it," "Fasten Seat Belts: State Law," and the anti-litter message, "Don't Mess with Texas!" I figured I was guiltless on all three counts, so maybe I'd make it through. Just when I was feeling unwelcomed, the "Welcome to Texas," sign came at last, but with the cryptic admonition, "Drive friendly, the Texas way." I would soon discover that means faster than I was willing to push the old Omni. In fact, I would hug the right lane for the next 500 miles across the state, passing two or three people who were probably asleep at the wheel, while thousands of Texans cruised by on my left.

Don't get me wrong. Texas is a grand and beautiful and wealthy state, and secretly, I admire the audacity of Texas. But having grown up north of the Red River, forever bent northward by the hot dry wind, I also admit a mixture of amusement and disdain toward Texans and their state, reinforced by an Army year at Fort Hood. But really, as Texan Molly Ivins is fond of pointing out, watching Texans can be fun.

In Oklahoma a joke made the rounds when I was a boy: As usual, Texas was too dry, and Texans looked greedily north at Oklahoma's abundant lakes and streams. But the question remained, how could Texas get some of that Oklahoma water. The answer: If you can suck as hard as you can blow, it shouldn't be a problem.

Like southern Oklahoma, northern Texas (at least half of Texas, in fact) is ranch country, though here, of course, the ranches are bigger. I had just traversed four of the top cattle producing states in the nation – South Dakota, Nebraska, Kansas, and Oklahoma. But Texas is by far number one, with over 15 million head. Native grasses – big and little blue stem, side oats grama, timothy and buffalo grass – still competed, but mesquite, sage, Johnson grass and forbs dominated over-grazed pastures. Texas was dry, and the cattle looked hungry.

The Census Bureau says the ethnicity of Montague County is mostly English, American and Irish, plus two lonely black people. Houses were few and far between, and so were trees and other travelers.

The first towns were Ringgold, Stoneburg and Bowie. Just outside Ringgold I pulled off at a roadside park, attracted by a grove of oaks. A historical marker, barely decipherable around high caliber bullet holes, said that in 1936 this stretch of the highway was paved with gold. Apparently the sand they used glittered, so the sand pit owner had the stuff assayed in Fort Worth and discovered that it did contain gold – about 60 cents worth per ton. Coronado never found the fabled seven cities of gold he sought here, but I crossed the 1849 gold-seekers' California Trail on a highway paved with gold.

Just north of Stoneburg, which looked fairly petrified, Herefords munched weeds amongst the speakers of a second long-defunct Chisholm Trail drive-in theater.

The official story in Bowie is that the town was named after Jim Bowie, popularizer of the Bowie knife, the long, single-edged hunting knife designed by his brother Rezin. According to novelist James Lee Burns, Jim Bowie was a slave trader even after the Compromise of 1809 made the practice illegal as well as immoral. Bowie joined the Texas revolutionary movement in 1830, disputing leadership at the Alamo with Col. William Travis. Apparently Bowie died unheroically of illness during the 1836 siege.

I stopped for a Texas-sized barbecued pork sandwich at the Crispy Chicken and Barbecue, where I talked with Andy Nored, a hefty retired oil man in bright red suspenders and matching face. I told him I'd read the town was named for Jim Bowie. Andy carefully plated a nacho with cheese, and munched it while he thought. "No," he drawled around the nacho. "Actually the boys downtown only saw the economic potential to be exploited by Jim Bowie Days about 1964. The truth," Andy said, "is that the town was named for a cattle driver of the same name."

After lunch I visited Pelham Park, the old Bowie Camp Pelham reunion grounds, 26 acres on the east edge of town bought in 1901 and preserved by the United Confederate Veterans to honor the Confederacy and its heroes. One big monument memorializes the confederates; another remembers men of Andy's generation who fought in World War II.

At Bowie U.S. 81 merges with a big four-lane coming from Amarillo, the first fast and heavy traffic since Wichita. Frequent fruit and vegetable stands and vendors of everything from antiques to jerky lined the road. I passed the Chisholm Trail Ranch, which offers trail rides for drug store cowboys, and encountered suburban sprawl 40 miles outside Fort Worth. From here to Mexico the Pan American Highway would be wide, smooth and fast.

I crossed the Saint Louis to El Paso Butterfield Overland Mail Trail at Decatur, and entered the suburbs of Fort Worth, once the territory of the Tonkawa and Waco Indians. Though the population of Fort Worth proper is just half a million, it is part of the 60-mile wide Dallas-Fort Worth metropolis of four million. Fort Worth began as a military camp in 1849, at the end of the Mexican-American War. It was founded by Gen. Winfield Scott, who in the 1838 marched the Cherokees to Indian Territory on the Trail of Tears, then invaded Mexico at Veracruz and conquered Mexico City in 1847. The town was named for another general, William Jenkins Worth, who also fought in Mexico.

Fort Worth is the county seat of Tarrant County, named for yet a third general, Edward Tarrant, who in 1843 attacked and wiped out a peaceable local village of Wacos, who lived in semi-permanent conical huts of willow and grass. Tarrant went on to attack other villages, but according to an incredible 1995 brochure from the Fort Worth Chamber of Commerce, "at the third village, the savages put up a spirited defense," making obvious the need of a fort here from which American soldiers might "pursue and punish the redskin raiders."

Special events in Fort Worth include the stock show and rodeo in January, the Chisholm Trail Roundup and Chief Quannah Parker Pow Wow in June, and Pioneer Days in September. (Quannah Parker was the last great war chief of the Comanche, son of a Comanche chief and a captive white girl, Cynthia Parker.)

Fort Worth is home to the world's biggest school of theology, the 4,500 student Southwestern Baptist Seminary. Billy Sunday, who played pro baseball for the Fort Worth Panthers in the 1880s, returned in 1918 to preach the biggest revival meeting in history, converting nearly a thousand. The city has the world's biggest revolving stage, Casa Mañana Theater, built as a centennial project in 1936. And of course, there's Billy Bob's, the world's biggest honkey tonk. The fact is that in Texas, most everything is the oldest or the newest, the biggest or the best, that ever was.

I found that Fort Worth isn't really that much of a cowtown anymore, in spite of its reputation. Meat-packing has been decentralized to smaller towns, and Fort Worth has become another sophisticated city, boasting not only the world-class Kimbell art museum, but also the Museum of Science and History, upscale restaurants, and all the accouterments of a swanky restored downtown on the banks of the Trinity River. A few years ago the Bass brothers bought and refurbished several square blocks of downtown, adding new hotels and condos. A private security force on bikes and foot control crime and make conventioneers feel safe. I arrived too late to tour the Kimbell, or to do the other high culture things one must do before five. Anyway, farm boy that I am, I appreciate lowbrow entertainment too. So after a stroll downtown, I headed for Cowtown.

The stockyards area was once a town distinct from Fort Worth, born when the railroad arrived from the east in 1876. It was incorporated in 1911 as Niles City, named for the Boston businessman who arrived in 1893, and reorganized the Fort Worth Packing Company in 1899. Swift and Armour came in 1902, and soon became the giants. Niles City was annexed by Fort Worth in 1923, but Swift and Armour ruled for another 40 years. The giants folded in the sixties, and the only cows sold in Fort Worth these days are for show. But Madison Avenue has nothing on these ex-cowpokes.

The entrepreneurs of Fort Worth have turned Cowtown into a major tourist attraction. Nobody wants to actually smell a cow or a pig or a sheep, or especially to step in what they leave behind. But tourists from all over love to buy fancy cowboy shirts, eat barbecue in old pig barns, and dance to country rock at Billy Bob's. Or were all these folks not tourists, but just Texans?

I had some wonderful Risky's barbecue, slow-cooked over mesquite, the desert bush that is overtaking pastures that Herefords over-grazed, pastures where longhorns, and before them buffalo, once ate grass. Risky's too is part illusion. It started as a little grocery where Polish immigrants Joe and Mary Risky eked out a Cowtown living. Now their grandson Jim owns several restaurants here, serving not only great barbecue, but Risky's oysters on the half-shell, and even Risky's Mexican food. I was getting closer to both the Gulf and the border. A neon Mexican beer sign in Risky's window flashed "Tecate," "Texas," "Tecatexas."

As a young man, manager Norman Heflin worked in the sale barn that is now Risky's — shoveling sheep manure in the same building where people now shovel down pig and cow ribs. Norman said the sale barn had pretty much shut down by the early eighties when he worked here, except for symbolic purposes.

I crossed the street to the oyster place to talk with Jim Risky himself, but he was going out the door as I came in. I did visit with four of Jim's friends. Large quantities of Risky beer had enhanced their memories of Cowtown. Wally Culps was the ring leader.

"I've been hanging out in Cowtown for 40 years," Wally proclaimed, "ever since I started shooting pool on Exchange Street. Every Saturday I'd tour both Swift and Armour. I ate free baloney at one and wieners at the other, and saved my money for pool." Wally recalled that after the big plants closed in the sixties, diminished cattle sales continued for awhile. He also told me, apropos of nothing, that both his older and younger brothers had polio. "I was so sorry, I couldn't get it," Wally said.

The entire packing town district is now packed with tourist attractions:

restaurants, mostly specializing in steaks or barbecue, bars, vendors of "authentic" western wear and artifacts, a fine museum, and of course the coliseum, built in 1908 and still going strong. The next weekend it was hosting the Coors Women's National Finals Rodeo. But the biggest attraction in old Cowtown is Billy Bob's.

Billy Bob's is truly huge. Texas-sized. It boasts two gigantic stages and dance floors, several bars and a restaurant, a whole section for games, including pin-ball and foosball, basketball, and a dozen pool tables. There's a real (though thoroughly dead and stuffed) bull on which a middle-aged, sagging-bellied couple from Colorado Springs were having their picture taken in poses of rapturous danger. And on Friday nights, professional bull riders (what other kind would there be?) ride professional bulls in a real dirt floor arena right in the middle of the honkey tonk.

And Billy Bob's draws the biggest names in country and western entertainment too: Billy Joe Royal, Hank Thompson, Tanya Tucker, John Conlee, Jerry Jeff Walker, Garth Brooks, Emmy Lou Harris, Charlie Pride, Jerry Lee Lewis, Conway Twitty, and Willie Nelson have played here. What's more, all of the above and many more have stuck their playing hands and signed their names into globs of wet cement, which subsequently dried, and Billy Bob has hung them all on the wall. Unfortunately, some adoring, or more likely drunken, fan had cracked Willie's down the middle.

Over the main dance floor a crystal saddle revolves, casting flickering diamonds of light on ceiling, walls and dancers, epitomizing the evolution from real cowboys and cows to dudes in shiny boots and dust-free hats, wheeling girls who've never been closer to a cow than hamburgers and ribs across a glistening hardwood floor. Cowtown is good tourist fun, and the place still retains enough aroma of the by-gone era to suggest authenticity. But in fact it's more Hollywood than reality, more glitz and pretend than guts and manure.

Early next morning I headed down I-35, which has mostly replaced U.S. 81 from Fort Worth to the Mexican border at Laredo. I was headed for Waco, where I had a date with Bubbles at the historic suspension bridge over the Brazos River. Waco is a city of just over 100,000, 12,000 of them students at Baylor, the world's biggest Baptist university, and Texas' oldest, founded in 1845. The Armstrong Browning Library at Baylor is a major 19th century research center, including the world's best collection of manuscripts of 19th century British poet Robert Browning, as well as manuscripts of Elizabeth Barrett Browning, John Ruskin, Charles Dickens, Matthew Arnold, and Ralph Waldo Emerson, housed in a castle built in the middle of the Great Depression. Baylor officials had just announced that after 150 years, dancing would be allowed on campus. Pres. Robert Sloan had concluded that dancing can be wholesome when "properly done."

Waco was also the home of Iconoclast publisher William Cowper Brann, who failed to ingratiate himself to his neighbors when he wrote things like, "Texas can furnish forth more hidebound dogmatists, narrow-brained bigots, and intolerant fanatics in proportion to population than can any other section of these United States." Brann was beaten by a mob of Baylor students in 1897, and assassinated on a Waco street in 1898. The marble monument to Brann, featuring a lamp of wisdom and light above his head, was defaced by bullets.

Other attractions in Waco include the Texas Ranger Hall of Fame and gun collection, the Texas Sports Hall of Fame, and the Dr. Pepper Museum, with samples of every Dr. Pepper sign and bottle ever made. The traveler can even enjoy a symphony or see a play at one of several theaters in this cultured college town.

Instead I had a long talk with an old college friend, Linda Walker, who as a ninth grader was "Bubbles" on a local Saturday morning TV show in Enid, Oklahoma. Bubbles drifted from her hat as she told stories and played with animals. For two decades Linda had been a professor of English at Baylor University.

We met in the middle of the 1870 suspension bridge, which bore cattle across the Brazos on the Chisholm Trail when Waco was known as "Six-shooter Junction." Later the bridge became a vital link in the Pan American Highway. It was designed by John A. Roebling, who four years earlier had designed the world's first and longest suspension bridge across the Ohio River at Cincinnati, and who later designed the Brooklyn Bridge, to be built by his son. The Brazos bridge remains in fine condition, having been retired from vehicle traffic since 1971. South of the bridge is downtown Waco. To the north is a mostly African American neighborhood (the most numerous ethnic group in McLennan County), and a booming new industrial park, spurred Linda said, by NAFTA, but offering mostly minimum wage jobs. She told me that gangs and drugs and crime had become big problems in Waco, with 14 murders in the small city in the previous year. We met between the two worlds, above the Brazos, Spanish for arms.

I asked Linda about Waco's reaction to the tragedy at Mount Carmel, the Branch Davidian compound. "The whole ordeal was heart-breaking for the community on many levels," she said. Linda said that few people supported the government assault on the Davidians. She said that for nearly a year it was the top story daily in the local media, but a year later, nobody talked about it at all. "The whole affair is repressed," she said, "like a bad dream, a trauma that never should have happened."

One of Linda's students asked at the time how society could judge whether David Koresh had any legitimacy as a "messiah." As a specialist in Henry David Thoreau, Linda has deep respect for the right to dissent, for the individual's right to keep pace to a different drummer, to "step to the music which he hears," as Thoreau put it, even the right of civil disobedience. Yet, she had no ready answer. The closest she could come was to recall the words of Jesus: "By their fruits you shall know them."

But the tragedy did put Waco on the map, and Linda predicted that someone would capitalize on the notoriety. During the stand-off with FBI and Alcohol Tobacco and Firearms agents, Linda had driven out to Mount Carmel to see for herself what was going on, but the entire area was cordoned off by author-ities, so she couldn't get close. Another day, just before the assault, she had gone for an allergy shot and found the hospital abuzz with activity, clearly preparing for an influx of patients. She knew something was about to pop.

I had a couple of hours left in Waco. I could have toured the Dr. Pepper museum, but I decided to look for Mount Carmel instead, to see where, depend-ing on one's perspective, the Waco Wacko led his flock to death, or where the ATF and FBI assaulted and killed 82 men, women and children who dared to live a communal life of separation and defiance, or perhaps both.

It took awhile, but at last I found Mount Carmel, the ruined Mecca of the Branch Davidians. I'm not sure what I expected, but just locating the place proved tricky. Linda gave me general directions, so I crossed the river again on I-35, where many of Waco's homeless people live, and where their "church under the bridge" was founded. Past Bellmead I stopped at a gas station for directions on FM 2491 to the former compound. I didn't know exactly what I was looking for, and was about to give up when I turned down a gravel road, perhaps by intu-ition, and there it was.

A prominent sign at the entrance to the property proclaimed, "Congratulations, you have found Mount Carmel," then listed the dates on which previous signs were stolen. Another sign welcomed me, but warned of dan-gers on the property, which looked like a bombed-out war zone: "Memorial and Ruin straight ahead. Hazards: Broken glass, nails, sharp metal, razor blade wire, deep water, open pits, unmarked washouts, rubble piles, and wildlife: Enter at your own risk." A woman who introduced herself as Amo had just returned from town with groceries. She invited me to look over the ruin and the Loud Cry Museum while she put them away.

I strolled through a recently planted orchard, 82 flowering shrubs and 82 small wooden crosses, one for each of the Davidians who died here, 18 of them children under the age of 10. On the perimeter of the ruin were two burned-out buses, two scorched motor homes, a twisted motorcycle, a couple of blackened cars, and scattered seared toys. There were mounds of bulldozed concrete, twist-ed metal, charred debris. The basements reeked of brackish water. A granite mon-ument placed by the Northeast Texas Regional Militia remembers the Davidians for holding out against federal forces for 51 days.

By coincidence, as I visited with Amo Bishop Roden outside the 8x10-foot plywood hut where she lives on the edge of the ruin, Congressional hearings began in Washington into the April 19, 1993 assault on the compound. Amo had been a Davidian since 1987, just before Koresh began his struggle for control of the church. She told me that someone (federal agents, local residents, she does-n't know who), steals signs as fast as she can put them up. She said the Waco Chamber of Commerce tells the curious that a crazy woman out here shoots at people. In fact, Amo welcomes visitors to Saturday Sabbath services under the spreading elm at what she called "the world's most persecuted church," a church

*Amo Bishop Roden at her home at the ruin of Mount Carmel near Waco (top), and the Stagecoach Inn at Salado.*

she said the government has been trying to destroy for 40 years.

Amo was a youngish-looking middle-aged woman, long blonde hair in a sagging bun that hinted of Seventh Day Adventist, from which the sect emerged. She wore a loose cotton dress, and in stark contrast to the setting, was sadly attractive. She was frustrated that someone didn't want people to find her and hear her story.

"David Koresh was an impostor," Amo said. The Branch Davidian Church began in 1955, she said, and local leader Lois Roden bought this 77-acre pasture and founded Mount Carmel in 1973. Amo said Koresh did a "hostile takeover" of the community by ingratiating himself to Lois, first becoming her driver, eventually marrying her, though he was 40 years her junior. Koresh then exploited that relationship to bring himself to power.

Amo said that in 1987 she had married Lois' son, George Roden, so that in a bizarre way, Koresh became her father-in-law. She said that in 1988 Koresh shot George, his rival for leadership, and that while Koresh escaped charges of attempted murder, George was jailed for contempt of court for expressing disrespect to the judge. Amo said Koresh was "a false prophet who destroyed a Mecca of God's people."

The Loud Cry Museum was a 12-foot square plywood hut, unprofessionally constructed and painted solid black. Inside I found twisted, burned bicycles, more charred toys and personal effects, and the photographs, news clippings, graphics, and posters which told the story of the attack on the Davidians. Large photographs showed army tanks from Fort Hood poking holes in the compound walls, filling the buildings with tear gas, and the entire compound in flames, fulfilling Koresh's apocalyptic vision. Another photo showed the government bulldozing the ruin less than a month after the fire, the purposeful destruction of all evidence of the life and death of Mount Carmel. The museum is surrounded by crosses.

Amo deplored the bombing of the Federal Building in Oklahoma City, and while Timothy McVeigh apparently did visit Mount Carmel about six months before the bombing, she said she never met him. She was angered by suggestions of a connection between McVeigh and the Branch Davidians. Neither did she blame militia groups for the Oklahoma City bombing. In fact, she said, the U.S. government is so "oppressive and dangerous" that she welcomed defense by the Texas militia, who installed the memorial beside the ruin. Amo said militias provide a "necessary balance of power."

I asked Amo about the future of Mount Carmel. Surely at some point the pain and embarrassment of Mount Carmel will wear off, to be replaced by the realization that there is a buck to be made. Bearing in mind that a wiped-out Indian village just down the road draws tourists, and the museum of guns and Texas Rangers is the biggest in town, I asked whether the time would come when Waco boosters would promote Mount Carmel as a tourist attraction. This sad-eyed woman laughed aloud for the first time. "As soon as they get rid of me," she said. "As soon as they change the management."

I drove away from Mount Carmel, thinking of Lawrence Ferlinghetti's poem, "A Buddha in the Woodpile." "If there had been only/ one Buddhist in the woodpile/In Waco Texas/ to teach us how to sit still/...just one saint in the wilderness/ of Waco USA/...Then that sick cult and its children/ might still be breathing/ the free American air/ of the First Amendment."

I left Waco by noon, driving south through Bell County, the home of Amanda "Ma" Ferguson, the first female governor of Texas, preceding Ann Richards by 65 years. I passed Temple, the "Wildflower Capital of Texas," where in the spring when the Texas state flower the bluebonnet reigns, the region is a blooming sea of blue.

Just past Temple is Belton, home of Baylor University's little sister institution, Mary Hardin Baylor, also established in 1845, but for women, when big Baylor was just for men. Though MHB did not officially go co-ed until 1971, as a soldier at nearby Fort Hood in 1968, I talked my way into Dr. Fussel's night class in modern fiction, over her strong objections. I needed three credits to complete certification for a teaching job I hoped to get after the Army, and Dr. Fussel needed to maintain the purity of her classroom. So our goals were in conflict. I won the first round, gaining admission, but from the first period on it was apparent that an "A" was not in my future. Dr. Fussel had devoted a lifetime to this institution, and she didn't like seeing the place polluted by men.

From MHB I turned the Omni west into the edge of the Balcones Escarpment, the fault which divides the Texas whose western edge I was skirting – humid, populous and wealthy – from the 60 percent of Texas west of the rise – arid, sparsely populated, and except for oil country, not so prosperous. Seven Texas rivers flow southeast from the escarpment to the Gulf. In the rocky hills ahead the Tawankoni once lived; I was headed for Killeen and Fort Hood.

Fort Hood was cattle ranches until 1942, when Camp Hood was established, named for Confederate Gen. John Bell Hood. Camp Hood was yet another spot by the highway where German prisoners of war were held. I spent a strange year of my life at Fort Hood, beginning in 1967. There I survived three attempts to ship me off to Vietnam, and from there I finally escaped to complete my service in Germany. At 339 square miles, or 217,000 acres, and as the only two-division army base in the United States, Fort Hood is billed as "the largest collection of soldiers and fighting machines in the free world."

The 1st Cavalry Division was joined at Fort Hood by the 2nd Armored Division, of which I was a reluctant part, in the fall of 1967. On December 12, 1967, Pres. Lyndon Johnson himself rode by in a jeep and reviewed my battalion as we stood at attention on the parade grounds south of Battalion Avenue, then wished us luck. Within three months, many of the men with whom I stood were dead in the Tet Offensive. I drove around the post, locating the places I used to work. The World War II barracks on 49th north of Battalion where I slept had become the Red Cross headquarters.

What I remembered better, though, was Killeen, which GIs in those days called "the armpit of the nation." In 1967, Army privates earned $95 a month, and if they were married, a small living allowance. Killeen was a den of slum lords and thieves, ripping off GIs on their way to Nam for every penny they could get for roach-infested apartments, junk furniture, and sordid entertainment.

Because my buddy Brad Fisher and I had nothing better to do in the evenings and on Saturdays, we took a moonlighting job with Pick Picklesimmer, the Pall Mall-puffing owner and proprietor of Capital TV and Appliance, on the railroad tracks. Pick's stock in the sagging warehouse he called a "showroom" consisted of scores of broken-down beds, moth-eaten couches, vertical hold-less TVs, and wobbly chrome dinette sets. Brad and I delivered these goodies to desperate fellow-soldiers and their families in an oil-burning '53 Chevy pickup. Pickelsmoker, as we took to calling him, rented out his goods at $10 per piece per month; we delivered them for $2 an hour.

Before long the horror of our enterprise took its toll on Brad and me, and gradually our work became less diligent. Then there was the moonlight night on the way back from delivering an inoperable console TV for the third time to a woman in Copperas Cove, when suddenly without warning my right foot turned to lead. The old Chevy groaned and clattered, inching its way up to 60, 65, almost 70. There was one long curve on the road between Copperas Cove and Killeen, and I took it at top speed.

Brad glanced at me nervously and suggested I slow down. Then he caught the malicious gleam in my eye, and broke into a sympathetic roar that still echoes somewhere through eternity. The big TV overcame the inertia of its wobbly legs, and began its final glide. It screeched across the bed, hit the edge, tipped on two legs for an everlasting second, and was gone. In the rear-view mirror, shards and tubes and splinters glinted in the moonlight for a wonderful moment, and subsided. I slowed the old Chevy down and we limped back to town, drying the tears of laughter from our eyes. I parked her under the street light in front of Capital TV, left the key in the ignition, and walked away.

For more than a quarter century I'd anticipated this return. I wanted to see if Killeen was still as nasty as I remembered. Now I was here, but I didn't recognize much. The town seemed a lot saner and less wicked, with the salaries of professional soldiers to absorb. And you could eat a different ethnic cuisine every night of the week, thanks to the army brides brought back from Germany, Vietnam, Thailand, Korea, and other exotic places. I drove by Luby's Cafeteria where in 1991 a madman gunned down 21 people and then himself. I looked in vain for a memorial.

I also looked in vain for Capital TV. Twice I thought I'd found a modern incarnation of the place, but the present tenants denied historical knowledge. I checked the phone book, but no Capital TV and Appliance, and no Picklesimmer. Not even a Picklesmoker. But after all, what did I expect? Pickelsimmer must have been in his 60s then, and surely a man of his moral fiber could not survive forever. And yet, somehow I was disappointed. I guess I'd hoped to peer into his shifty eyes once more, to confess details of that night in the moonlight. Why? Just to see his face blaze red, I suppose, to hear him sputter defenselessly over his busted TV.

Denied this sadistic indulgence, I headed back to the highway, and south again to Salado. Salado, Spanish for salty creek, began in the 1860s as another stop on the Chisholm Trail. The old Shady Inn Villa, later renamed the Stagecoach Inn, still stands beside the highway under the arms of the huge live oak which gave the place its original name. Its guests have included Sam Houston, Jesse James, Robert E. Lee, Jr. and Col. Custer, all of whose names were recorded in the guest book, stolen in 1944 and never recovered. The Stagecoach Inn is still welcoming guests, but now well-heeled tourists who pay $10 for lunch in a historic place. I looked the Inn over, then settled for a bowl of soup up the street.

Across from the Stagecoach is yet another museum with artifacts from the cattle drive days. In fact, the whole town has the feel of a museum, which tourists seem to love. And I actually spotted the state bird, the mockingbird, singing his myriad tunes in the state tree, a pecan. But Salado also has a place in progressive Texas history: the first farmers' Grange in Texas, an organization founded to fight for farmer's rights, was established here in 1873.

On down the interstate the Omni rumbled, taking me past Jarrell, which would soon be destroyed by a tornado, then Georgetown, and into Austin. Austin became the compromise capital of the Republic of Texas in 1839, and like Fort Worth, is home to about half a million. It is named for Stephen F. Austin, who led the fight for Texas independence from Mexico. Before 1839, it was Waterloo. And before Europeans moved in, Tonkawa, Comanche and Lipan Apache peoples lived in the hills of the Balcones Escarpment to the west and in the valley of the Colorado River.

A big storm was moving in fast from the southwest, and I sped through miles of glass-faced suburban office buildings reflecting the roiling clouds, looking for shelter before the deluge. It was Halloween night, and I wanted to be on 6th Street for the "Nation's (you guessed it) Biggest Halloween Party." Along with all the goblins of Austin, I hoped it would not be rained out.

Much to my chagrin I had to take a room at a high dollar joint – Motel 6. It cost me enough to stay a week of nights in Central America, but by now it was pouring rain, and anyway, I probably couldn't have found anything cheaper in this rich town. I read and wrote awhile, and when the rain finally let up, I headed down to 6th Street for the party.

Austin is perhaps Texas' most cosmopolitan city, promoted as the "Jewel of the Lone Star State." And owing to its more than 100 live music clubs, including such famous places as the Armadillo and Threadgills, they also call Austin the "Live Music Capital of the World." It is of course home of the Texas state capitol building (seven feet taller than the U.S. Capitol, as one might expect), and of the 50,000 student University of Texas, whose endowment is second only to Harvard's. (Texans must lie awake at night worrying about being second in something.)

The Chamber of Commerce claims that Austin is the most highly-educated U.S. city of over a quarter million people, and having become a new "silicon valley" in the 1980s, the most computer-literate city in the nation. They say Austin has the most restaurants, bars and movie screens per capita, and is the best place in the country for interracial couples to live. (I'm not sure how they measured that.) *Money* magazine had ranked Austin along with Grand Forks and Fargo, North Dakota as among the top five places in the country to live, with the added advantage that Austin isn't frozen solid half the year. But most impressive of all is that Austin has more bats than any other U.S. city, 1.5 million of them, most living under the Congress Avenue Bridge over the Colorado River, south of the Capitol.

Apparently, when engineers designed the reconstruction of the bridge in 1980, they unwittingly created the ideal bat house by leaving 1x16-inch crevices between the girders under the bridge. Since bats migrate north from Mexico looking for a summer home, and since Austin has plenty of insects, including mosquitoes, their favorite food, over a million bats moved in. At first, I presume, city fathers must have been horrified, given the undeserved bad reputation of bats. Should they torpedo the bridge? Poison the creatures? But cooler heads prevailed. Environmentalists, led by Bat Conservation International, pointed out that bats are gentle and generally harmless, and that the horde could consume several tons of insects every night. Then in the true spirit of the dauntless Texan, some fertile mind at the C of C found the proper spin: The bats could be yet another tourist attraction, further evidence of the superior quality of life in Austin. Unfortunately, they forgot to tell the bats it was Halloween, a holiday in their honor, and only a few stragglers had not migrated south for the winter.

The rain stopped, and along with 25,000 gorillas, ghosts, ghouls, painted ladies, corpses, mummies, giant chickens, nuns, Martians and even a few creatures recognizable as Austinians, I made it down to 6th Street, live music street, for the Halloween shindig. I ate Tex-Mex enchiladas at Calle Ocho, then strolled 6th Street awhile before settling on a blues joint, Headliners East, where I sipped locally-brewed Shiner beer and grooved to the slide guitar of Brian Robertson and the Juke Joint Blues Band, the drummer of which wore a gigantic pig nose for the occasion.

Between songs I talked with an electrical engineer from Vancouver Island about the nearly successful secession vote in Quebec the previous day. John explained that the separatist movement was mostly emotional, stirred by political demagoguery. He was glad his fellow Canadians voted to remain in the union, but he expected the separatists to continue their campaign to establish a French country in America. What a contrast, I thought, to the peaceful cohabitation of many diverse cultures in Winnipeg, where my journey began.

Next morning I strolled around the Capitol, admiring the beauty of the 1888 native red granite structure, but appalled by the three monuments to oppression and division which surround the capitol, memorials to those who fought for separation from Mexico, partly to establish slavery, and to others who fought for separation from the U.S. in order to maintain it.

I watched a press conference put on by half a dozen grocery giants before a backdrop of delivery trucks, in which the death of food stamps in Texas was proclaimed. Food stamps would be replaced by credit cards for the poor, designed to make the food stamp business more efficient for retailers.

On the UT campus, I rode the elevator up the 307-foot limestone tower from which student Charles Whitman gunned down 14 fellow students on August 1, 1966. Again, no memorial. The woman at the information desk said the incident was something everybody was trying not to remember. Then I viewed the exhibits in the Lyndon Baines Johnson Library on the east edge of campus. Historians have painted LBJ as an enigma, a mass of contradictions, and visiting the library and museum reinforced my own mixed memories of the man.

There was the president whose first election to Congress involved alleged voting irregularities, whose five-year presidency was dominated by the fiasco of the Vietnam War, and whose announcement in 1968 that he would not seek reelection I, as a soldier at Fort Hood, truly welcomed. But there was also the president who dreamed of a "Great Society," who declared war on poverty, who believed in education and the obligation of society to take care of its less fortunate members. The president whose administration established Medicare and federal aid to education. The man who signed the Civil Rights Act, the Voting Rights Act, and more laws designed to make America a land of freedom and equality and humanity than perhaps any other president in our history. In fact, it is essentially Johnson's Great Society that Newt Gingrich and his Republican counter-revolutionaries later attempted to dismantle.

Before leaving Austin, I had lunch at the Cactus Cafe with poet Tammy Gomez. Tammy was a diminutive chicana, 33, short black hair and proud eyes. She made her living at the University Bureau of Business Research, but her passion was poetry, and using poetry to help her people – women, people of color, people of compassion – take full possession of their place in the modern world. Tammy talked about her family, about the community radio program she produced for KO-OP, about her "spoken word band," La Palabra, about Austin, chicano politics and NAFTA, and of course about her poetry, which she performed with the band. Tammy gave me a copy of her chapbook, *Seis Huesos*, or six bones, six poems hard and tough as stones, but tender as marrow at the center, poems mostly about women defining themselves, defending themselves and the planet, de-phonying sexist lies, defying whatever stands in their way.

In "Manslaughter" Tammy takes the word apart, revealing the ugly "man's laughter" behind spousal and domestic abuse. In "FALSIES" she playfully builds a concrete breast of breast images, then deflates ten "falsies" under which women have lived concerning their breasts: "Silicon breast implants are a safe and viable option for women /... If you're not a 38-C you can't be sexy/ Better to have falsies than to be flat."

Tammy and La Palabra had just completed a coffeehouse tour of Colorado and New Mexico, but her favorite gig was for her extended family gathered in a living room in Abilene, Texas, where part of her family still lives. Tammy said that with the death of singer Selena, young Chicanos were looking for artistic role models. Tammy saw Tejano music as easy-listening and romantic, a music that combines Mexican and western traditions, but safe music, music which lulls. She was alarmed by its popularity, which suggested complacency, acceptance of the status quo. She hoped her brand of rebellious and anarchical poetry would wake young people up to injustice, to the need to struggle for change.

I asked Tammy about NAFTA, about the economic crisis in Mexico and the resulting increase in Mexican immigration to the U.S., and about the fact that Mexicans and Mexican Americans had become the top ethnic group in Travis County. She said NAFTA was battering Mexicans, keeping wages low and flooding Mexico with imports with which Mexican industry was not prepared to compete. She said NAFTA was also adding low-wage jobs in Texas. I suggested that perhaps a low-wage job is better than no job. "You should never choose for someone else something that is worse than you would anticipate or expect for yourself," she said.

Tammy said that in 1995, the Texas property rights group, Save Our State (SOS), and others worked to copy California's Prop 187, hoping to thwart the influx of immigrants by taking away social services. Otherwise, she said, relations between whites and Chicanos/Mexicans in Texas were generally more congenial than in California.

We also talked about Texas itself. Tammy said that many Texans are "texocentric," feeling that Texas has everything they need: good winter weather, small towns, big cities, ocean shore, mountains, forests, deserts, factories and farms. Why go elsewhere? She has a poem about this phenomenon: "Texas bred, Texas fed, Texas wed, Texas dead." But Austin, she said, is a cosmopolitan island of diversity, where she had found an arts and activist community that was global in perspective. They "extend their boundaries" through networking, through local organizations and the collectively-owned KO-OP radio and through the worldwide web.

Tammy had to get back to work, having already extended her lunch hour, and I had to make time to San Antonio to pick up South Dakota filmmaker Doug Sharples at the airport, so we said good-bye. Doug and I would retrace Beat writer Jack Kerouac's 1950 journey down the Pan American Highway from San Antonio to Mexico City, celebrated in *On the Road*. Doug would shoot highway scenes and Kerouac haunts in Mexico City for his film "Go Moan for Man."

I was running late, so I cruised past San Marcos, where the San Marcos River rises from Aquarena Springs in the middle of town, and where LBJ went to college at Southwest Texas State. I also had to bypass the ethnic German town of New Braunfels, founded in 1845 when Prince Carl de Solms-Braunfels of Wassau, Germany brought a colony of immigrants. Though the town now has more residents of Mexican than of German origin, New Braunfels still celebrates its German heritage twice a year with Volksmarsch and Wurstfest.

As I crossed the Guadalupe River I turned on Public Radio's "All Things Considered" in time to catch a story about the laundering of Cali Cartel drug money by Panamanian banks. I would remember the story again in Panamá City, the downtown of which bristles with newly-constructed skyscraper banks, adjacent to a ghetto. U.S. investigators claimed that Panamanian bankers were recycling $2 billion a year in Colombian drug money. Didn't Pres. Bush tell us that removing Noriega would take care of that problem?

I met Doug at the airport on the north edge of San Antonio and drove to the home of Tom and Lori Lobe, who had recently immigrated from South Dakota to San Antonio to teach political science. Tom and Lori offered us beds for the night.

European contact in San Antonio dates back over 300 years. In 1691, the Payaya Indians called the place Yanaguana, for the clear water of the river. Spanish explorers Terán and Massanet arrived on May 19, Saint Anthony's birthday, and thought nothing of changing the name of the river and the place to San Antonio. By 1718 Spaniards had established the Mission San Antonio de Valero, later known as the Alamo (Spanish for cottonwood), the site of the 1836 massacre of independence fighters by the forces of Mexican Gen. Santa Anna. In 1731 the Spanish established a Villa here, the structure of state following that of the church. San Antonio remained a stronghold and outpost of the Mexican government until the Texas Revolution.

San Antonio was the biggest city yet on the highway, almost a million. Half the residents are of Mexican descent, a percentage that increases from here to the Rio Grande. The city has several major universities, and as many military bases. I had driven down from Fort Hood for the Hemis-Fair in 1968, an event and exhibition which symbolized San Antonio's status then and now as a transitional city, half Mexican and Spanish, half North American and English. Many neighborhoods in San Antonio are virtually indistinguishable from barrios in say, Monterrey. Spanish speech, Tejano music, Mexican food and tropical flora reign. Jack Kerouac said of San Antonio in 1950, "We were already almost out of America and yet definitely in it."

Doug and I drove downtown to check out the river walk and to hear some music. The idea of taming, confining and exploiting the San Antonio River for entertainment and tourist appeal was promoted by architect Robert H. H. Hugman in the 1930s. Hugman designed the present river walk, tree and restaurant-lined sidewalks curving along both sides of the river 20 feet below street level, past the Alamo and through several blocks of central city. The river walk was quiet that Wednesday evening, a calm and relaxing place to sip some suds and watch the not quite so clear anymore Yanaguana flow by.

From San Antonio all the way to Monterrey, Mexico was once Coahuiltec country. It is sparsely inhabited, flat sage brush land, with pockets of irrigated farms. At San Antonio the Pan American Highway parts from the old Chisholm Trail, which went southeast to the King Ranch. U.S. 81 veers southwest, roughly following the old Upper Presidio Road, the Spanish route from Laredo. This was the 1950 route of Kerouac and fellow travelers Neil Cassady and Frank Jeffries (Dean Moriarity and Stan Shepherd in *On The Road*), and the road I remembered from the sixties. Interstate 35 now skirts the towns of the old highway, but we pulled off to visit several – Devine, Pearsall, Dilley, and Cotulla.

In Devine, cattle country history is evident at the almost century-old Stroud Blacksmith Shop, where hundreds of area cattle brands are on display. The next two substantial towns, Pearsall and Dilley, are respectively, the peanut and water-melon capitals of Texas. But Pearsall is not limited to peanuts, and in fact, the six-foot fiberglass peanut beside the highway looks a lot more weevil-eaten than when I first saw it in 1967. Pearsall also produces cotton, corn, grains, vegetables, cattle, hogs, goats and honey. And to top it off, they even have a Potato Festival every year. Our timing was off, and we missed the excitement. But I did find refreshingly honest the mimeographed sheet from the local Chamber, which states, "there's not a lot of shopping in Pearsall because everyone goes to San Antonio for that."

Dilley lies just south of the Frío River. (How did a river in south Texas get named cold?) The big black diamond watermelon on Dilley's Main Street has survived three decades in better condition than Pearsall's peanut, the cut-out quarter still revealing juicy red meat and glossy black seeds. Dilley watermelons allegedly find their way to every state in the union, having long since replaced the lowly onion as the chief crop of the region. The annual Watermelon Festival the second Sunday of June epitomizes the town's motto, "a slice of the good life." But now Dilley also has a slice of the biggest growth industry in Texas; in 1992 the state opened a 1,000 "bed" prison here which employs 300 people. Just to the west is Crystal City, home of Mexican Americans I'd met in North Dakota and Nebraska.

Mostly though, I remembered Dilley as the place where Jack Kerouac, return-ing *On the Road* from Mexico in the fall of 1950, was "standing on the hot road underneath an arc-lamp with summer moths smashing into it," hearing "the sound of footsteps from the darkness beyond, and lo, a tall old man with flow-ing white hair came clomping by with a pack on his back, and when he saw (Kerouac) as he passed, he said, 'Go moan for man,' and clomped on back to his dark." Kerouac took the cryptic message as a commission from a higher realm, a definition of his task on Earth, a guiding principle in his spiritual quest. As he turned out half a dozen books in as many years, the old man with flowing hair was never far from his shoulder. Hence, the title of my filmmaking companion's work. Of course we stopped to shoot some footage in Dilley, as we would all along the road Kerouac took before us.

Down the highway a piece, Cotulla languished in the desert sun for half a century before somebody dammed the Nueces River for irrigation. After 1836 the Republic of Texas considered the Río Grande its border with Mexico, but Mexico considered the Nueces its fall-back northern border. Now Cotulla calls itself the "Hub city of the Winter Garden South Texas Brush Country." And except for cleared and irrigated farm land, brush it still is – mesquite, creosote bushes, cactus, and scrub tamarack trees. In spite of the town's cultivated garden image, the phone directory lists more hunting-related businesses than anything else – 11 hunting ranches, "havens," and guide services. In March Cotulla hosts a javelina hunt and Wild Hog Cook-off. (The javelina isn't really a hog, of course, but a peccary.) The town deserves a couple of other historical notes: Before the Texas Rangers arrived in 1874, Cotulla was known as "the sheriff's deadline," beyond which the law did not reach. And LBJ had his first teaching job here; a photo in the Johnson Library shows the teacher with his students. The civil rights president is the only white person in the picture.

Gaunt and lonely cows lurk about windmills, and tiny communities dot the brush: Artesia Wells, Encinal, Cactus, Callaghan, and Webb. Then Laredo comes into view, and the Río Grande is near. Old Laredo, on the Texas side, is home to nearly 200,000, half of whom are under age 26. It is a historic city, established by Don Tomás Sanchez, a captain in the Spanish colonial army. Sanchez was granted land in 1755 to set up the Villa de San Augustine de Laredo. Laredo was an important outpost for successive governments in Mexico for almost a century, and the object of Apache and Comanche raids in 1821.

Whereas the rest of Texas has lived under six flags, Laredo knew a seventh. In addition to Spain, France, Mexico, the Republic of Texas, the Confederacy, and the United States, for nine months in 1840 Laredo was capital of the separatist Republic of the Río Grande, declared in the border region by people who resisted the 1836 revolutionary government of Texas. A memorial in the central plaza marks the site of a major battle between the Botas (those with boots) and the Huaraches (the sandal-clad peasants) for control of Laredo. Mexican novelist Carlos Fuentes has described the Río Grande as the center of a thousand-mile-wide border region: To the north lies "Baja Oklahoma," and to the south, "Mexamerica."

The U.S. annexed Texas in 1845, and declared war against Mexico. Mexico surrendered in 1848, and the Treaty of Guadalupe Hidalgo established the border at the Río Grande (aka Río Bravo on the Mexican side). The U.S. had taken nearly half of Mexico's territory. Thus the first of many refugee waves crossed the river, Mexicans fleeing south to build Nuevo Laredo.

By 1881, tensions between the two countries had eased, and it was possible to ride the new Texas-Mexico and International Great Northern Railroad the 700 miles to Mexico City in 36 hours, just twice the time it takes today. In 1889 the first bridge connected the two Laredos, and eventually Laredo became the busiest landlocked port of entry in the United States.

The flow of refugees north began during the 1910 Mexican revolution. Newly installed President Carranza's federales attacked Nuevo Laredo in 1914, and the border region was hot for a decade. Migration both ways across the border has been common ever since, though increasingly immigrants have come north, seeking jobs and financial security. Today, Laredo is the second-fastest growing city in the United States.

Doug and I stopped in Laredo for various border preparations. I removed the front license plate, and smeared the rear plate with mud. By now the entire car had acquired an obscuring coat of dust and grime, an effect I hoped to cultivate. I purchased vehicle liability insurance, since U.S. coverage ends at the Río Grande, and traded dollars for pesos. As it turned out, we changed too many. We weren't prepared for how serious the economic crisis in Mexico had become, and just how much a dollar would buy. We filled up with dollar gas, and headed for the river.

We inched our way across the international bridge, idling semis jockeying for position at the Mexican aduana. Automobile and electronic parts and textiles move south, and finished products, assembled with cheap Mexican labor, flow north. But customs officials on both sides of the river will soon be busier. As free trade grows, drugs and people may cease to dominate their attention. The tide of heavy trucks at the border will multiply, and traffic jams at the bridge will grow.

# Northern Mexico

*"We had finally found the
magical land at the end of the road."*

*~ Jack Kerouac, On the Road*

We entered Mexico on November 2, el Día de los muertos, the Day of the
Dead. At the customs office, the slouching, sticky-palmed quasi-official of the
past had been replaced by a professional young woman, who gave me a receipt
for my $11 vehicle entry permit, and told me about the maquiladoras. She said
Nuevo Laredo has them all – chemical, electronic, clothing, everything. In fact,
scores of international corporations have assembly plants here, she said, sprawling into the desert beyond the city fringe. I wanted to visit a maquiladora, and
she told me how to find them.

I asked what the workers are paid. "The minimum wage," she said. "150 pesos
a week." Since the peso had plunged from three down to seven to the dollar in
the previous year, that was $21.

"How would you like to work all week for $21?" she asked. She wanted to
know my work and how much I earned. I thought a moment; hesitant to
acknowledge the gulf between us, I gave a vague and deflated estimate of a couple hundred a week.

"That's a lot of money," she said, almost reverently.

"Yes," I said, "it is."

The maquiladoras, several thousand manufacturing and assembly plants
owned by U.S. and international corporations, are concentrated along the northern Mexican border. They employ a million workers, mostly women, assembling
clothing, car parts, computers and other electronic gadgets, producing asbestos,
PCBs, and pesticides, including materials banned in the U.S. Mexican environmental and worker safety laws are weaker than those north of the Río Grande,
and enforcement is lax. New shanty towns had sprung up around the "industrial
parks," the young official said. Like the plants themselves, the impromptu towns
lacked adequate water supplies and waste treatment facilities. Attention to worker and resident health and safety was minimal. The century-old words of Mexican
dictator Porfirio Díaz are still profound: "Poor Mexico, so far from God and so
close to the United States."

I asked the young woman what she thought of NAFTA, whether it would
improve the lives of Mexicans. She was skeptical. With the recognition that

NAFTA was producing jobs in Mexico, I'd been asking working people all down the highway, especially people from Mexico, what they thought. Nobody seemed to think it would benefit anybody besides the corporations who employ workers for $21 a week. I remembered Tammy Gomez's words about not wanting for somebody else what you wouldn't want for yourself or your kids.

We mounted the Omni and bumped through Nuevo Laredo on Mexico 85, the Pan American Highway to Mexico City. We passed the plaza de toros (bull ring), and the first of many monuments to the great Mexican heroes Simón Bolívar, hero of the fight for Latin American Independence from Spain, and Benito Juárez, the Zapotecan Indian president whose new constitution prohibited slavery, guaranteed freedom of speech and the press, and greatly restricted the power of the church. Juárez's stony eyes gaze north, toward the United States.

On the fringes of the city we drove through squalid neighborhoods of minimum wage workers, emerging at last at El Jardín de Los Angeles, the garden of angels. Here the upper crust of Nuevo Laredo are buried, a city much finer than that inhabited by most of the living. In fact, I'd never seen a more beautiful cemetery in Mexico, or for that matter, anywhere on U.S. 81. Rows of tall cylindrical junipers separate isles of graves, neatly tiled with paving stones, as if to safeguard the dead from the cares of the world above. And on the Day of the Dead the place was at its finest, with millions of flowers, mostly marigolds, artfully arrayed. Families in their Sunday best swept graves and washed tombstones, eating tacos and chicken, visiting with each other, preparing to spend the night with lost loved ones. I wondered which Mexicans had it better, the real dead of the class who lie in the garden of angels, or the living dead who are buried in the factories of the giants of international industry, who labor long days and years for the stale crust of life.

We had entered Mexico in the panhandle of the state of Tamaulipas. This was still Coahuiltec country, but like most of Mexico except the isolated mountain regions, it is mestizo, mixed Spanish and Indian. The country is dry and forbidding, producing the same mesquite and sage and cacti as the other side of the border, though on this side the Drug Enforcement Agency hadn't sprayed the peyote cacti with herbicide. Lance Henson told me back in Oklahoma that representatives of the Native American Church must now cross the border to acquire sacramental peyote buttons.

Most names here are Spanish, the blood and language and customs an imprecise mixture of Spanish and Indian, the people united by poverty. But those with enough to eat don't necessarily consider themselves poor; in fact, in important ways most folks with Cadillacs wouldn't understand, they are rich. Perhaps the Mexican perspective is broader than that of more sophisticated North Americans. As Beat writer Carolyn Cassady put it in her book *Off the Road*, Mexicans "weren't going anywhere but had already been and were resting before the next creative cycle occurred."

A few miles beyond Nuevo Laredo, around the Nuevo Leon state line, 20-

foot Joshua trees thrust up from the lower vegetation. We stopped at one of the frequent roadside shrines, a far more typical commemoration of the dead than at the cemetery. A small cement cross with a figure of Jesus, placed as a recuerdo de sus hijos, a remembrance by his children, noted the place where Juan Casas Vásquez, aged 32, died in a car crash November 1, 1983 – All Saints Day. The head of Jesus was broken from his body and reposed on his shoulder.

The Sierra Madre Oriental came into view, a broad swath of mostly arid mountains that parallel the Sierra Madre Occidental to the west. The two ranges merge south of Mexico City and continue south, linking the Alaskan Rockies to the volcanoes of Central America. In the shadow of the Sierra Madre we pulled off for a cold drink in the picturesque old mining town of Vallecillos. The precious minerals may be gone, but the rock remains. The entire town is built of stone, all the houses, all the walls. In most pueblos the streets are dust or mud, depending on the season, but in Vallecillos even the streets are paved with stone.

At the town entrance is a bronze Benito Juárez, so well-known in Mexico that identifying him by name wasn't deemed necessary. An official sprawled on a chair against the Municipal Palace wall said the only work here is quarrying the rock, formerly the waste product of mining, now sold as building material. Many of the old stone houses were abandoned, probably by folks who'd fled north. I imagined rolling out my sleeping bag in one, staying the night, or the rest of my life.

We idled through the town, past a bunch of kids playing soccer in the plaza. Juan Ramón, an enterprising chap of 11, peeled off from the group and ran to meet us, hoping to score a refresco. Doug, Juan and I sat on the steps of a little store-front house with our drinks, and within moments every kid in town had gathered, the boys hovering and trying out their half dozen words of English, the girls giggling shyly behind their hands. Juan Ramón wanted to see my tape recorder. He flipped out when I recorded his voice and played back "Me llamo Juan Ramón."

I'd planned to stop in Ciénaga de Flores (marsh of flowers) to visit with Tomasa, the sister of my new Oklahoma acquaintance Elvira Vásquez. Tomasa and her husband ran a highway chicken restaurant called Crunch, but Crunch was closed on Thursdays, and anyway we'd lingered long with the kids in Vallecillos, and darkness was creeping up the mountains, so we pushed on to Monterrey. We came over the last ridge, and the city sprawled before us, a broad puddle of light between the 7,800-foot Cerro de la Mitra on the west and the lower, saddle-shaped Cerro de Silla to the east. Riding low in the saddle's sky was the Southern Cross at last.

Monterrey is the big city of the north, in fact the first city of over a million on the Pan American Highway. It is also the point farthest west anywhere on the road from Winnipeg to Panamá.

Monterrey was founded in 1560. North of the border, 18th century was old; here things ranged from ancient to old when the 18th century rolled around.

Monterrey was named for the Count of Monterrey, Viceroy of New Spain. During the Mexican-American war, partly a by-product of the North American struggle over slavery, slave-owning Gen. Zachary Taylor, Old Rough and Ready, occupied Monterrey in 1846, just as Henry David Thoreau was going to jail in Concord, Massachusetts, for resisting slavery and the Mexican War. Gen. Taylor defeated Santa Anna in 1847, and rode his war exploits into the White House.

Doug and I got a room in the Nuevo León Hotel near the bus station. I went looking for a taste of cabrito, roasted kid goat, the plato especial here. Then we headed downtown to see the Gran Plaza, the cathedral and the state capitol, the steps of which were littered with wilting flower remains of the Day of the Dead. We followed the strains of classical music the half mile up the Gran Plaza, hoping to find a concert in progress. Instead, in a little closet off the foyer in the capitol, a state employee played compact disks, the music booming out across el centro from huge speakers mounted above the capitol columns.

Next morning I stopped at a farmacia for a supply of anti-malarial chloroquine tablets, recommended for travelers to the tropics. I got a two-month supply for $1.50, which suggests the kind of mark-up we pay for drugs in the U.S. We breakfasted on pan de muerto, the bread of the dead, specially shaped in skull and cross-bones, eaten to defy the grim reaper. The bread was now day-old, but not bad as warmed over death. We washed it down with 35 cent half-liter glasses of fresh orange juice, and headed south, through Santiago, past the old landmark cafe with the 35-foot sombrero roof at El Alamo, past the goat ranch of the "king of cabrito," through Allende, and into the orange capital of Montemorelos.

Beside the road south of Montemorelos I bought a bag of at least 50 freshly-picked naranjas (oranges) for 75 cents, 20 pounds or more, an investment I would enjoy and share all the way to Guatemala. Near Linares I supplemented the fruit with home-made sugar cane candy from a stop sign vendor. We crossed the puente de muerte, death bridge, left the state of Nuevo León, and reentered Tamaulipas. I had planned to leave the highway at Hidalgo for the village of La Piragua, but somewhere beyond Villagrán, Doug and I fell into a deep conversation about God and forgot where we were for 20 miles. Should we go back? I really wanted to meet the family of Santiago Vásquez, my parents' friend in Hennessey, so we turned around.

Back at the cottonwood-shaded plaza in the pueblo of Hidalgo, I asked directions to the ejido La Piragua. The road to La Piragua was really more of a trail, five or six miles of rocky one-lane dirt, with frequent fords through what in the just- passed rainy season would have been streams. La Piragua is a pueblito of perhaps 40 or 50 people, mostly "Vásquez or married to a Vásquez," Elvira had said. When I'd asked Santiago how to find his parents' home, he just laughed. "Ask anybody," he said.

I rattled into town and asked a boy how to find Sr. Ramón and Sra. Dolores Vásquez. He pointed me down a rocky trail. I stopped again where a family was sitting down to eat under a thatched shelter in their yard. I told the woman I knew Santiago and had come to visit his parents. She trotted over to the Vásquez house to announce our arrival. I left her an armful of oranges.

Sr. Ramón Vásquez greeted us at the gate — dignified, gray-haired, wrapped in a blanket serape. The yard was encircled by a barbed wire fence; two small structures shared the enclosure with a patch of corn. Like most houses in the ejido, the Vásquez house was small, a cement block foundation with vertical pole walls and a thatched roof. An open-air cooking room, the cocina, stood nearby.

Ramón opened the gate and invited us in. He introduced us to Dolores, who had joined him in the yard. We stooped and entered the low doorway. The day was raw and damp, but it was cozy inside. I gave Ramón and Dolores a picture of Santiago and Elvira and their boys, and they asked for news. I told them Santiago hoped to visit, maybe at Thanksgiving. Ramón's eyes glowed with pride as we talked of his Oklahoma son. He pulled two chairs near the bed and we sat down. Moments later Dolores went out, gathered an armful of sticks, and disappeared into the cocina.

The main house was a single room, divided in the middle by a cabinet. Behind that stood a large ornate bed of rich dark wood, probably an ancestral heirloom. Near the door were another bed and the chairs. A mouse ran across the roof beam, a common guest in an open house, and a finch fluttered in for a visit. Despite its openness to the elements, the house was clean and orderly, reflecting the lives of its inhabitants.

Another of Ramón and Dolores' sons, young Ramón appeared at the door to say hello. Word had traveled through the little town that we had come. After all, we'd seen no other cars here, so the arrival of a clattering, dusty old Dodge, while not exactly out of place, attracted attention. Thirteen Vásquez children grew up in this tiny house. Several had gone to Monterrey for work, and Santiago to Oklahoma. Only this son remained in La Piragua.

La Piragua is one of hundreds of ejidos established as communal farms after the revolution of 1910 — part of the land redistribution demanded by peasant general Emiliano Zapata. I asked Ramón and his son about the ejido, about their crops and land, and about the local economy.

La Piragua was established in the twenties, just after the revolution, Ramón said, and was farmed collectively for many years. Now much of the land was in private plots, but some was still farmed communally. "I liked the unity that collective land generated," Ramon said. "Today the people are less equal than they once were." Ramón and his son grew corn and beans on their plot near the San Antonio River. Ramón said their crops were pretty good that year, but prices were very low. When men here work for others, they earned about 20 pesos a day, or $3. But usually no work was available, and neither man thought NAFTA would help.

Before long Dolores announced that la comida was ready, and we went to the cocina. We sat around a sloping table and ate frijoles (beans) and spaghetti and fresh hot tortillas and homemade salsa. ¡Muy rico! A better meal I hadn't had on this journey, nor better company.

I wanted to be in Ciudad Mante by dark, and the afternoon was fading. We poured out a couple dozen oranges and said good-bye. Ramón gave me a warm abrazo (embrace) and told me if I saw Santiago to pass it on. We bumped our way back to Hidalgo, back to what by contrast seemed a major thoroughfare, though the Pan American Highway here is not more than 20 feet wide, about like a county road in South Dakota.

Our route took us through Ciudad Victoria, renamed in 1825 for Mexico's first president after independence, Guadalupe Victoria. We looked in vain in the Juárez Plaza for Izcuinán Tlazolteotl, the Huastec goddess of human desires I'd read resided here. But we did find the Municipal Palace where in January 1991, on our way back from a filming trip to Mexico City, we'd listened to a local official promising the "car thieves union" that the government would go light on them. Our bus had been stopped for an hour south of Victoria by men who had barricaded the highway with parked cars and logs to protest a Mexican government crackdown on thieves who imported stolen U.S. cars. A man in the crowd told me then that local officials drove new Lincolns and Cadillacs. We didn't see any car theft, then or now, and the dirtier the Omni got, the less I worried about such possibilities.

Just south of Ciudad Victoria we crossed the Tropic of Cancer. There was no magical change at the line, and unfortunately most of the tropical forest that once grew here has been cut down. But still a gradual change had come; the world had grown lush. When Kerouac and his buddies came through in 1950, they pulled off nearby to sleep, Kerouac on top of the car, where mosquitoes mixed his blood with the sweat "clotting up thousands of dead bugs into cakes" on his skin, and he realized that "the jungle takes you over and you become it." For the first time he felt that "the weather was not something that touched me, that caressed me, froze or sweated me, but became me. The atmosphere and I became the same." Indeed, there is no escape from the atmosphere of a tropical night. One can only hope for a big-bladed ceiling fan to stir the dank air of a hotel room. We drove through the sugar cane fields that replaced the selva, our windows open for breeze.

By Ciudad Mante, darkness had fallen. We got a room in Hotel Gomez, and at a little grill called El Asadero just off the plaza had a wonderful meal of two bowls of bean and cilantro soup and two alambres (skewers of tender beef, onion and peppers, grilled just right) and two beers, all for 24 pesos ($3.50). Doug being a vegetarian, I got all the meat, the first time I'd pigged out since Fort Worth. Then we retired to Chicharra's Bar, where a guy named Jerasmo took a long draft of Superior, hugged a battered guitar to his chest, and scratched out tunes in classical style, singing songs of love and lost love for the dozen men gathered with as much soul as any star who ever faced thousands at Carnegie Hall. When he finished, Jerasmo offered us the triple handshake and sat down to talk. He welcomed us to the land of the Huastecs; he said that some people here still speak the language, especially toward the coast. Up in the Sierra Madre to the west is Tarahumara country, he said. Most of the men in Mante make sugar.

Next morning we hit the road early, stopping at a cafe for huevos tibios (poached eggs) and bread and coffee. Limón dulce was served with the eggs, as it is with meat, fish, beer, most everything in this region. I like the lime-like limón, and tried it on everything with which it was served. Strangely enough, it made everything taste – like lime. We left unexplored one of Mexico's biggest sugar factories, where the men with whom we'd spent the evening worked. I had traveled from sugar beets in North Dakota to sugar cane in Tamaulipas, both harvested and worked to sweetness by Mexican men.

We crossed more irrigated sugar cane and mountains and ranches and valleys, through little pueblos with names like El Abra, Antiguo Morelos, and Laguna del Mante, now in the state of San Luis Potosí. Just before Ciudad Valles we were stopped for a thorough search by the notorious Judicial Police, known as much for drug trafficking as for drug control. The agent said he was looking for cocaine. "Sorry," I said. "We don't have any." The big scavenger, the crested caracara, circled overhead, flashing white tips on wings and tail, conducting his own search for something to eat.

We stopped awhile in the heart of Huastec country at Ciudad Valles, established in 1533, the oldest Spanish city in San Luis Potosí. At the market we bought avocados and bananas. A ten-foot pile of left-over zempasuchiles (marigolds), the flower of the dead, wilted beside the street. We found the Huastec museum, but it had closed for the Day of the Dead, and though it was now mid-morning of the 4th, the museum had not come back to life. We peered through the windows at the pottery of the ancients.

Tropical flowers, pink and lavender and orange, are reflected in the colors of houses here. Brilliant birds flitted among banana groves. Twenty-five foot bamboo had become common, and as tropical foliage grew thicker, so did men carrying machetes along the road. Women bearing pots or bags of anything and everything on their heads trudged from home to market or back. Tiny huts were surrounded by gardens more exotic than any grown in the U.S. on the richest of estates with the best of gardeners. We had arrived where mother nature is in her prime.

We gassed up at PEMEX, the government monopoly. For the first time ever, my tank was filled by a Mexican girl. Not only at the customs office, but even in gas stations women were breaking into jobs formerly reserved for men. The price of fuel was the same everywhere in Mexico, regulated by PEMEX at just over 2 pesos per liter, just over $1 a gallon, about the same as in the U.S. I was glad to see that unleaded was now slightly cheaper, the government's price structure discouraging the use of lead. Now if they could do something about those smoking diesel buses and trucks.

After the villages of Las Armas and Pedro Antonio de los Santos, we climbed into the hills and approached Tamazunchale, a Huastec town on the Río

Moctezuma. We were at the foot of the big wild mountains we must cross to Mexico City. Tamazunchale had beckoned to me for years – the quintessential mountain Indian town, far from anywhere, inaccessible from the outside world before construction of an earthen Pan American Highway in the 1930s. Even with the highway paved, we would find it so steep and winding, and at times so foggy south of Tamazunchale that for at least a hundred miles we could travel no more than 30 miles per hour. Years ago I flew over these mountains and towns, looked down from six miles up and said, someday I have to go there. Now the town lay beneath us in the valley.

Before our descent we pulled off in a cliff-side grove of tall, flying buttressed ceiba trees to look at the town and the Moctezuma River, its brown body winding through the verdant valley below. There we met Venustiano and his son Javier, wood carvers who live suspended on the edge of the mountain, far above river and town. For 40 years Venustiano had carved the masks of Huastec and Olmec figures from local cedar and mahogany and sold them from the little lean-to where his son Javier had joined him as partner in Artesanas del Patio. "I tried Michigan in the United States and Ontario, Canada when I was young," Venustiano said. "I found both too cold, in more ways than one, so I came home." Venustiano spoke three languages – his native dialect of Nahuatl, Spanish, and English – and he had survived in all three worlds. In well over 2,000 miles from Winnipeg south, Venustiano and Javier were the first artists I found who lived, and made and sold their work beside the highway. From here south there would be many.

Venustiano and his family cling precariously to the majestic mountainside, a hundred feet from the Pan American Highway but secluded from its rumble, above the town but not in it. Venustiano told us about the Huastec and Olmec gods, and about his years on the mountain where he seemed perfectly happy to be. He offered two of his finest Olmec figures for $4 each. We took them, figuring we'd worry later about how to get the ten-pound objects home. When Doug caught a plane in Mexico City a few days later, I was greatly relieved when he offered to transport mine to South Dakota.

We crossed the Moctezuma River into Tamazunchale, got a 70-peso room in the Hotel Virrey and set out to explore the town. Tamazunchale consists of two main streets, curving along the narrow river valley, the highway the upper street, the lower street doubling on Sundays as the market place. I climbed to the top of the town, where a gnarled barefoot woman solemnly tended a grave on a ledge above me. I had a couple of tacos at one street-side stand and a pineapple pastry at another. Doug and I strolled down to the plaza to see the marigold-bedecked skeletons suspended among the trees, mocking death. The 16th-century church is dedicated to Saint Judas Tadeo, the "advocate of difficult and desperate cases."

Located in the mountains and on the river, Tamazunchale is rich in fruits and flowers, butterflies and birds. The town's name in Huastec means "place of the governor," the hotel clerk told us. The most famous governor here was a woman,

*Javier and Venustiano and their carved Huastec masks, beside the highway in the Sierra Madre mountains (top), and decoration for the Day of the Dead in Tamazunchale.*

Tomiya. The clerk said that on holidays the danza del gavilán, the dance of the sparrow hawk is performed here, a version of the famous voladores, or flying pole dance which originated with the Totonacs on the Gulf coast and which I once experienced across the mountains at Teotihuacán. Four young men leap from atop a towering pole, tethered to unwinding ropes which bear them back to earth, an ancient ritual performed to bring rains, a good harvest, and the harmonious turning of the four seasons.

But Tamazunchale's history and charm have not relieved its poverty. The road is long and difficult, not likely to attract many tourists. In fact it occurred to us that we hadn't seen another gringo since Monterrey. Most of the traffic to Mexico City now goes west from Monterrey to Saltillo, then south to the capital on Mexico 57. So the shops in Tamazunchale were nearly empty, and nobody was buying. The mountain economy moved slower than the muddy Moctezuma. In the plaza a group of boys were engaged a wild game of dice. Two wore baseball caps, one an L.A. Dodgers and the other non-descript, both turned backwards, as on boys north of the border.

It was Saturday night; I had timed my visit to catch the Tamazunchale market on Sunday morning, said to be among the best. I was sure that then the town would come to life. But this evening things were slow, even at the Pequeño (little) Bar across from the hotel. The few men there were watching some Hollywood adventure movie on TV, and the only women were blondes in bikinis, plastered on the walls. I wondered what would convince Mexican men that dark-skinned women are as beautiful as their blonde sisters. As if to accent my thoughts, a black swallowtail butterfly with three-inch wings fluttered into the Pequeño and lighted on the wall above Doug's head, choosing a spot barren of posters. It was still clinging there, flaunting its Mexican beauty, when we finished our beer and left.

Because our hotel was on the highway, buses growled most of the night, but by now I was growing accustomed to that. We got up with the marketers and were in the street as the booths opened. On the market's fringe in a muddy street by the river a farmer sold piglets from a little portable corral, suspending them by the hind legs so prospective buyers could feel the flesh and test the weight. When the bargaining was done he deposited the pig in a burlap bag, exchanged a handshake for pesos, and called out for his next customer.

We left Tamazunchale about 9:00 and continued our climb, soon entering the state of Hidalgo, named for the "liberation theologian" priest who led the 1810 revolution against Spain. He was executed by the Spanish the next year, after the rebels were temporarily subdued.

I had worried about the Omni's performance in mountainous terrain, but it ran well, a hungry Omnivore, clattering and whining around the curves. The 225 miles to Mexico City would be an all-day trip; the first 90 miles took three hours plus stops, very slow going, but so enchanting I didn't want the mountains to end. We passed a couple of truckloads of charcoal, bound for Mexico City to toast the tacos of street vendors.

We stopped for a better view of the vast deep valley, the Moctezuma sliding along a thousand feet below. A young family, a man, a woman and a little boy, were walking by to town. I asked them about the local fruits, bananas, oranges, and mangos, and the coffee and nuts. The man asked me about the value of the dollar and about work in the U.S., whether there were jobs and how much they paid. He said there were "no jobs here, nada, none."

Just north of Los Duraznos we were stopped by a crowd with a flag-draped rope stretched across the road, a high pressure and presumably unorthodox method of taking a collection for the local church from whence they had just emerged. Doug gave them a few pesos, and we moved on. This was but the first of several shake-downs by the Catholic church that Sunday.

South of Los Duraznos the highway reaches 7,900 feet, and butterflies were profuse and various. Then we dropped fast through a hardwood and pine forest into a very different ecological zone, the other Mexican world, the desert. The shift from flowers and bananas and misty tropical forest to parched earth is sudden and profound — almost no transition at all.

Down at the 450-year-old pueblo of Zimapán the earth is a dusty crust, the vegetation cactus, the animals the lizard, the goat and the burro. Suddenly I was dodging burros at every bend. Boys herded flocks of sheep and goats, looking for a little grass in the roadside ditch. The rocky lavender earth is barren of most else, but the cacti include the maguey, which the Otomí who live here use for food, fiber and drink.

For at least a millennium, the Otomí culture has revolved around the now ruined city of Tula. And for all that time, the maguey has sustained the Otomí economy and way of life. Every part of the succulent plant is used: Houses are built of the stalks and leaves; the thorns become needles and nails; the fibers are used for washing pots and making thread and rope and cloth; the pulp becomes soap; the hearts are roasted for food; the bent leaf is a drinking cup; the juice is fermented for pulque wine; even the larvae which live in the plant find their way into the bottle.

We reached the Río Arenal valley, a ribbon of profuse and diverse vegetation winding through the arid hills, and pulled off in dusty Ixmiquilpán to see the huge and elaborate but now decaying 1550 Dominican church and convent. The interior decor is ancient faded frescoes; the stone steps of the convent are cupped two inches deep by the now-stilled feet of nuns. Near the church stands an incongruous statue of Don Quixote and Sancho Panza. Against what windmills does the man from La Mancha tilt in Ixmiquilpán?

Just north of the old mining city of Pachuca we passed a monument to the Pan American Highway itself, erected by North Americans living in Mexico. We forked southwest for the last 50 mile stretch, four lanes no less, lined with wheat and corn and stone teepee granaries and vendors of snow cones and booze. Just outside Mexico City is Teotihuacán, the ancient Place of the Gods. Founded 24 centuries ago, Teotihuacán was the first great city of central Mexico. Its estimated population of a quarter million exceeded that of classical Rome, and its largest structure, the Pyramid of the Sun, rivals the great pyramids of Egypt. The temple of the plumed serpent, Quetzalcóatl, is faced with fine stone carvings of the serpent, and of Tlaloc, the god of rain, whose favor is always sought in this parched land.

Glimpsing the snow-capped peaks of the twin volcanoes beyond the broad valley of Mexico, we headed through Texas-style traffic into the haze of the biggest city on Earth. We turned down Insurgentes, passing the Basilica of Our Lady of Guadalupe, where on December 9, 1531, the Virgin Mary reportedly appeared to a poor Indian man, Juan Diego. Three days later the apparition reappeared, permanently etching herself on Juan's poncho. Today Mexicans ride a people mover through the church, pondering the Virgin's peaceful face, which gazes out from what the church insists are the tattered remains of Juan's cloak. Like Juan Diego, they too hope for miracles.

# CENTRAL MEXICO

*"We fight for the land and not for
illusions that give us nothing to eat."*

~ *Emiliano Zapata, 1918*

We arrived in Mexico City at a good time. On Sunday evening the city's infamous traffic is at its lowest ebb. The moon was rising full, ambered by the haze. But the air was the cleanest I'd seen in the city in years. Not that breathing was healthy, but the weekend rest from workday pollution and a brisk north wind had purged the vapors of the vast metropolis.

Mexico City was in several ways the symmetrical apex of my journey. It lies almost exactly half way between Winnipeg, Manitoba and Cañita, Panamá. Its estimated population of 20 million probably equals the total of all the other cities on the route. And it is the highest city on the highway, 7,240 feet. So in Mexico City I felt relief that I'd made it half way, the Omni was still running, and I still had money in my pocket.

We got a room at the Monte Carlo on Uruguay, a place I'd stayed a couple of times before. The Monte Carlo is in a 1772 Augustinian monastery, just three blocks from the Zócalo, the city center. It's an easy walk to Alameda Park and the Palace of Fine Arts, the Cathedral, the ruins of the Aztec Templo Mayor, the chapel of Jesús Nazareno where Hernán Cortés lies, and my favorite restaurant, the Café de Tecuba, a setting of both Carlos Fuentes' novel *Christoper Unborn* and Elena Garro's story "Blame the Tlaxcaltecs."

Doug and I had enchiladas at the Casa de Azulejos (the House of Tiles) near the Palace of Fine Arts. In 1662, it was a Franciscan convent. It became a palace in 1735, and a restaurant early in the 20th century. Not exactly a U.S.-style throw it up in a month type place.

Walking back to the hotel, we stopped for a beer at La Faena Bar on Carranza, a block north of the Monte Carlo. The glory days of the old bull-fighter bar had passed. But encased in glass around the walls of the big hall still hung the costumes, capes and swords of a dozen revered matadores. I remembered booming times, but tonight the place was almost empty. The economic crisis was apparently profound.

In Laredo we'd gotten over seven pesos to the dollar. Now we learned that on our second day in Mexico a rumor of a military coup had driven the peso even lower. Many people were too busy looking for their next tortilla to talk, but those who were talking in Mexico City were focused on la crisis, the peso's plunge to 40 percent of its value in just a year. Accompanying the loss of buying power were price increases, interest rates which made borrowing out of the question for most people, and escalating unemployment.

The mariachi band Shadows of Michoacán came to our table and played for us the classic "Malagueña" for 25 pesos. Sure, $3.50 is steep for a song, but I had a pocket full of pesos, and everything I was buying in Mexico was so cheap it was almost criminal. Anyway, even musicians have to eat. The patriarch of the group, Santiago, was from the state of Guerrero, the rest from Michoacán, all struggling to live and eat in the big city. After the song, Santiago sat and talked of hard times for awhile, then abruptly pushed back his chair, extended his hand for the triple saludo we'd been getting since La Piragua, and moved on to hustle his next gig.

Early next morning I climbed the stairs to the roof. The snow-capped volcanoes in which this great seething cauldron lies were not yet eclipsed by smog, and above the city's din, I found solitude to write. I remembered D. H. Lawrence, who wrote *The Plumed Serpent*, his novel inspired by the Quetzalcóatl myth, here at the Monte Carlo.

After breakfast across the street at Poncho's, I strolled down to the Zócalo. I stopped by the 1528 church of Jesus the Nazarene on Pino Suárez to visit the bones of Cortés. The conqueror was buried in the floor of the church in 1547, and moved to a crypt beside the nave 400 years later. No longer can Mexicans savor standing on his grave.

From Nazareno I walked north past the bronze sculpture in-laid in tile on the southeast corner of the Zócalo, the depiction of the origin of Tenochtitlán, the old city conquered by Cortés. An Aztec family watches the eagle light upon a cactus at this very spot, a writhing snake in its talons and beak, the sign that this was the place to build the sacred city.

Across the street the National Palace houses the legislature and the president's office. The palace was erected for Cortés in 1523 on the foundations of Aztec ruler Moctezuma's destroyed palace. It is believed the invaders' conquest was made easier because the Aztecs associated the light-haired Spaniard with the mythical hero Quetzalcóatl, whose return from the east they anticipated. The palace was crawling with soldiers, higher security than I'd ever seen here. Everyone who entered had to surrender identification, driver's license or passport. I was there to see again the living murals of Mexican history, the work of Diego Rivera.

Rivera's extensive frescoes, painted 1929-51, vividly depict the beauty and structure of the pre-Aztec agave (maguey)-based cultures of Mexico, the Tarascans, Totonacs, Zapotecs, and Huastecs. Other panels portray the grand canaled Aztec city of Tenochtitlán, the arrival of Cortés in 1519, the ruthlessness of the conquistadors and the complicity of the Catholic Church, the fight for independence from Spain, and the modern struggles for land and justice. My favorite panel pictures authorities of church and state in all their finery, bickering over a bag of gold, torturing enslaved Indians, driving them to build the Spanish city on the ruins of Tenochtitlán. Even the horses and mules are muzzled so they can neither eat nor protest. Rivera's paintings truly capture the horror of conquest. I chuckled to recall that in 1933 John D. Rockefeller commissioned the great artist to produce the mural "Man in Control of His Universe" in the Rockefeller Center in New York, but had it painted over when he discovered the face of Lenin in his shrine to capitalism. Rivera duplicated the vast mural in the Palace of Fine Arts in the Mexican capital, calling it "Man at the Crossroads."

I reclaimed my passport from the soldiers at the door and fell into conversation with a group of men whose plight demonstrated that not much had changed in Mexico since Rivera's day. Thirty sanitation workers from the state of Tabasco had been camped against the palace wall for four months in a huelga de hambre, a hunger strike, demanding better wages and working conditions. "We're still waiting for somebody in the government to talk with us," one man told me. I heard their story, gave them a few pesos for food, and wished them luck.

Just north of the National Palace, next to the cathedral, lie the ruins of Templo Mayor, the sacred center of Tenochtitlán, the 300,000 strong capital of the Aztec world that Cortés destroyed. The ruins were uncovered 35 years ago during construction of the subway system. The various levels of the foundation have been restored, demonstrating how, like the Maya, the Aztecs rebuilt their temples every 52 years, another layer upon the old — a renewal act the opposite of their sacred serpent, which periodically sheds its skin. Between Templo Mayor and the cathedral, a long line of street vendors sold items supporting the Zapatista rebellion: books, audio tapes, photographs of Subcomandante Marcos, EZLN pins, and t-shirts bearing the images of Zapata and Marcos.

It took nearly a century to build the cathedral, from 1573 to 1667; it was constructed of stones from the destroyed Aztec temple. Like the Palace of Fine Arts, the cathedral has sunk several feet into the earth in this former lake bed. Its foundation is so irregular you feel the incline as you cross the floor. The perennial work to save and restore the massive listing structure was at a fever pitch, but the cathedral retains its golden opulence in spite of its earthquake-induced trauma. Outside, I talked with tradesmen who lined the fence west of the cathedral, waiting for work.

Dozens of men, most young to middle-aged, able-bodied and strong, carpenters, electricians, plumbers, and handymen, sat along the wall next to the monument to Xochimilco lake, which once covered this mountain valley to an estimated depth of 12 feet. Tool boxes and bags before them, the men were eager for work, calling out their services as I walked by. "The best I could hope for would be 100 pesos for a full day's work," a carpenter named Miguel told me. "If I could find it." But when I passed that way again in late afternoon, many were still there, nervously shifting tools and expressions, dreading the long walk home, empty-handed except for a now heavier bag of tools.

For those who wait too long without work, there is the National Pawn Shop across the corner, built where Moctezuma died. Here workers can pawn their tools when their children grow too hungry. Established by the government so the working class could borrow money, the National Pawn Shop is now crammed full of tools, not to mention wedding rings, musical instruments, household goods, and the other necessities of life which become luxuries when there is no food.

In the afternoon Doug and I filmed three houses in the city where Jack Kerouac lived at various times, and where he wrote several books. At Cerrada Medellín 37, Kerouac wrote the first part of *Desolation Angels*. He also stayed with William Burroughs and other Beats at 210 and 212 Orizaba, where he wrote *Doctor Sax* and *Tristessa*. While Doug filmed Kerouac's shack on the Orizaba roof, I pulled a Spanish translation of *Tristessa* out of my back pocket and read a piece to three young residents, who passed a joint as I read, oblivious to Kerouac's ghost.

Later we went to Tlatelolco Plaza, also known as the Plaza of Three Cultures. Most dramatic are the sprawling ruins of the Aztec ceremonial center, excavated in the 1940s. Here the final battle in the conquest of Mexico was fought on August 13, 1521. An interpretive panel at the archeological site states that military leader Cuauhtémoc neither triumphed nor was defeated, but that his suffering gave birth to a new mestizo culture — another reminder of the truth of Simone Weil's observation that "history is the propaganda of the victors."

On this site on October 2, 1968, the Mexican Army shot down an estimated 300 students who were demonstrating against government infringement on the traditional autonomy of universities. Though the 1968 killings caused the U.S. Army to cancel a leave it had granted me to attend the Mexico City Olympics, and though a memorial beside the church confirms the carnage, a security guard I talked with denied any knowledge of the killing.

Immediately adjacent to the ruins stands the 1609 Santiago Apostle Church, which houses the embalmed body of Padre Sebastián. Sebastián was born in Spain in 1502, came to Mexico in 1533, and died in Puebla, Mexico in 1600 at age ninety-eight. Padre Sebastián is displayed for all to see, just inches behind glass. Sebastián fathered the road which took Catholicism from Veracruz through the capital to Zacatecas in the northern desert, and brought back silver in return. Hair in the nostrils, dirt under the nails, calluses on his feet, Padre Sebastián is either the best-preserved four-century-old corpse I've laid eyes on, or a very good wax model and a massive hoax by the church. I haven't confirmed which I saw.

These two cultural artifacts, monuments of the Aztecs and the Spaniards, are surrounded by those of the third culture, the high-rise apartment buildings of modern mestizo Mexico. Clogging the median of Reforma Avenue just south of Tlatelolco we found a fourth, the homeless and the unemployed, beggars, windshield washers, and vendors of everything from lottery tickets to brushes to candy. A middle-aged man was selling Chiclets by the pack, a job once the province of little boys, a measure of the depth of the economic crisis. When the light turned red, a fire-eater swallowed flames, hoping for tips from less-jaded travelers.

I had hoped to meet with several people in Mexico City, including Nobel Prize-winning Guatemalan indigenous rights activist Rigoberta Menchú, who lived in exile here. But when I called the night before I found she had just flown back to Guatemala. The man I talked with, Hugo Benítez, told me to read *La Jornada* for details, which I did. Rigoberta's sister's two-year-old son had just been kidnapped by two gunmen, and Rigoberta had returned to Guatemala City to search for him. The Guatemalan Human Rights Commission, which I planned to visit in Guatemala City, had appealed to the Secretary General of the United Nations for help in the search. The kidnapping story was on page 55. On the front page, besides Yitzhak Rabin's funeral, were three stories about the economic crisis — one about businesses not paying their taxes, another about a 20,000 strong protest rally in Morelia, the third about people substituting pasta for meat in their diets.

I did arrange a late night meeting with actor/director Luis Cisneros of El Tecolote (The Owl) Cultural Center and Theater on Sullivan, near the U.S. Embassy. I had stopped at Tecolote in 1991 on my way to a demonstration against the Gulf War at the embassy. Mexicans were demonstrating then, not only because they export oil to the United States, and the war illustrated how far the U.S. would go to preserve its "right" to other people's oil, but also because of their long history as a U.S. doormat.

At El Tecolote I helped Luis and the actors ready the theater for their next production, "Tu quieres lo mismo" (I love you the same) by Mexican playwright Jorge Garvín, a historical play about the importance of the railroad to Mexican history. "Without the railroad to transport rebels," Luis said, "there could have been no revolution in 1910."

El Tecolote has existed since the early 1960s; Luis had been associated with the theater as actor, and later as director, for 20 years. A nocturnal creature, the owl is able to see even in the dark. As in the United States, the owl is venerated for its wisdom.

Luis said that in this metropolis of 20 million, 15 percent, about 1.7 million, were unemployed, part of the 10 million unemployed nationwide. Another 30 percent are under-employed in the "informal economy," street vendors and hustlers of every sort. He said there were three "minimum wages" in Mexico, in three zones. Rural workers earned as little as $2 for a day's work. In Mexico City the minimum was 19 pesos per day, about $2.50. In the maquiladoras near the border they got "high wages," Luis said with a bitter laugh, $3 to $4 a day. The devaluation had of course hit the lowest-paid workers hardest. Prices had not dropped, while the peso had lost over half its purchasing power in a year. Obviously, most Mexicans could not buy manufactured goods imported from the U.S., an assumption upon which NAFTA's promise rested.

"Look, let me put these grim statistics in the day-to-day perspective of the

Mexican worker," Luis said. "In the United States, a minimum-wage worker can buy a three-pound chicken with less than an hour of work. His Mexican counterpart must work all day, and still won't have enough to buy the same chicken. Almost half the households in Mexico City somehow exist, or fail to exist, on less than $2.50 per day."

Like most Mexicans I talked with, Luis had no confidence in the Institutional Revolutionary Party (PRI), which had ruled for seven decades – longer than any other political party in the world – but which would fall at last to PAN's Vicente Fox in 2000. He said President Ernesto Zedillo, the last minute replacement for assassinated PRI candidate Luis Donaldo Colosio, was "bland and ineffective." Zedillo had just flown to Washington to make a $700 million pre-payment on the U.S./IMF bailout loan with money borrowed from German banks at exorbitant rates. Mexico would surprise her critics, however, by paying off the entire loan, as well as cutting inflation in half, in the next year.

Luis welcomed the Zapatista uprising, and noted that massive demonstrations in Mexico City had shown wide-spread support for the rebels' demands for more jobs, better wages, fair elections, and political, judicial and land reform. "Unfortunately," he said, "so many in the Mexican working class are so overwhelmed by the daily struggle to stay alive that it is difficult to engage them in the movement for change."

By now it was nearly midnight, and I wanted an early start in the morning. I hadn't revisited some of my favorite places in the city, the world-class Museum of Anthropology in Chapultepec Park, the museums of history and the revolution, the Frida Kahlo Museum in the suburb of Coyoacán where Frida and husband Diego Rivera lived and created art, the nearby house where in 1940 Leon Trotsky was murdered by Stalin's agents with an ice pick, not even the Palace of Fine Arts or the 250,000-student National Autonomous University. But I would return another day. Two days of big city and bad air are enough at one time. I said good-bye to Luis and his friends and headed back to the Monte Carlo.

Doug and I left the hotel next morning at 8:00 and reached the airport by 9:00. I dropped him off, and by 9:30 I'd been lost, nearly asphyxiated, and robbed by a cop. First I made a wrong turn and headed north instead of south on the inner loop and had to go four miles to turn around. Back at last to Zaragoza, which heads east out of the city, I encountered a major traffic jam at the exit. I inched toward the intersection, buses puking petrol fumes in my face. The light turned green and I turned left onto Zaragoza. A uniformed cop with a gun stepped in front of me and waved me over.

The officer opened the door and got into the car. He asked to see my license, and of course I complied. He said he'd have to write me a ticket for an infraction, for failure to stop at the light. I said I did stop, but he only chuckled, and whipped out his ticket book. "This will cost you 300 pesos," he said, pen poised pregnantly above the pad. I reiterated that I'd done nothing wrong, and said I wanted to see the chief. "So you don't want a ticket?" he asked. No, I didn't. "OK then, just pay me half, 150 pesos," he said, "and I'll let you go."

"No way," I said, "I didn't run the light. I want to see the chief."

He patted his gun. "You'll have to pay," he said.

"So what you really want is a soborno," I said, a bribe. His face spread into a sweaty smile.

"Now you understand," he said. I dug in my pocket for a 5 peso coin. I thrust it at him, looking him square in the eye. He considered for a moment, took the coin, and got out.

Mexicans encountering authority often pay much more. The national Judicial Police, for example, are charged with enforcing drug laws, among other things. But it is well-known on both sides of the border that these officers are as likely as not to be corrupt. Many are involved in drug trafficking, and some are guilty of murder, but few have been prosecuted. The Judicial Police also serve as enforcers for the ruling party. It was they who shot down 17 farmers who were protesting clear-cutting of timber in their watershed mountains in the state of Guerrero on June 28, 1995. Compared to those official thugs, traffic cops are small potatoes, supplementing meager wages with extortion. Zedillo promised to clean up police corruption, and began by firing some high-ranking cops. But it remains to be seen whether anybody in Mexico has the power necessary to complete the job. Meanwhile, official corruption spawns general distrust and disrespect for law, and as despair mounts, even the violent crime rate is rising fast.

At the next stop light another policeman headed for me, attracted no doubt by the silver tourist sticker that border officials had stuck on my windshield. "You ran the red light," he began.

"Bullshit," I snarled, in English, letting him translate if he wished. "I got shook down by your buddy at the last light and it's not going to happen again." The light turned green. I yelled "adiós" and stomped the accelerator to the floor. He slammed his fist into the fender as I zoomed by, and I resolved to keep moving whenever possible, especially in the presence of cops. I did keep moving, out of the worst of the smog, through the sprawling eastern ghetto where in 1977 Norma and I rolled for half an hour by train through the cardboard and tin shacks of hundreds of thousands of homeless people. Out of the Federal District, I entered the state of Mexico, back into the corn fields and amongst the hardworking campesinos, herding their sheep and shocking their corn.

I turned off the main highway at Chalco for a detour through Amecameca, hoping for a closer view of snow-capped Popo and Itza. Popocatépetl and Iztaccíhuatl are twin volcanoes east of Amecameca. (Spellings of the names vary, and apparently Mexicans have trouble pronouncing them too, and have settled on nicknames.) At 17,845 feet, Popo is 550 feet taller than Itza. Between the two is Paso Cortés, the route of the conquistadors to Tenochtitlán. The volcanoes had been dormant for two centuries. But if economic collapse, rampant corruption, civil unrest, a major earthquake and two hurricanes weren't enough for Mexico to endure that year, the long quiet Popo had begun to smoke again. Perhaps even

Mother Nature is not a friend of Mexico.

According to Aztec legend, the two mountains are a pair of lovers, a warrior and a princess. The ruler sent Popo to battle his enemy, but while he was gone, a rival reported Popo's death in order to gain Itza's hand. When Popo returned triumphant, the princess died of a broken heart. Popo carried the dead princess to the mountains, where the pair were converted to volcanoes; thus Popo kneels forever over his sleeping lover. I drove a few miles east of Amecameca until I saw the jagged glaciered top of Itza, but smoke and clouds enshrouded Popo's summit. I'd have to leave him for another day, hoping he wouldn't blow his top before my return.

Behind me in the city, the millions were now lost in haze. I drove south through fruit and honey country on Mexico 115 to Cuautla, then southwest to the pueblo of Anenecuilco, Zapata's home. I wanted to see where Emiliano Zapata was born, lived, loved, fought and died.

Even before the fame rekindled by the Zapatista rebellion in Chiapas, Anenecuilco was obviously proud of her native son. In the plaza, Zapata stands handsome and brave, defending tierra y libertad, land and liberty. In the shadow of his statue is another monument, constructed of 150 blocks of granite. Each is inscribed with the name of an ejido in the state of Morelos, a reminder that Zapata's struggle continues for just distribution of land.

A big sign at the corner of the plaza directed me past the school named for Emiliano's brother Eufemio, to the Zapata house and museum on the west edge of town. At the museum entrance, a bronzed Zapata in broad sombrero and drooping mustache tells the visitor, "The earth is for those who work it with their own hands." The museum consists of three parts. A round building houses the photographs and documents of Zapata's life and the history of the 1910 revolution. An awninged wall bears a 10x70, five-panel mural by Cuernavaca artist Roberto Rodríguez Navarro, depicting the revolutionary struggle for liberty and land, the last panel illustrating the at-least-temporary triumph. The centerpiece of the museum, sheltered by another round-domed structure, is the stone and adobe three-room house, formerly thatched but now roofless, where in 1879, Emiliano was born.

I was welcomed at the door and shown through the museum by Necéfaro Hernández, a man of about 30 who, though slightly-built and mustache trimmed, bore an uncanny resemblance to Zapata himself – the dark Indian skin, the perfect features, the flashing eyes of the people's general. "Many residents of Anenecuilco still bear Zapata's name," Necéfaro said. "Many more claim his blood, and most his spirit."

I drove back to Cuautla, had a torta for lunch, and went to find Zapata's grave. An elderly man selling snow cones from a three-wheeled cycle pointed it out on the south edge of the plaza, beside what is probably the grandest of the many Zapata statues I'd seen. It was here in the heart of his beloved Morelos, amongst the campesinos for whose life and dignity he had fought, that they

*Detail from the mural by Cuernavaca artist Roberto Rodríguez Navarro, at the Zapata museum in Anenecuilco (top), and Martín, sacristán at the 16th century church in Yanhuitlán*

brought Zapata home to rest when President Carranza had him murdered in 1919. Like Sandino in Nicaragua a decade later, Zapata was lured into a death trap, in the pueblo of Chinameca, by the promise of land and peace. But Zapata didn't really die. Not for the people of Cuautla and Anenecuilco, not for the Maya peasants of Chiapas, not for those who fight for justice and liberty everywhere in his name. A young campesino asks at the end of John Steinbeck's 1953 screenplay *¡Viva Zapata!*, "Can you capture a river? Can you kill the wind?"

Still high on my visit to a long-time hero, I headed south toward the sugar town of Izucar de Matamoros. But half way, in the tiny town of Tepexco, I hit what must have been the thousandth tope of the day, and suddenly, nothing. The Omni had succumbed to one tope too many. For those who've never had the pleasure, a tope is a speed bump, a six to eight-inch-high roll of asphalt or cement across the highway, which must be crept over at under five mph to avoid taking out the exhaust system, not to mention more vital equipment. Anyway, the faithful Dodge was dead as a dawdling burro. The starter wouldn't make a sound.

I got out in the sweltering sun and pushed the errant beast toward shade, an arching tree beside a tiny store in front of which a sign announced "Mecánico Eléctrico." What luck! I thought. Two men playing checkers with Corona and Dos Equis beer bottle caps on a concrete slab in the shade got up to see what was the problem. "Unfortunately," one said, "the mechanic starved out and went to Chicago."

Though the checker players weren't much more mechanically gifted than I, we tinkered awhile, and agreed the problem was in the ignition. So what to do. I checked the battery, the lights, the cables, even tore out the ignition switch. Then one of the men remembered a friend with mechanical skill, and set out to find him.

I was imagining sleeping in the back seat beside the road when Jorge showed up with his little bag of tools. Part magician and part miracle-worker, Jorge within a minute traced the problem to a broken wire, and within five had the Omni running again. I gladly paid him the 30 pesos ($4) he requested, which I imagine he thought was highway robbery. I thanked Jorge profusely, and hit the road.

By now it was getting late. I knew I couldn't make it to Huajuapan de León as I'd planned; there were far too many burros, cows, goats, dogs and people on the road to even think about driving after dark. So I raced the setting sun, through onion fields and sugar cane, into the state of Puebla and past Izucar de Matamoros. There I turned southeast and rejoined the Pan American Highway, Mexico 190. The map showed that from this cross-roads to Panamá my journey would be more east than south.

Beyond Izucar the mountains were covered with 15-foot prickly pears and multi-trunked, tree-sized pitayo (organ) cacti. I squeezed through a steep rocky gorge, and pulled into the pottery-making Mixtec town of Acatlán, where I got a room at the Plaza Hotel. There I spent a pleasant evening, milling about town amidst hundreds of plastic banners for PRI, PAN, PDR and PT. Next Sunday was election day, and the campaign was in full swing.

The churchyard was shady and full of lovers, and the market was closing. I had a beer and talked Mexican politics with Sergio, owner of Don Sergio's Restaurante Marisco on the ever-present Calle Emiliano Zapata. "Most Mexicans, myself included, have little confidence in any of the parties," Sergio said. Though he liked leftist Cuauhtémoc Cárdenas and the Democratic Revolutionary Party, Sergio planned to vote PRI once again. "Only the PRI can deliver locally," he said, "being aligned to the party in continuous national power." He said the PRI had the most local support, that the Republican-oriented PAN was second, the leftist PDR third, and the PT (Workers' Party) had little strength. I did observe, however, that PT banners hanging across streets and in the plaza rivaled those of PRI. I went back to the hotel for a dinner of fish fried with vegetables in butter and garlic, wrote till everything was quiet, and went to bed.

When I set out next morning, I hoped this day would be less eventful than the last. It's a long mountain road from Acatlán to Oaxaca, and though there is a new toll road part way, I would avoid the temptation, sticking faithfully to the old Pan American Highway. From Acatlán I followed the Río Mixteco valley to Huajuapan de León, birthplace of Gen. Antonio de León, hero in the battle of Molinos against the 1847 U.S. invasion. Most of Huajuapan was destroyed by earthquake in 1980.

In addition to palms, from which textiles are made, maguey plantations had become frequent. Distilling mescal, the maguey fire water, is a major regional industry. Though a local expression has it that "para todo mal mescal, y para todo bien también," (for the bad times, mescal, and for the good times too), I exercised the good sense to leave it alone, worm and all. Instead I had rolls and coffee at Mary's Restaurant, a tiny cement block room with a single table. Along the highway boys herded goats and burros in the ditches. Several burros lay dead, casualties of the road. One boy zinged rocks at his flock with a sling shot, simultaneously keeping his goats in line and himself entertained.

After Tamazulapan the road descends into the valley and straightens out at last. I stopped at Yanhuitlán to visit the 460-year-old Dominican church and convent, a huge structure of big blocks of limestone, towering more than eight stories high, far above the little town. The convent had been restored, and could be toured for a dollar, but the church was still not open to the public. But Martín, a middle-aged sacristán in a Houston cap, whipped out a foot-long key, and for three pesos opened the ancient creaking door and let me in for a look. Unlike the Santo Domingo church I would visit a few hours later in Oaxaca, this church is not especially remarkable, except for its size. If the surrounding houses were inhabited by Lilliputians, Gulliver could stroll about the sanctuary with ease.

But there is an appalling piece of history associated with the church. In 1642, agents of the Holy Inquisition tortured several Indian chiefs until they confessed to ceremonial use of hallucinogenic mushrooms, then burned them in the churchyard for their sins.

As I left Yanhuitlán I picked up a young man named Raymundo Cruz Cruz. (Both parents had the same last name, so Raymundo had been "double crossed," so to speak.) A photography student at the technical institute in Oaxaca, Raymundo was working on a book of photographs of small Mexican towns. We had a nice talk as we rode along, and he gave me a word I'd been searching for. I learned I'd been grabbing voices for days. To tape record, in Spanish, is grabar, he said.

I left Raymundo in Nochixtlán, the town where, unlike all the sane travelers, I by-passed the new toll road and stuck with my free highway, even though Raymundo warned me it had a few hoyos (holes). The old road would take me to the valley of Oaxaca through the tiny mountain settlements of El Palmer, Cuesta Blanca, El Cortijo, Llano Verde, and 8,200' El Tejocote, towns where houses cling precariously to hillsides and people to life. It was this area, Raymundo told me, that the Spanish explorer had in mind when the king asked him what the state of Oaxaca was like. The explorer picked up a sheet of paper, crushed and crumpled it into peaks and valleys and handed it to the king. "That, your majesty, is a map of Oaxaca," he said.

On the loneliest stretch of road, up in the pines near the mountain-top town of Cuesta Blanca, I suddenly came upon the policía, a pickup truck with two officers in front, and two more, with rifles, in back. They were moving slow, about 30 miles an hour, very strange behavior for police, I thought. Paranoid after yesterday, I wanted no more encounters with cops, so I slowed to 25 and dropped back, but they slowed down too. I followed for a couple of miles, not daring to pass, fearing that by passing I'd be guilty of another "infraction." I could pass the police, drive 25 all the way to Oaxaca, or stop. I pulled off for lunch at a mountain-top comedor.

When I hit the road again it was clear, not only of authorities, but of all other travelers. How much longer, I wondered, could this little comedor stay open. Business couldn't have been worse if they'd been in coffin repair. All the traffic is on the new highway now, and the only visible means of income is cutting firewood. Most of the locals travel by burro or by foot, and when they get where they're going, they have no money to spend. And I had thought I-29 was drying up communities on old 81 in North Dakota. By comparison, those little farm towns are booming.

# SOUTHERN MEXICO

*"Here we are, the dead of all times, dying once*
*again, but now with the objective of living."*

~ *Subcomandante Marcos, Zapatista Army of National Liberation, 1994*

At last I descended to the valley of Oaxaca. Negotiating the most congested traffic of the trip, I arrived at the Hotel de Valle west of the plaza, a place I'd stayed before. The city is colonial, and the streets narrow, not built for the hordes of cars and smoke-belching buses which clog them. William Phelps Eno, whose motto was "ex chaos ordo," Latin for "out of chaos order," would have hated Oaxaca's streets, for out of order has come chaos. Eno was the highway engineer who began studying traffic issues in 1899, wrote four books on the subject, and proposed and lobbied for what became the traffic rules and patterns by which we live in the United States. Eno had a chauffeur and footman, never had a license to drive, and probably would have sold insurance had he foreseen modern Oaxaca.

Oaxaca is the capital of the state of Oaxaca, the principal city of the Indian south. No two sources agree on the city's population, but upper estimates are close to a million. It's a wonderful place to visit – on foot. Oaxaca was the birthplace of two famous Mexican presidents, the great liberator Benito Juárez, a Zapotecan Indian born in the little town of Guelatao north of the city, and 33-year dictator Porfirio Díaz, overthrown at last by the 1910 revolution.

I stowed my things at the hotel and headed up the mountain to Monte Albán, one of the great cities of ancient America. Monte Albán lacks the vast pyramids of Teotihuacán near Mexico City, the towering temples protruding from the jungle at Guatemala's Tikal, and the elaborately carved stone of Uxmal in Yucatán. But its unique majesty begins with the site itself, a mountain top leveled and first built upon perhaps 2,500 years ago by people influenced by the Olmec. The lofty city overlooks Oaxaca to the east, and several pueblos to the west. Monte Albán was a sacred city – for its first builders, then for the Zapotecs, who erected most of the existing structures, and still later for the Mixtecs. My favorite feature of Monte Albán is the Danzantes, the dancers, a file of four-foot figures frozen in bas relief, kicking up their heels and madly flailing their arms for 2,500 years, a crazy dance that, though possibly depicting sacrificed captives, could have inspired the twist.

I managed to stay ahead of an amoebic torrent, a large French tour group.

Besides French I heard German, Japanese, British English, and of course Spanish, the most diverse assortment of people I'd encountered since Winnipeg. For a day I had rejoined the tourist trail. I scrambled over the pyramids and temples, then relaxed with a drink and a genuine banana-leaf-wrapped mole tamale, that unique blend of chili, chocolate, sesame and secret seasonings that is at its richest and best in Oaxaca. So fundamental is mole to the local cuisine that whole shops are devoted to this product alone, available in dozens of variations. I bought a turquoise necklace for Norma from a jewelry maker named Adelina, and came down from the mountain.

Back in Oaxaca I visited the Regional Museum to see the jade and gold and other treasures gleaned from the tombs of the ancient rulers of Monte Albán. Next door is the baroque 1550s Santo Domingo church, perhaps the richest in all of Mexico. This Dominican church is not as large as the one in Yanhuitlán, but virtually every surface is paved in gold – the high vaulted ceiling, the santos and crucifixes and scrolls, the walls themselves, gilded with elaborately ornamented gold leaf. Many of the 27 historic churches in Oaxaca are rich in gold, but in Santo Domingo, no point on ceiling or wall is more than six inches from the gleaming metal. How many hours of slave labor mined the gold, built and embellished the church? All for the glory of God? The king? The priests? Such wealth, amidst such poor people. Of course this church and all its gold must be preserved for future generations, not only as a sanctuary, but as a creation of incredible beauty and art. But it is also a monument to slavery and official greed, and I couldn't repress iconoclastic thoughts about how many tamales all this gold would buy for the beggar woman who passes her days at the door, and for the millions of Mexico's poor.

I walked to the Zócalo, the main plaza, where I found even more tourists than on Monte Albán. Europeans and North Americans were eating and drinking in the swanky sidewalk establishments east of the plaza. It reminded me of Santa Fe, where tourists have virtually driven the locals from their own city center. The few Mexicans who ate and drank on the east side were light-skinned and well-dressed. I found a little taquería on a side street for supper.

When I returned to the plaza, the music had begun. Mariachis ambled and sang amongst the tourists; marimba tones tinkled from the southwest corner. I settled in at a little place on the north side, where five men and a woman who called themselves "Los Ultimos de Tacuara" played Andean-accented music on flutes, guitars, and various drums. Eight-year-old Gato (cat) and his five-year-old brother came to my table, selling Chiclets and generally trying to scare up a peso. It was almost 11:00, when little boys should have been in bed, but these dirty urchins, like so many others, were still hustling. Gato and I played several games of tic-tac-toe, and try as I might to let him win, either I or the other cat took every game. He just didn't get it. Finally he cheated and won. I gave Gato and his brother a peso each and told them it was time to go home to bed, hoping to God, but afraid to ask, if they had a home to go to. The boys went out, and the latest and utmost from Tacuara took a break. Band member Erasco joined me for a drink and I bought a tape of their music.

Later yet, I strolled to the south side of the plaza, where a protest rally was in progress. The local teachers' union was on a 24-hour sit-in strike. In light of 43 percent inflation in the past year and the devaluation of the peso, they were demanding a salary increase. A 50-foot, five-color banner spanning the columns of the Municipal Palace demanded "end the repression," admonishing strikers that "united and organized we are invincible." A 10-foot man thrust aloft an assault weapon, the banana clip emblazoned with the letters EZLN, Zapatista National Liberation Army.

I talked with fifth grade teacher Francisco, a handsome man in his thirties, who told me the teachers earned $280 per month, or $2,500 a year. "The teachers are united in the strike," he said. "And most of the students support us too – whether out of principle or for a day off," he added with a grin. Francisco said most teachers, students and other workers in Oaxaca also back the Zapatistas, seeing them as the vanguard of a Mexico-wide struggle against corruption, for democracy and economic reform.

When I last visited Oaxaca in 1991, the same spot fronting the Municipal Palace was occupied by another group of demonstrators, that time campesinos who had camped on the plaza for weeks, demanding roads, potable water, and agricultural loans. I wondered if those farmers got anything they needed then, and whether Francisco and his colleagues would make progress toward equitable professional salaries now. Compared to Mexicans earning the minimum wage, the teachers are well-paid, but like those earning the minimum, their salaries are perhaps a tenth of what their counterparts earn north of the border. The pressure for Mexican workers in all occupations to go north – assembly workers in the maquiladoras of Nuevo Laredo, the mechanic who fled Tepexco to Chicago, or the teachers in Oaxaca – is understandable.

Next morning I continued south, as usual. Actually southeast, but I couldn't shake the presumption I'd lived with all my life that it was south to which I drove. My first stop was at Santa María del Tule, the only town I know that is named for a tree. Santa María is very old, but when the first stone was laid, the tree was already here. The tree is "El Tule." There are, of course, many tule trees, also known as ahuehuete, or cypress. In fact, in the same churchyard looms another tule with a 20-foot-thick trunk, a tree which anywhere else would be regarded as a giant. But beside El Tule, it is an upstart, el hijo. For its father is THE Tule.

I had visited El Tule three times before, but its majesty never diminishes. El Tule is said to be the oldest and grandest living thing on earth, and I know no rivals. By official estimate, El Tule is 2,000 years old, though some sources say much older. Compared to the breadth of its trunk, the tree is not tall, a mere 13 or 14 stories. But the trunk of this gigantic cypress is over 52 feet in diameter, wider than a large house! I timed a stroll around the tree, which took a minute.

The estimated weight of El Tule is 63,000 tons. El Tule still seems healthy, showing no signs of distress. Fortunately, since my last visit the Pan American Highway had been rerouted a block away from the tree, so it can now breathe fresher air again.

My rumination was shattered by the arrival of a Winnebago, from which two North American couples emerged. It cost a peso to go inside the churchyard and get close to El Tule. Indignant at the request for 15 cents each to look at a tree which they could view through the fence, the driver stuck a thousand-dollar video camera between the slats, zoomed in for a few seconds of tape, fired up the $50,000 motor home, and roared away. When the dust had settled, I swallowed my despair, put from mind the many shrines to death I had encountered, and lost myself in meditation before this most wondrous shrine to life.

Just south of Santa María del Tule, I visited the ancient ruin of Dainzú, partially unearthed in 1967. Dainzú is unique among American antiquities I have seen, built not in a valley or on a mountain top, but terraced into the western slope of a hill. Lizards scurried among the bas relief figures which decorate the few exposed foundations. Higher up the hill is a ball court much like the one at Monte Albán.

When Dainzú was built two millennia ago, El Tule was perhaps a sapling. When Dainzú was abandoned sometime before the conquistadors arrived, El Tule must have looked pretty much as it does today. Taken by itself, though a minor ancient work of man, Dainzú is impressive. Beside nature's magnificence up the road, it is an interesting pile of rocks, laid together by long-forgotten men. As Paul Theroux said in *Riding the Iron Rooster*, "nothing puts human effort into better perspective than a ruined city." Unless it's El Tule.

My next stop was a pueblo I'd long heard about, but never visited, Teotitlán del Valle, a famous village of weavers just beyond Dainzú. Teotitlán lies in a valley a couple miles north of the highway. Its low, unpainted adobe houses and winding cobblestone streets look unchanged for ages; indeed from a jet traveler's perspective, the town might seem a mere swelling of the earth from which it is made.

Most of the residents are traditional Zapotecan weavers, many selling from shops in their homes. For the price of a 10-minute call home, I bought half a dozen small woolen weavings from a tiny young woman named Carmela, just west of the plaza. She called them servilletas, or table napkins. I called them works of art, and brought them home as gifts for special friends. I couldn't imagine spilling ketchup on a weaving fine enough to grace the walls of any gallery.

I'd spent most of a perfect morning at El Tule, Dainzú, and Teotitlán, and now I had to make some time. I wanted to be in San Cristóbal de Las Casas by next afternoon, and in Guatemala by election day. So I had to be somewhere in the isthmus by night, with several essential stops along the way.

In the 700-year-old village of Tlacolula, a softly-sobbing young woman led a little son through the chapel, caressing every sacred object, then fondling her face and body and that of her son, as if to transfer some much needed blessing from the lifeless icons to her own troubled life. I went to the Banomex across the street and changed money, getting almost eight pesos to the dollar. The economic crisis had continued to deepen. If not her contact with icons, what could ease the suffering of this young woman and her countrymen?

The next pueblo in the Oaxaca valley is Mitla, Zapotecan for "place of rest." Zapotecan kings were buried beneath the ruins of this ancient city long before it was conquered by the Mixtecs in the 10th century. The archeological ruins of Mitla feature intricately-mosaiced stone work, reflected in the creations of the weavers and other artisans who sell their work beside the ruins. And the dusty streets leading from town to ruin are lined with the tiny shops of vendors of locally-distilled mescal, cheaper and more plentiful here than any place I know.

The highway continues its serpentine southeasterly course, climbing high into the Sierras through the villages of Totolapan, Las Margaritas, San José Viejo, El Camarón, and San Bartolo. Then I plunged fast from a mile high to 800 feet at the riverside town of Magdalena Tequisistlán. Now in the lowlands, the palm-lined valley was hot, and getting hotter. I stopped and sipped a cold drink in Magdalena with a truck driver who was hauling a load of agave hearts to the next town, Jalapa, where they would become Presidente tequila.

Canyon walls south of Magdalena range from orange to pink to lavender. Past Jalapa del Marqués lies the Benito Juárez lake, formed by damming the Tehuantepec River. Then came the final descent, and I crossed the river and entered the first of two famous Tehuana cities of women, Santo Domingo Tehuantepec and Juchitán de Zaragoza. Now almost at sea level, I was sweltering in the sub-tropical sun. Only a slight breeze from the Pacific made the atmosphere breathable.

These Tehuana cities on the Isthmus of Tehuantepec have much in common. The Tehuana culture is to a great extent matriarchal, and the women of both cities have the reputation not only for stately beauty, but also for aggressiveness in personal and business affairs. I spent some time in both towns, but especially in the plaza and market of Tehuantepec. Atypical in this patriarchal country, the principal statue in the plaza is that of a local woman, a matronly teacher, Señora Juana Romera. The market is run almost exclusively by women; the few men were engaged primarily in menial labor, such as sweeping the floors. A butcher delivered a long-winded denunciation of the PRI government and its "gringo accomplices," perhaps for my benefit, accenting her points with sweeping slashes of a broad carving knife.

I bought a handsome hammock from a big woman named Teresa, whom I strangely seemed to meet at every turn, her price declining with each encounter. Teresa was a bit of a tease, but she could afford to be. She weighed at least 180, and she had lots of hammocks to sell. Some sources claim that the women here actually hoot and whistle when a handsome man passes, but I know this not to be true; I strolled down every isle of the market place, and drew some stares, but

*"El Tule," the world's largest tree, at Santa Maria del Tule (top), Teresa, hammock maker at Tehuantepec (bottom left), and Geraldo, shoe shine boy in Comitán.*

not a single whistle.

I drove northeast for the first time, into the isthmus toward Juchitán de Zaragoza, where I had thought to spend the night. But a couple hours of light remained, and the low lands were still very hot, so I pushed on, toward the higher town of San Pedro Tapanatepec. En route I met the biggest snake I've ever seen outside captivity, a ten-footer as big as my arm, slithering across the steaming blacktop. At the narrowest part of the isthmus, I passed La Ventosa Junction, famous for its wind, as the name suggests. Near La Ventosa, at the turnoff to El Porvenir (the future) I passed a farm of generators, big blades slowly cranking out electricity from the wind. Perhaps the presumably accidental conjunction of the wind generators and the sign to the future is an omen.

I had one more stretch of 60 miles before Tapanatepec, and plenty of daylight, I thought. I was cruising at a good 50 through flat land and 12-foot sugar cane, when suddenly ahead, traffic ground to a halt, a long line of cars and trucks and buses ahead of me. Word came down the line that a road crew was replacing a culvert — without a detour — and we'd have to wait. People piled out of the bus behind me, and the driver and several passengers came to lean with me on the grimy Omni. I dragged out my bag of oranges, still a third full, a woman from the bus produced a pan of tamales, and we had a party right there in the road, the bus driver, the tamale woman, a couple of nurses from Australia on their way to volunteer service in Honduras, a family with a baby and a little boy, and me.

When traffic moved again it was dark. An hour and a half's worth of vehicles from each way meant a congested road all the way to Tapanatepec. I got a room at the only hotel I found, the Casa Blanca on the parque. (Somewhere along the way from Oaxaca, plazas had become parks, which they would remain throughout much of Central America.) Besides a bed, my room came furnished with the two essentials for a hotel room in the tropics — a ceiling fan, and a lizard on the wall to eat insects. The young man at the desk recommended the Comedor Económica Lupita down the street.

For $2, Guadalupe Mosce Rascado filled me up with fish, salad, rice, tortillas and beer, all delicious. While I ate she talked. She told how she won first prize in a cooking competition in Tehuantepec. On the wall was a poster-sized color photo of Guadalupe, holding her big golden crown before her ample breasts, the smile of triumph on her face. "Come back for breakfast," she said. "Any time after 6:00, and you can have flan." Flan, that rich Latin American caramel custard for breakfast? Why not? I promised to return.

Next morning at 6:30 Guadalupe was busy. While I inhaled two cups of the most succulent flan ever made, she brought smoking coals from someplace in back and ignited the fire in her cook stove. Then she splashed buckets of water on the outside wall and scrubbed away yesterday's dust with a broom. She was moving slightly slower than the night before, but the restless rhythm of her big muscular arms and legs never seemed to pause.

At Tapanatepec Junction, Mexico 190, the Pan American Highway, goes northeast to Tuxtla Gutiérrez, on to San Cristóbal, and south again into the highlands of Guatemala. Mexico 200 splits off and heads southeast along the coast. All the way to San Miguel, El Salvador, these alternate routes parallel; in Central America they are CA 1 and CA 2. The 1949 *Rand-McNally Atlas* shows the coastal route as the Pan, or "Inter-American" Highway, but once the highland road through Guatemala was paved, the mountain route took the honor away. I headed back into the mountains.

As I left Tapanatepec I passed a school bus with a "di no a las drogas" bumper sticker, say no to drugs. In just four miles I crossed the continental divide amidst pine forests and purple morning glories and verdant grasses. Soon I was in the state of Chiapas, the sign to which was riddled with bullet holes. I had passed through Chiapas once before, on my way to Guatemala in 1988. I was glad to be returning for a more extended visit. I hoped to learn more about the Zapatistas, and about the conditions that had prompted their 1994 rebellion. Mexican officials had conceded just a month before that the nation's indigenous peoples deserve some kind of autonomy, but details remained to be worked out. The Zapatistas had also demanded better living conditions and an end to political corruption and fraudulent elections. I was eager to see if progress could be observed.

The first thing I found when I crossed the state line was road work. A massive project to rebuild the Pan American Highway through the mountains was underway, perhaps partly to employ rebels or would-be rebels, temporarily defusing a major cause of the uprising, a lack of jobs. An improved highway would also facilitate army access to Chiapas. The primary task was to construct concrete shoulders and gutters to handle the rainy season run-off, which had washed great chunks of the road away. Hundreds of men were at work, most with pick or shovel or wheelbarrow. Trucks brought in materials, but the work of preparing the bed and of mixing, pouring, and finishing the concrete was all done by hand.

When traffic stopped for awhile I got out and talked with some of the workers. "We work from 6 a.m. to 7 p.m. with half an hour for lunch," a young man called Alberto told me. "We earn 25 pesos a day." That would be $3, or 25 cents an hour for all day on a pick or a shovel in the punishing sun. I thought I was living cheap, sleeping in $6 hotels, spending $6 a day on food and drink. I was taking care of only myself on $12 a day, and many of these men had large families to feed on $3 a day. How much, I wondered, did that leave for shelter and clothing and medicine, and for fun. There seemed to be no shortage of workers, and the men toiled mightily to keep their jobs. Yet there are those in both Mexico and the U.S. who fail to understand the Zapatista rebellion.

I was now in Zoque Indian country, having passed from the ancient Zapotecan sphere to that of the Maya. I drove through Lázaro Cárdenas and Cintalapa and Ocozocoautla before reaching the state capital. Lázaro Cárdenas was renamed to honor the president who in the 1930s stood up to the U.S. and nationalized Mexican oil. Tuxtla Gutiérrez is the capital of Chiapas, having replaced San Cristóbal a century ago. Tuxtla is a trading and agricultural center on the big and clean-looking Río Grijalva, a city of a quarter million. A few miles north of Tuxtla is Sumidero Canyon, where the Chiapan Indians, driven to the canyon edge by invading Spaniards, fought to the bitter end, and when they could fight no more, perhaps a thousand men, women and children leaped to their deaths in the canyon rather than submit to Spanish enslavement.

The other mountain town before San Cristóbal is Chiapa de Corzo, founded on the site of an Indian village in 1528 by conquistador Diego de Mazariegos. The huge 16th century church speaks of the colonial past in this city of 20,000. The Moorish fountain in the plaza links the city to the Moors, the Arabic-Berber Africans who conquered Spain in the eighth century. The fountain is a 75-foot, eight-sided pavilion, supported by eight pillars, built of red Mozarabic brick in the shape of the crown of the Catholic Kings of Spain.

On each of the eight pillars, a plaque relates a chapter in the history of the place: The Nandalumi, who lived here from time immemorial, the invasion of Capt. Luis Marín in 1524, successfully repelled, followed by that of Mazariegos in 1528, which succeeded. The Chiapan warriors fought valiantly, but defeated, moved with their women and children higher into the mountains. Having expelled the rightful owners, the conquistadors founded the city of Villa Real, later renamed Chiapa de los Indios. By 1552, Chiapa had become the regional economic capital, and in 1562, the Moorish fountain was finished, the only one of its kind in the Americas. In 1888 the town was given its present name, Chiapa de Corzo, in homage to Angel Albino Corzo. The "castle," as the fountain is called, fell into disrepair, but was reconstructed in 1944, and today remains a marvel. The extent to which the lives of the Chiapan people have been rebuilt was not immediately apparent.

At a restaurant on the plaza I had tacos al pastor (kid goat) — greasy, full of onions, and tasty — and headed on east. Increasingly, road signs and other available surfaces had been overpainted with EZLN. Huge ceiba trees are common here, hovering over adobe and stick houses. Morning glories were profuse, and a bright yellow flowering bush that looked like a rose but was probably an annual plant, completely covered one mountain top. I climbed steadily to a summit, marveling that anyone, even someone as set on conquest as the Spaniards, could have gotten over these mountains, accomplished their mission, and had the tenacity to stay.

I passed women with great bundles of fire wood strapped to their backs, toiling up the mountain road toward San Cristóbal. Incredibly steep slopes are planted to corn, as they are in the highlands of Guatemala. This was definitely Maya country, the most beautiful mountains I had seen, and the people the most colorfully dressed. Younger women, their elaborately woven huipils (blouses) predominately red, carried babies on their backs, other burdens in their arms. An old woman wove a huipil as she guarded goats on a pinnacle of grass beside the road

It must be fewer than 20 miles as the vulture flies from Chiapa de Corzo to

San Cristóbal, but it was well over an hour by road, high, twisting, and narrow. In a 200 foot ravine down a 45 degree cornfield lay a crushed car, a crowd of people gathered around the bodies. In the town of Nachig a convoy of armored vehicles loaded with combat-ready soldiers was parked beside the road. School was out, and the most exotic children I've ever seen trudged past the convoy on their way home. What a mad contrast, what a farce, like the stark irony of an Orozco or a Rivera painting, these drab soldiers here to subdue such resplendent children and their parents. I itched to take a picture, but many Mayas believe that photographs diminishes the subject's soul, so I kept the camera in its case.

Passing the road to Zinacatán where men traditionally wear pink shorts and breech cloths and wide flat straw hats with ribbons, tied if married, loose if not, I descended to the historic 7,000-foot valley city of San Cristóbal de Las Casas. Most of the 73,000 people of San Cristóbal are Maya, the Chamulas the prominent group. Most speak a Mayan dialect, either Tzotzil or Tzeltal.

As all the 16th-century Dominican churches I had encountered from central Mexico south would indicate, the Dominicans dominated the religious life, and to a great extent the political life, of colonial Mexico. Scores of extravagant edifices were constructed and filled with gold, essentially with forced labor. Many in the church hierarchy were accomplices of the conquistadors in the relentless destruction of indigenous cultures and the subjugation of peoples. For example, the second Catholic Bishop of Yucatán, Fray Diego de Landa, launched an almost completely successful campaign in 1562 to burn the Maya codices, which contained the historical records and the mythology of the ancient Maya world. Only a few texts remain, including the *Popol Vuh*. But San Cristóbal de las Casas honors a man who defied the destroyers and exploiters, denouncing their deeds.

In 1524 the Spaniards defeated the Chamula here at what was then called Jovel; they established the city of Villaviciosa, vicious city, in 1528. When Dominican missionary and Bishop Bartolomé de las Casas arrived in 1545, Indians were still abused and killed with impunity; rape and slavery were standard Spanish practices. Las Casas condemned these atrocities, challenging the authority of Spanish Gov. Enrique de Guzmán, earning the hatred of the conquistadors. Las Casas had preserved and edited the diaries of Christopher Columbus, and had himself as a young Dominican priest lived by the labor of slaves on the island of Hispaniola. But soon he saw that the church's vision for converting the "new world" had been corrupted to horrible genocide.

In a 1511 sermon, Las Casas had demanded of colonists, "With what right, and with what justice do you keep these poor Indians in such cruel and horrible servitude?" In 1542 Las Casas wrote *A Short Account of the Destruction of the Indies*, published in 1552 and dedicated to Spanish Prince Philip, a far-ranging indictment of Spanish abuse of native peoples from Hispaniola to Peru. Another 20 years would pass before the king of Spain would issue "New Ordinances Governing the Treatment of Indians in the New World," and even then the injunctions were largely ignored. In fact, in mid-20th century, Indians were still forbidden to walk on the sidewalks of San Cristóbal.

I got a room at the Real del Valle, a well-preserved colonial hotel just off the plaza, and set out to see the town. On my way into town I had discovered that the cobble-stoned streets of San Cristóbal are even narrower than those in Oaxaca, not designed for cars, an unpredictable maze of unmarked one-way lanes, a nightmare for the uninitiated. I decided to walk.

The plaza and the city center are well-maintained colonial Mexico at its best. The cathedral and the 1547 Santo Domingo church are grand, and the plaza is surrounded by tidy hotels and quaint restaurants in colonial structures. Until the Zapatista uprising, San Cristóbal was on the tourist trail. There were still a few North Americans and Europeans around, but most restaurants were almost empty. No doubt the tourist business was suffering, though to some extent the usual crowd had been replaced by journalists and delegations of international observers. For a dollar I bought a colorful woven barrette, featuring a boy, a girl and a fish for my daughter Laura from a Maya woman named María. María was pleased when I told her my mother shared her name.

Like his predecessor Las Casas, Samuel Ruiz, the Bishop of Chiapas had defended Indian rights, serving as mediator between the Zapatistas and the Mexican government. He was out of town, so I went looking for others with insight. I found a young man named José at the Human Rights Commission, Margaret O'Shey at Casa de Paz (Peace House), and Associated Press photographer Scott Sady, who for the past year had covered both the conflict and the negotiations in Chiapas.

Margaret came to San Cristóbal from California to manage the Peace House set up in 1994 by North Americans who had joined Bishop Ruiz in a protest fast at the cathedral. The Peace House had maintained an international observer presence, coordinating North American delegations to Chiapas. Margaret had just returned from a speaking and fund-raising tour in the United States, having stopped in Tuxtla Gutiérrez on her way back to visit Zapatista political prisoners. The men had supposedly been named by an anonymous EZLN deserter as leaders of the rebellion, but after several months in prison, they still faced no specific charges, Margaret said. I went for my car, and Margaret and I talked as I drove her to a non-descript house on a dirt street near the edge of town to deliver "a ton of money" she had gathered in support of those impacted by the turmoil. But most of the emergency aid coming to the region was from the European community, Margaret said.

The government had agreed in recent autonomy negotiations with the Zapatistas to recognize traditional Maya models of justice and decision-making, the self-governance that has always existed in the villages, but underground behind the facade of the local PRI government. "But I'm very skeptical that the government will really allow much autonomy in Chiapas," Margaret said. "Indigenous peoples in other states such as Guerrero would soon make the same demands. I'm afraid that the peace talks were cynically calculated to buy time for the government while they plan other strategies to control the people of Chiapas." In fact, in 1999, the next Mexican president, Ernesto Zedillo, would be making the same pledge, but again without substantial results.

North American solidarity activists were not immune to intimidation and violence. Just a few days before my visit, Cecilia Rodríguez, the U.S. director of the Committee for Democracy in Mexico, was traveling with her husband south of San Cristóbal when they were stopped and abducted by armed men, who then sexually assaulted Cecilia, Margaret said. A big demonstration by Mexican women at the U.S. Embassy in Mexico City demanded that the U.S. government investigate the attack.

"The real strength of the EZLN is not military," Margaret said, "but the ability to bring attention to the conditions of life for indigenous peoples and the poor, and to shape national and international opinion." Locally, their strength lay in the sympathy of the villagers, though many Protestants, themselves victims of Catholic discrimination, did not support the rebellion. Subcomandante Marcos and other leaders issued communiqués every couple of weeks, Margaret said, and when negotiations were in session the leaders held frequent press conferences. They had become adept at focusing attention on their struggle, wielding influence well out of proportion to actual numbers.

I shared a beer with photographer Scott Sady, a young man with a long ponytail. Scott said his film had been confiscated by soldiers that very afternoon as he photographed the forced eviction of refugees from a squatter camp outside San Cristóbal. Scott was preparing to leave for the pueblo of San Andreas, where peace talks were about to resume. He said the EZLN leaders were hiding in the Lacandón selva, but that Zapatistas were everywhere, going about the normal routines of life, no doubt at work on the Pan American highway, awaiting the outcome of the talks, ready to resume armed struggle if necessary.

In the evening I visited Na Bolom Center for Scientific Studies, established by Danish anthropologist Franz Blom and his wife Gertrude, an archaeologist, linguist, photographer and writer who came from the Swiss Alps to Mexico as a journalist in the 1940s. Gertrude Blom first went to the Lacandón Forest in 1943. She fell in love with the forest and its people, the most isolated and non-westernized in North America, and became good friends with Lacandón spiritual leader, Chan K'in. With her husband, she devoted the next half century to the preservation of the Lacandón Forest of Chiapas and the Lacandón people.

Na Bolom (Lacandón for "the jaguar") is a most interesting place. I arrived too late to meet Gertrude Blom, who died in 1993 at age 93. Her husband Franz, who first came to Chiapas in 1919, had been dead for 30 years. He is best remembered for his exploration of the Maya ruins at Palenque, and for his definitive 1950 two-volume work, *La Selva Lacandón*. The Bloms' home, originally a colonial seminary with lovely courtyard and gardens, is now a museum of Lacandón history and culture, a guest house where Lacandón people may eat and sleep free of charge, and headquarters of an ecology project and tree nursery whose goal is to preserve forest and to replant 60,000 trees in the Lacandón rain forest each year Most of the forest has already been cut down by loggers and ranchers and by set tlers relocated by the government from other parts of Mexico.

Though as I would discover on down the road, forest destruction is occurring at an alarming rate throughout Central America, Mexico was suffering deforesta tion at the second fastest rate in the western hemisphere. A LANDSAT satellite photo published by *National Geographic* in 1989 illustrates well what had already happened to the forest of Chiapas. The Guatemala border is distinctly obvious a a glance. The photo shows heavy forest on the Guatemalan side, but only scattered patches of trees on the Mexican side of the border. Only deep in Lacandón terri tory, especially in the Montes Azules Biosphere Preserve, is the forest protected from exploitation. The Lacandón believe that when a tree is cut without permission from their chief god, Hachakyum, the sky the tree is holding up will fall. Except fo the small biosphere preserve, most of the Lacandón forest is gone. The Lacandón sky is sagging very low.

The next day was November 11, Veterans' Day in the U.S. I turned the vener able Omni south once more and headed for Guatemala. I stopped for awhile in the Tzeltal town of Comitán de Domínguez which, when the Spaniards arrived, wa Bulumcanán (New Star), the most populated Quiché Maya kingdom in the region Five hundred varieties of orchids are native here, though I saw only a few. Besid the six-pointed Moorish star kiosk in the Comitán plaza, a little boy named Geraldo polished my battered sneakers.

Comitán is the childhood home of Mexican writer Rosario Castellanos. Born to privilege, Castellanos returned Indian land she inherited and worked for May cultural preservation with the National Indigenous Institute. In her book *City of Kings*, Castellanos tells the stories of the subjugation, exploitation, and continued struggle of indigenous peoples. The stories suggest that outsiders can never full know the Maya, nor can even well meaning people help if they come laden with the baggage of unquestioned assumptions and cultural superiority.

Between Comitán and the border lie the camps of refugees from Maya village in Guatemala, driven out by government forces in the 1980s. Some refugees had returned, but tens of thousands remained. En route to Guatemala as a delegate with Witness for Peace in 1992, Norma stayed with a family in nearby Maravilla camp She slept on a board spanning two barrels, above the pigs and other creatures on the dirt floor.

The highland mountains of Guatemala loomed just ahead, a forbidding natur al frontier. The last town in Mexico is Ciudad Cuauhtémoc, named for an Azte leader killed by Cortés. To the north is yet another Emiliano Zapata, and to th south, just inside Guatemala, is Tecún Umán, named for the hero of Guatemala resistance to Spain. How ironic that in these border towns named for long-dead heroes of resistance, the cycle of oppression and struggle continues, unabated.

# GUATEMALA

*"What hurts Indians most is that our costumes are considered beautiful, but it's as if the person wearing it didn't exist."*

*~ Rigoberta Menchú, 1992 Nobel Peace Prize Laureate*

I entered Guatemala at La Mesilla, crawling through potholes, waiting my turn to be fumigated. I paid seven pesos to an official who sprayed under, around, and even inside my car with some noxious chemical, the name of which he couldn't tell me. Then he swung open the pine pole gate and I entered CA-1, which I would follow through six nations to the Darién Gap. Next was the passport check. Though I already had a visa, issued by the Guatemalan Consulate in Washington, I paid $2 to get it stamped by a man in a U.S. Army t-shirt, which he said he got from his nephew in the states. His assistant gave me a plug of the sugar cane candy he was eating.

Next was the aduana, customs, where I needed official permission to import my car. "This will cost you 150 quetzals," said a young man behind black shades.

"That's outrageous," I said. I explained that official information from the Guatemalan tourist bureau states the cost of entry should be about $5.

"O.K., make it a hundred," he said, "or $20."

"Show me in writing the official charge for vehicle transit," I said. He came down to 75 quetzals, $12.50, which I finally paid. Only then did he remove the black glasses from his scowling eyes, peck out the permit on an antique Corona, and stick a big orange stamp on my windshield. What was much worse, they were giving a Guatemalan peasant behind me the same treatment.

"Hey, we've got to eat too," protested the other customs official, the best-dressed man around. I'm sure the campesino was impressed.

Now it was the National Guard's turn. I'd crawled about two blocks up the mountain through a maze of money changers and refugees, overloaded pickups and smoking buses, when a soldier rapped on my window. He told me to park and get out with my papers. "I've already paid three times," I said. "I hope you don't want more money."

He hesitated. "No. Just an official check." This was the first of five military roadblocks I would encounter in 100 miles to Quezaltenango. And all for what? They didn't even check my trunk to see if it was loaded with assault weapons or drugs. When I was free of the border at last I ascended into the mountains, to the town of La Democracia. I'm sure that's one of the things the residents wish for.

Almost as unpleasant as the border officials were Guatemala's roads.

Through 30 years of war and strife, the country's infrastructure had been neglected, and through the mountains, the road was at times nearly impassable. The political parties seemed to have plenty of money to paint mountain cliffs with hands, keys, doves, targets, flags, cowboy hats, airplanes and other party symbols, but those in power apparently had nothing for road repair, even at election time. In the first hundred miles of mountain highway I would pass at least a dozen landslides or wash-outs, the "temporary" passages murderous on vehicles and dangerous to cross. If anything, the road was worse than when I traveled it in the war year of 1988. The biggest chasms are generally toward the edges, so trucks and buses barrel down the middle, without regard for oncoming cars. The center line is just a suggestion, not a rule. You can get over or get smashed. And that was before Hurricane Mitch.

At the turn-off to Huehuetenango, a Club de Liones (Lions Club) sign welcomed me to the city. But the street into "Huehue" was mined with unwelcoming craters a foot deep, no doubt a world record, I thought at the time, though I would discover more of the same ahead. If they'd simply scraped off the remaining asphalt and smoothed the earth it would have been a vast improvement, at least in the dry season. Only three kinds of traffic moved faster than 10 miles per hour – bicyclists, who artfully dodged the chasms, buses and trucks with wheels large enough to span some of the holes, and fools, whose cars would soon be in the junk yard. The elevated tope of Mexico had been replaced by a new kind of speed bump, the convex principle replaced by the concave, unintentional, far less predictable, but even more effective in controlling speed.

In el centro at last, I got two tacos and a pineapple pastry for lunch. I had finished one taco when an old woman came in asking for food, and I gave her the other. When she was gone the waitress asked if I wanted a replacement. I said no thanks, but when she tallied my cuenta she knocked off the price of the second taco. I left a tip of the same, and jolted back to the highway. The Maya ruins of Zaculeu are just north of the city, but I lacked the nerve just then for more miles of moonscape.

So if it's that bad, why visit Guatemala? Because it is the land of perpetual spring, of mountains that elevate the spirit as do El Tule or the tallest redwoods. The people are among the most genuine and resplendent on earth, their cultural heritage profound. Among other accomplishments, the ancient Maya were masters of mathematics and astronomy, even predicting solar eclipses within hours. They developed an accurate calendar 2,000 years ago. They built the tallest, most complex, most enduring aboriginal structures in the Americas. Their descendants still populate Guatemala in more that two dozen cultural groups, each with its unique traditions and patterns of dress. Most Mayas speak Spanish, as well as one or more of several living dialects of the Mayan language.

The Maya culture is, and always has been, centered around corn, not just the staff of life, but the sign of God's pleasure. Growing corn on ancestral land is the core of cultural and spiritual life. In her "cultural autobiography," *I, Rigoberta*

*Menchú*, Menchú says "our people are made of maize ... Maize is the center of everything for us. It is our culture." Menchú says the Maya always ask the earth's permission before they plant their corn, because "the earth is the mother of man." According to Chicano playwright Luis Valdez, who calls himself a "neo-Maya spiritualist," the Maya word for work also means to believe, to create, and to do with love and pain. The four directions, the four colors, and the four roads common to the mythology of indigenous Americans were features of ancient Maya mythology, and though Lakota holy man Black Elk saw the north-south road as the good red road, Valdez says the Maya believe that no one is complete without traveling all four.

An afternoon of exquisite mountains and cratered road later I arrived at San Cristóbal Totonicapán, the turn-off to Quezaltenango, a six mile, half-hour drive from CA-1, not counting the military search. All the traffic between Guatemala's two largest cities, Quezaltenango and the capital, is routed through the town of Salcajá on a narrow one-way street, another street whose pavement is worse than dirt. This must be the bottom circle of hell for the people who live here – putrid exhaust, choking dust, bouncing buses and trucks, a decibel level that obliterates the songs of birds and the unlikely laughter of children.

Emerging from Salcajá, I encountered the first earnest inspection. Two teen-aged soldiers pawed through everything, books, tapes, dirty clothes, food. They even found my laptop computer, which I thought was safely stashed beneath the seat. But they were most interested in my army canteen. They wanted to know if I got it in Vietnam.

I reached Quezaltenango, known locally by the pre-Spanish name of Xela, at dusk. My destination was the Colegio Seminario San José, serene on a hill west of the choking city. Like Mount Marty College back in Yankton, San José is a Benedictine school, but with the unique purpose of educating Guatemalan men for the priesthood. When I arrived, the priests and seminarians were in the chapel for evening vespers. I waited outside, watching the stars define themselves and the lights come on in the city below. The hulking cone of Santa María volcano blackened against a purple sky.

Padre John Brahill emerged and welcomed me. He invited me to bring in my bag, then took me to the dining room for an awesome dinner of fresh vegetables and fruits. Later we retired to the recreation room to talk. The facility was new, the seminary having moved here from Sololá just four years earlier. John was the college prior. A trim man of 46 with short graying hair, he came to Quezaltenango from Chicago when the new campus was built. He took a crash course in Spanish at one of the city's three colleges, and spoke the language well, with a Chicago accent.

It was Saturday night, the eve of national elections, so I asked John about the political process in Guatemala and whether he thought the voting would produce progress. Pres. Jorge Serrano Elías, who assumed dictatorial powers in 1993, had been driven from office and from the country, and Congress had replaced him with former Human Rights Director Ramiro de León Carpio. "The new president has attempted to improve respect for human rights," John said, "but he is up against a brick wall, the fact of continuing military supremacy." Yet, unlike previous elections, John said, there had been less pre-election violence, and he expected the election to be relatively fair. He said that of the 19 candidates, Alvaro Arzú of the National Advanced Party (PAN) seemed most popular, but that with such a splintered electorate, a plurality would be unlikely in the first round of voting.

Perhaps the greatest farce was that Guatemalan Republican Front candidate Alfonso Portillo was running as a defender of human rights. Portillo had actively campaigned with former Gen. Efraín Ríos Montt, whose military dictatorship of the early eighties was among the bloodiest in four decades of strife, second in brutality only to that of his predecessor, Gen. Romeo Lucas García. John said many Guatemalans wondered whether Portillo was merely a front man for Ríos Montt, who came to power by military coup in 1982. According to the Organization of American States, the Inter-American Commission on Human Rights, and several church sources, the government's war against the indigenous people in the highlands killed at least 100,000 civilians and destroyed 440 Maya villages between 1981 and 1983.

I asked John about the economy, and about the plight of refugees. "The real issue," he said, "is economic and social, which for the Maya means separation from the land. For all campesinos the situation is grim, but especially for returning refugees, whose land in many cases is now occupied by others, either by the rich, or by other displaced people." I remembered words about the Maya and their native land in the *Popol Vuh*: "We have always lived here: We have the right to go on living where we are happy and where we want to die. Only here can we feel whole; nowhere else would we ever feel complete, and our pain would be eternal."

John said that for indigenous people, whose entire culture is tied to possession of land, the transition to a capitalist industrial economy, even if decent paying jobs were available, would be difficult. "Such a shift would involve a transformation in ways of thinking," he said. "And it would produce devastating social changes. But as in Mexico, both land and jobs are in short supply, and in both countries population growth is exponential."

I asked whether, given Guatemala's tremendous economic problems, continuing political chaos, corruption, military domination, crumbling infrastructure and environmental degradation, there were reasons for optimism about the country's future. John took a long breath and blew it slowly through his teeth. "I'd like to be hopeful," he said. He noted that the level of political violence and intimidation had been reduced, that soldiers who murdered seven repatriated refugees the month before had been arrested and prosecuted, and more significant, the minister of defense had been forced to resign, which probably would not have happened in the eighties. He also said that the government was beginning a campaign to promote ecological awareness, though no concrete programs were yet in place to combat air and water pollution. John ventured that in spite of limited experience with democracy, the Guatemalan people were inching forward in that direction. But "it's like inventing the wheel when you don't have the tools," he said.

I picked up *La Prensa Libre* and saw that Rigoberta Menchu's nephew had just been released by his kidnappers in Quiché province, where I was headed in the morning. I went to bed, praying that Father John's hopes and those of the Guatemalan people would bear fruit, that tomorrow's election would be a step toward peace, justice, and a better life for the beautiful people of this tortured land.

I rose early election morning and went out to watch the clouds clear from Santa María. I shared a traditional silent breakfast with the men of the community and hit the road. I wanted to see how the voting was going. I stopped on the edge of Quezaltenango for a look at Parque Minerva and its neo-classical Temple to Minerva, one of many such replicas of the Greek temple honoring the goddess of wisdom built during the 22-year presidency of Manuel Estrada Cabrera, 1898-1920. The brutal and dictatorial Estrada, the subject of Guatemalan novelist Miguel Angel Asturias' scathing novel *El Señor Presidente*, apparently thought the classical temples would inspire a desire for education. Unfortunately, he failed to build schools where young Guatemalans could fulfill that desire. Most of the temples had by now been damaged or destroyed by earthquakes or other forces, but this one remained intact, impressive but incongruent, yet another monument to European culture built on Guatemalans' backs.

I filled the gas tank for about $1.50 a gallon, which I would find a typical Central American price, and reentered CA-1 at San Cristóbal Tetonicapán, near the place on the Xelajú plains where in 1524 Tecún Umán died in single combat with conquistador Pedro de Alvarado, and where his wife Alxit then committed suicide. At the intersection I offered a ride to Manuel Jesús, a traditional Quiché Maya man of about 40, hitching to his hometown of Nahualá to vote. Manuel was a weaver of woolen skirts and serapes, which he sold in the market in Nahualá. He wore the traditional attire of men of his pueblo, toeless leather shoes without socks, a straw hat, a black wool serape he himself had made, and a black and white checkered knee-length woolen skirt. Manuel bought the yarn for weaving from a local spinner, who got her wool from three different herders, each with a different breed of sheep.

Manuel told me about life in his village, and about the crops they raise and eat in these mountains: the Maya staple, corn, but also wheat, beans, potatoes, apples, peaches, strawberries, oranges and grapes. He said in the countryside workers earn from 10 to 15 quetzals per day, about $2. Everyone in his pueblo speaks Quiché, but most also speak Spanish when necessary.

Manuel talked of the horror his pueblo lived and died through in the early eighties, when the Guatemalan Army "depopulated" villages they suspected of sympathy with the rebels, killing indiscriminately, burning whole towns to the ground, driving survivors out of their mountains to Mexico. "Many young men from my village were murdered then," Manuel said, "We lost at least a thousand people. Now the violence has lessened, and many refugees have returned. But still people sometimes disappear." In those days, he said, the American artery flowed with blood.

As we rode and talked, I came to see that though Manuel's work and experience are so very different from mine, our values, fears, and dreams were the same. His mountains are the antithesis of my plains, but we alike enjoy the fruits that they produce. We both know that the earth sustains us, that our highest duty is to sustain her richness for generations to come. Manuel felt the same pain at the senseless deaths of sons and neighbors that I would feel, and a just and peaceful world are the aims we shared. How I wished to introduce Manuel to others I'd met along the road, Bud Hanzlick and Jon Piper back in Kansas, Lance Henson in Oklahoma, Tammy Gomez in Texas. I would wind them up and let them talk. What we could learn about ourselves, about each other, about the one world we share.

Far more people were walking the Pan American Highway than riding in cars. When I let Manuel out, a young couple got in. I took them as far as Chichicastenango, where I was headed for the Sunday market. They were on their way to vote in the next town, Santa Cruz del Quiché, where Menchu's nephew had just been released. Like everybody else I'd met, they expected PAN's Arzú, "the candidate of the rich," the man said, to win. They supported a minor human rights candidate. The woman was glad Menchú's nephew was freed, but said it was only the activist's prominence that pushed the government to a full-scale search. "If it had been my son," she said, "they wouldn't have done anything." Like Padre John and Manuel Jesús, she said the human rights situation was improving in Guatemala, but not necessarily for the indigenous people and the poor.

Amazingly, the road off CA-1 to the major tourist destination of Chichicastenango was new. In "Chichi," Confradías, religious brotherhoods, paraded the crucified Christ through the Sunday morning streets, accompanied by drums and fireworks. I entered the white-stuccoed Santo Tomás church, where a hybrid Catholic-Maya mass in the Quiché language was in progress. A tiny, aged Maya woman, a prayer leader, trudged the church steps, swinging a tin can with a wire bale, an incensor of copal clouding the steps and door with pine resin smoke. Inside the church, scores of candles added their smoke and scent to the copal. Pine boughs littered the floor; the altar was crowded with offerings of flowers and corn. Then I hiked up the hill to see the pre-Catholic Maya ritual at Pascual Abaj, shrine to Huyup Tak'ah, god of the Earth.

Back down in the plaza, people stood in line at the Municipal Palace to vote. An official in ladino clothes and dark glasses who reminded me of the border glared silently behind the desk. What a contrast, these mestizo officials hiding

*Maya women market their wares on the steps of Santo Tomás
Church in Chichicastenango.*

*Tomás, maker of Tecún Umán masks in Chichicastenango.*

behind opaque lenses, to the open and frank Mayas who, even if they're pulling your leg or bargaining hard, will look you straight in the eye and betray any guile with a smile. I bought a pair of Tecún Umán masks from a wood carver named Tomás, and a handful of woven pouches from two ancient toothless ladies whose next meal probably depended on the sale. From a girl named Ana I bought a table cloth, hand-woven by her mother. Despite her dark skin and intricately woven huipil, she reminded me so strongly of my own daughter Laura that I wanted to hug her.

After noon I headed toward Guatemala City. But I couldn't get the image of Laura from my head, and when I reached the turn off to Lake Atitlán, I didn't turn. I'd planned a day of leisure in lake-side Panajachel, but without warning loneliness had overwhelmed me, and completing my journey and returning home now seemed more important. I pushed on toward the capital. I'd spent a week in Panajachel and Antigua in 1988, and remembered them fondly and well. For now there was more new world down the highway.

I did pull off to gaze across the mountains to Lake Atitlán, the 1,000-foot deep blue caldera, a jewel amidst volcanic pomp. Southeast was Antigua, and beyond Antigua, the twin volcanoes, Fuego and Agua, fire and water. Fuego smoked, and Agua steamed, just as when I climbed her in 1988, climbed through her mist to the old man who showed me the insignificance of measuring time.

In Panajachel I'd met a North American artist who was in Guatemala gathering material. She complained that the Maya children of Chichicastenango had been corrupted by commercial values, expecting a quetzal to have their picture taken. Oblivious to contradiction, she bragged that in Washington, DC, she would sell her paintings from those photographs for $1,000.

Suddenly a cluster of small and very dirty children appeared from nowhere, hawking lame yarn versions of the sacred quetzal bird. I didn't want any, but I checked my bag of oranges and found five remaining, just enough to go around. They peeled them greedily with grubby hands, the juice of Mexico dripping from their elbows. I thought of all the children I'd seen that day. One boy pulled a little car along the street by a string, but I could recall no others at play. Some sold Chiclets or crafts their mothers had made or fruit beside the road. Others herded goats or sheep, or pushed, pulled or shouldered heavy loads. Among the great tragedies of poverty is that kids don't get to be kids. Play is a luxury that many third-world children never know. When not working, they often gaze with hollow eyes, perhaps stoically, perhaps only in hunger.

I stopped at Chimaltenango for another election check. A few people were voting at the school, but far more were being harangued by a preacher who promised them hell over a blaring loud speaker that disturbed the peace for everyone seeking Sunday afternoon rest in the park. He was backed by a phalanx of eight men in suits, arms folded across their chests, faces grim. I bought a Pepsi from a woman who said she didn't have time to vote because she had to sell Pepsis.

Designs and hues of women's huipils gradually shifted as I drove, from reddish to lavender to pink, each as complex as the one before. Most of the men and some of the women walking the road carried machetes, the all-purpose tool. With a machete you can clear a trail, split a coconut, kill a snake, drive a burro, or defend yourself. From the beginning of Maya country in Chiapas, the beast of burden was no longer a burro. Now it was a human being, most often a woman.

As daylight faded I entered Guatemala City, largest capital in Central America, and at two million, second biggest city on the Pan American Highway. I got a shanty room on the roof of the Capri, a dumpy hotel on 9th Avenue, and walked up town. From 1988 I remembered 6th Avenue as booming and prosperous, justifying its alternate name, Calle Real, or royal street. Unfortunately that's not what I found. Fashionable hotels were transformed or closed, and good Guatemalan restaurants were gone. In their place I found three Chinese places that smelled like the market and the same American chains I'd avoided since Grand Forks — Burger King, McDonald's, Wendy's, Pizza Hut and Taco Bell. I chose a place that looked like the chains but had an unfamiliar name, Two Amigos. Not even dos amigos. The biggest capital in Central America, and on Calle Real I couldn't find an authentic place to eat. Being election day, beer was not for sale either, so I couldn't try a Gallo or a Cabra — a rooster or a goat. It was either questionable water or a Coke.

The downtown streets were a darkening pit, election day litter added to the usual grime. It began to drizzle, and homeless people huddled in doorways. The stench of urine singed my nostrils. People hacked and spat the pollution they'd breathed. Vendors lurked in the shadows, selling everything from tacos to single cigarettes from a pack of Lucky Strikes. I'm rarely squeamish about darkening city streets, but this night I tasted apprehension. Guards with shot guns and assault weapons stood in the doorways of banks and restaurants. Even Two Amigos had two gunmen at the door. They didn't look like friends.

Sixth Avenue was browned out, but once I left the main drag, the streets were positively dark. Even the Zócalo was dim, half the street lamps out. If Mexico is the third world, this had to be the fourth, the product of poverty and neglect, corruption and misrule, militarism and dictatorship. Dwelling in advanced decay, a people in purgatory waited to drop through the floor to hell, their faces betraying scant hope of seeing paradise. Somewhere in this vast city, I knew there must be neighborhoods with clean light streets, inviting restaurants, and well-fed children. But not here. The election was over, but misery stalked the streets of the capital. It was hard to see how anything would change, whatever the results.

Next morning things looked brighter, as things will do in the morning. The rain had stopped and the sun was warm. Street cleaners had begun their work, swishing their long branch brooms in wide arcs, pushing paths through the debris. I had coffee and fried bananas and picked up *Prensa Libre*. As predicted, Arzú of PAN appeared the big winner, taking 61 percent of the vote thus far counted. Arzú would face a run-off with Alfonso Portillo of Ríos Montt's right-wing Guatemalan Republican Front (FRG), who garnered 17 percent in early returns. Left-leaning Jorge Gonzales del Valle of the New Guatemala Democratic Front (FDNG) came in third with eight percent.

*Prenza Libre* reported that fewer than half the registered voters went to the polls, about 46 percent. Perhaps Guatemalans have as little faith in their electoral process as we citizens of the United States. The paper said the capital had grown even darker as I slept. Electrical power mysteriously failed across the country just after midnight, shutting down vote-counting computers, throwing the entire process into confusion. With all the votes counted two days later, Arzú's lead slipped dramatically to 36 percent, and Portillo's total rose to 22 percent, putting them in a close race between right of center and extreme right. In January Arzú won the run-off and the presidency by the slimmest of margins, 51 percent.

Amazingly, in 1999, after Portillo admitted killing two men in Mexico in 1982 and fleeing Mexico to escape trial for murder, he became president, elected with the help of the poor, who had made no gains in four years of Arzú's rule.

As John Brahill indicated, pre-election violence had been minimal, but I now found that even as he and I spoke on election eve, the Guatemala City office of the United Nations' Human Rights Mission in Guatemala (MINUGUA) had been sprayed with automatic weapons fire, a chilling message that if international observers were not safe in Guatemala, certainly citizens who stood up to power were in danger. MINUGUA stated bluntly that "impunity (army and police forces remaining above the law) is the most serious obstacle to the respect of human rights in the country."

I finished the newspaper and set out looking for Casa Alianza, Covenant House as it's known in the U.S. I didn't have the precise address on 8th Avenue, but I knew it when I saw it. A knot of unwashed, long-haired boys lurked outside an iron gate, obviously wishing to be on the other side. A man with a key opened the gate and let me in. I talked with Guadalupe Espinoza, who works with homeless and in trouble kids. The 30 or so boys inside, aged six to 16, were clean, trimmed and polite. Unlike the boys outside, they'd had breakfast.

Casa Alianza opened its doors in Guatemala City in 1987, Guadalupe said, responding to the growing multitude of hungry, homeless street kids, kids who had turned to petty theft and to sniffing solvents and glue to alleviate hunger. Police sometimes murdered troublesome boys, an easy way to solve the problem when you operate with impunity. Thanks to 195 law suits brought by Casa Alianza against 123 cops and 48 soldiers, authorities had become a little more careful. But the suits made Casa Alianza and its staff some enemies, and according to *The Internationalist*, several of the workers were threatened and beaten and one killed.

Casa Alianza was located in a seedy part of downtown, a couple of blocks from my shabby hotel. This particular facility, a formerly stylish villa with a big open courtyard, was a 24-hour a day crisis center. Other facilities provided temporary homes for girls and older boys. In Guatemala, Honduras and Mexico,

Casa Alianza took in 4,000 street kids that year, Guadalupe said, providing food, shelter, medical care, and counseling. Casa Alianza was funded principally by donations from U.S. citizens. Guadalupe said boys could stay there for three months, while more permanent solutions were found. I asked about Casa Alianza's success rate. Guadalupe shrugged her shoulders, a gesture which conveyed both hope and recognition of reality. "Some of the kids can be saved," she said, "turned around, educated, made into productive adults. Others will end up back on the streets, hungry, in trouble with the law, maybe dead."

As I left the refuge a dozen boys were still hanging on the gate. One followed me and asked for bread. I gave him the sandwich I was carrying for lunch. I walked across downtown to the Center for Legal Action for Human Rights on 6th Avenue. I was hoping to talk with Frank LaRue, a human rights lawyer whose father helped build the Pan American Highway in the 1930s. Unfortunately Frank was in Quezaltenango, from whence I had just come. Instead I met with Eugenia Myangos, an attractive woman in her thirties in a bright flowered dress. I asked Eugenia what the election meant for human rights in Guatemala. She said not much. The abstention rate indicated that the Guatemalan people weren't impressed with their choices – or that they were still afraid to vote. Anyway, Eugenia said in the now familiar tone of near despair, with the problems Guatemala faced, it was difficult to see how even a well-intentioned politician could change very much. She said the PAN candidate was "perhaps the best of the worst."

Eugenia said the minimum wage in Guatemala City was 400 quetzals, about $66 per month, while in el campo (the countryside) men earned about $1.60 per day. The fincas, the big plantations, paid even less. She said Guatemala had the maquiladora syndrome too, factories moving to rural areas where wages were lower. The sweatshops employed mostly women, and workers were expected to take the pill so work time wouldn't be lost to pregnancy. Eugenia said the Guatemalan economy was "on the same plain as Haiti."

The Center for Legal Action took a wide variety of cases, Eugenia said, representing human rights, worker rights and women's rights. They also worked with international groups trying to exhume the bodies of people killed by the army and death squads. The Center supported a four-year, four-point program, promoting respect for human rights, development of the democratic process, respect for the Maya cultures and languages, and land reform.

I asked Eugenia about the kidnapping of Rigoberta Menchú's nephew. She said the abduction now appeared not to have been political, but rather a family conflict. I told her about my border crossing and the frequent police and army checks. She said "excess control" was a problem, but thought the frequency might have been election-related. But border corruption, she agreed, was rampant, a fact I would reconfirm that afternoon when I left Guatemala. I would pay quasi-officials to get out, just as I had to get in.

I said good-bye to Eugenia and walked to the National Palace on the plaza, a grand and ornate one-block-square three-story building of green granite, built in the 1940s by dictatorial president, Gen. Jorge Ubico. The magnificent palace, now more gray with soot than green, was heavily guarded by soldiers with M-16s, but one escorted me inside to see the fine frescoes of Guatemalan history painted in 1944 by Alberto Gálvez Suárez.

An interesting feature of the National Palace is the bronze plaque by the palace steps, paying homage to the heroes of the "Glorious Revolution" of 1944, the men who overthrew palace builder Ubico and installed Dr. Juan José Arévalo, the first of two popular and progressive presidents. The second was Jacobo Arbenz, whose efforts to distribute banana plantation land to peasants, Pres. Dwight Eisenhower couldn't abide. Eisenhower sent the CIA to dispose of Arbenz in 1954, returning Guatemala to military dictatorship, setting off decades of bloodshed from which Guatemala has only begun to recover.

It was on these palace steps that U.S. lawyer Jennifer Harbury starved herself for 32 days in November 1994, demanding that the Guatemalan and U.S. governments release information about her kidnapped, and presumably army-murdered husband, Efraín Bámaca Velásquez (Comandante Everardo of the Guatemalan National Revolutionary Unity, URNG). Failing to get results in Guatemala City, she resumed her fast on the Capitol steps in Washington, DC, finally forcing the U.S. government to admit that the CIA both knew about and was involved in this and other political murders in Guatemala, including that of U.S. citizen Michael DeVine. Congressman Robert Torricelli revealed in March 1995 that Bámaca had been captured, tortured and murdered, allegedly at the order of U.S. Army School of the Americas graduate Col. Julio Roberto Alpírez. Alpírez was on the CIA payroll at the time of the murder.

Back home I would continue to follow Guatemala news. In January the car of Harbury's lawyer, José Pertierra, was fire-bombed, and the next day a shot was fired at the house where Harbury had stayed in Washington. Pertierra was pressing the Organization of American States to investigate the murder of Harbury's husband, a move strongly opposed by the Guatemalan military. Pertierra told National Public Radio that a U.S. intelligence source told him his name was on a death list in Guatemala. The FBI supposedly assigned 25 agents to investigate the attacks as possible terrorist acts, but no arrests were made.

Harbury returned to Guatemala City, working to exhume the remains of her husband and hundreds of other victims of the Guatemalan Army she believed were buried on a military base. She told NPR she'd been informed she too was on a death list. The only thing keeping her alive in Guatemala, she said, was the "political awareness of the situation and the pressure from Washington." Col. Alpírez was eventually prosecuted.

The new president did address the issue of police impunity. One of Arzú's first actions was to fire 118 police officers and agents, almost half of them station chiefs. The rebels declared a cease-fire March 20, and on December 29, 1996, a "final peace accord" was signed, ending the 36-year civil war. Tax increases on the rich would fund education for the poor, and Guatemala was recognized as a multi-cultural nation. But Army, CIA and guerrilla fighters guilty of atrocities went unprosecuted.

By noon I was longing for countryside again; I headed for El Salvador. Once beyond the city, the colorful Maya dress faded to the "western" dress of the ladino Maya people work on fincas in the south, but their domain is the north. I passed pineapple stands with big luscious fruits for 30 cents. If I'd had a car full of helpers I'd have stopped for a feast.

I did stop at Cuilapa, the little town that claims to be the geographic center of the Americas, from Alaska to Argentina. Under a huge ceiba tree in a dirty little plaza north of the market I found the marker, long neglected, barely legible. Under the arch proclaiming the town's prominence lies what was once a beautiful fountain, the floor an inlaid tile map of the Americas, Cuilapa highlighted in the center. Many tiles were broken and missing, the fountain watered only when it rained, the town's one chance to attract a few visitors long-neglected and virtually forgotten. But after all, how many visitors could there be in a country for three decades at war, accessible only by the crumbling Pan American Highway?

I stopped for military checks only twice south of Guatemala City, the last near the border, a thorough search and examination of papers. But the road proved very slow. The O.K. stretch of highway near the capital had been an aberration, and a few miles out of the city it was back to pot hole purgatory. The maximum speed most of the way to the border was 35, often much less. Even at that snail's pace, constantly risked destruction of the Omni's vital elements. Even where it passes the big stone-arched wall of the Jutiapa military base, the road was rough, but by El Progreso and Asunción Mita, it was hardly passable. I was genuinely surprised to arrive at the next border with the tough old Omni still intact, rattling a bit more than in Texas, to be sure, but somehow still going. I was beginning to understand why there was no book in print about life along the great American artery.

# EL SALVADOR

*"The streets of San Salvador will never disremember.*
*They know how to count their dead."*

> ~ *Jaime Suárez Quemain, "The Streets of San Salvador"*

Three more border ladrones pocketed 60 quetzals ($10), raising the grand take at Guatemala's borders to $25 before they opened the gate and let their Salvadoran counterparts at me. The Salvadoran side proved different in three ways. First, it took even longer, an hour and a half to work my way through the most Kafkaesque rigmarole imaginable; second, instead of dealing directly with border officials, I now was conducting business with the ununiformed "officials" indirectly, through a passel of understudies who wanted their cut; but third, at least Salvador cost less, only a nominal $5 to get the necessary stamps. I'd gone from highway robbery to a bureaucracy that would confound Joseph K.

I got through at sunset, and hit Salvadoran CA-1 toward Santa Ana, second largest city in the smallest, most densely populated country on the continent. Believe it or not, Salvadorans were at work rebuilding the road, as in Mexico. At one point before Santa Ana, the roadbed had been scraped down to dirt, the smoothest surface the Omni had encountered all day.

I cruised through the deepening dusk, thinking about ancient migrations. The Olmec empire extended this far south from the Mexican gulf 4,000 years ago, and later the Maya came. The Pipil, descendants of Nahuatl-speaking Aztecs, still live in remote towns such as Nahuizalco, a few miles south. Other indigenous groups include the Lempa, the Pokoman and the Matagalpa. But Alvarado more effectively crushed the native peoples here than in Guatemala, and most of Salvador is now mestizo.

It was mid-November, coffee harvest time, and the bright red berries glowed beside the twilight road. The giant coffee fincas of El Salvador were no longer all owned by the famous Catorce, the 14 families. Now over 200 families held great wealth here, but two percent of the population still owned 60 percent of the land, and 90 percent were poor.

I arrived in Santa Ana at last light. As usual, the few street signs bore not some simple and easily readable name like 3rd or Elm, but all four names of some long dead Spaniard – difficult to grasp even in daylight from a passing car. I finally found a room at the Roosevelt Hotel, where I learned a new word, sábana (sheet), which my bed didn't have. I hoped the Roosevelt was named not for rough-rider Teddy, but for his cousin, Franklin, who saw the wisdom of pulling U.S. troops out of Nicaragua in 1933 rather than suffer further losses to Sandino's guerrillas.

FDR declared a "Good Neighbor" policy, forging links to connect the American nations; I'd just crossed two 1937 steel bridges with plaques recalling U.S.-Salvadoran cooperation in their construction. In the thirties, the U.S. helped the Central American nations build the Pan American Highway. In the eighties we funded regional armies which bombed bridges and mined the road. In the nineties we mostly turned our backs on the region's despair.

But though he built bridges, FDR is not blameless; his administration also approved installation of the notorious Somoza family to replace U.S. Marines in Nicaragua. Somoza might be a son of a bitch, FDR is quoted as saying, but at least he was our son of a bitch. After all, Somoza and his kind would keep the new road open for U.S. cotton and banana companies. Nor was the U.S.-funded construction of the highway through El Salvador as clean as it might sound. The president was Maximiliano Hernández Martínez, the general who took power by military coup, and whose army killed 30,000 peasants in the infamous 1932 matanza, or massacre. A Salvadoran woman named Gloria told me the highway was built with chain gang labor.

I was now at 14 degrees latitude, a good 3,000 miles south of Winnipeg, and the period of daylight was considerably extended. But I was also far east in the central time zone, so it was quite dark by 6:00. I wouldn't see much of Santa Ana until morning. I walked to el centro for enchiladas at a restaurant that advertised itself as "authentic Mexican." The enchiladas bore only a faint resemblance to anything I'd ever eaten, either in Mexico or at home. The tortilla was thick and hard, fried in grease and smeared with a thin layer of beans and a little sauce. It was quite tasty, however, and may have been good Salvadoran cuisine, but it made Taco Bell look like "authentic Mexican food." The authentic cerveza Suprema was.

In the morning I returned to visit the cathedral by daylight, the first Gothic church I'd seen since the Río Grande. Like so much else in this volcanic cauldron, most of the church had been destroyed by earthquake. Only the stone Gothic front was original; the rest was rebuilt of red brick, another most unusual feature. Across the street in Parque Libertad (at the intersection of Independence and Liberty) I found a small replica of the Statue of Liberty. A taxi driver idling by the plaza told me that before the Spaniards changed everything, Santa Ana was called Cihuatehuacán, which in Nahuatl means "place of holy women." At least the Spaniards who named the country for "the savior" renamed this town for a female Catholic saint.

Even the act of naming, I had come to realize, provides insight into the arrogance or the humility of the immigrant. The Frenchmen at Winnipeg, the Quakers I would meet at Monte Verde in Costa Rica, and many others, adapted themselves to the new place, adopting descriptive or indigenous names. Joseph

Nicollet's 1839 map of Dakota country, for example, bears native names.

Many Dakota and Nebraska towns, on the other hand, are named for new-comers, pioneers or railroad men, and not a few places in Texas honor generals. From San Antonio south, Catholic saints lent their names to the places Spaniards claimed. The choice of names — native, descriptive or newcomer — is an exercise in power that tells much about the namers.

En route to San Salvador I stopped in a little town east of the highway to visit a priest I'd met in South Dakota years ago. He had subsequently founded an orphanage for the children of people killed in the 12-year Salvadoran civil war. With an estimated 75,000 dead, there were plenty of orphans. When I first met the padre he was touring the U.S., telling North Americans what their tax dollars were doing to El Salvador. U.S. Agency for International Development statistics show that for years, the Reagan Administration pumped $1.5 million per day into this tiny country, most of it directly to a corrupt and brutal army with close ties to the death squads which nightly executed and mutilated anybody the right wing labeled "subversive." In all, Reagan sent about $4 billion to the Salvadoran generals. So there were thousands of orphans in Salvador, most of them teenagers. But since the killing, political and otherwise, continued, there were many younger orphans too.

In the eighties this liberation theologian priest worked directly with the Farabundo Martí Front for National Liberation (FMLN); eventually he was driven underground by death threats. Even now it is necessary to protect his identity. An aging man with pot-belly and missing teeth, his tired eyes remain penetrating. His heart, and his voice of empathy and command, of discipline and love, recall Jesus as much as any man I've ever met. So I'll call him Padre Jesús.

Padre Jesús continues a long tradition, albeit a minority one, of courageous leadership by Salvadoran priests, from Padre José Matías Delgado, who issued the first "grito," the cry for rebellion against Spanish repression in 1811 by ringing the bells of El Rosario church in San Salvador, to Father Rutilio Grande, who organized Christian "base communities" in the villages and was murdered for his efforts in 1977, to Archbishop Oscar Romero, gunned down by assassins as he said mass in 1980, demanding in the name of God that his government stop killing its people.

But in spite of his defense of the poor, which in Salvador has meant opposition to brutal power, somehow Padre Jesús had survived, not by keeping Jesus inside the church, but recklessly carrying his master's message of brotherhood to the fields and the streets. Survived beyond retirement age in the palm of God's hand, insisting that fellow men take seriously Jesus' message that love requires justice. Yet Jesús had no plans to retire. The youngest of the boys to whom he was father and brother, teacher and priest, nurse and provider, counselor and friend, was only six, so many years of love and work lay ahead.

Padre Jesús began his work with Salvadoran orphans many years ago, "doing justice," he said, "for all the injustice these people have suffered." Then, a decade ago he inherited money, with which he bought a piece of land and built a couple of austere buildings to house the boys he was taking in. Later he helped establish a similar facility for girls.

The colonia surrounding the orphanage is a squatter town of refugees from war, the poorest neighborhood in town. More than half the adults were unemployed, and drugs and violence were epidemic. Many youth had joined maras, neighborhood gangs, and boys as young as 12 were involved in violent assaults and murder.

The home was a shady oasis in the midst of this depressed neighborhood. The boys cleared brush and planted bananas, plátanos, oranges, mangos, avocados and vegetables. The padre's rule was that if they cut down a tree, they replace it with three. The boys themselves built a chapel, and a technical skills facility was under construction. Their animals included a donkey which some of the boys called "mother superior," and a dog which came to die, but which the boys nursed back to health. The boys called her Angustia (anguish) because of her condition when she dragged herself in, and the name stuck. The padre was for putting Angustia out of her misery, but the boys begged to try to save her, and he agreed — exactly what he was trying to teach them.

The orphanage was bursting at the seams with more than 50 boys. Jesús said he could fill another facility immediately if he had the funds. The boys ranged in age from six to early 20s, including 11 in the local university and one who had just graduated. He was training the older boys to run the orphanage. One of the university students did the daily food marketing, another kept the accounts, a third was in charge of vehicles and maintenance. All were big brothers to the younger youths, taking them on Sunday outings, helping them with studies, keeping them in line.

When Jesús began this home, he made a strategic decision. "Instead of preparing my boys for a trade, as most orphanages do, I would give them the chance to become professionals," he said. He hustled the donation of a room full of used computers from supporters in the U.S., and all boys become computer literate. Besides academics, the boys pursue art, sports, and music; Ten boys play the organ in the chapel. And every boy who is capable will get a chance at higher education. "The goal is for these boys not only to lift themselves out of poverty, but to become leaders in the struggle for peace and democracy," Jesús said.

The boys also cleared a piece of land and planted pasture grass, developing the best soccer field in town. For the previous four years they were undefeated, the best team in the region. People from the neighborhood join them in their open air church on Sundays, and the technical facility provides employment skills for other youth of the town.

As in most of Central America, the Salvadoran economy is sorely depressed, and recent austerity measures had deepened the misery of the poor. The government had reduced its subsidy of rice and beans, and prices had shot up. Jesús said many of the women in the colonia were widowed mothers who carried a basket of bananas or other fruit on their heads to the market every day, earning from 6-10 colónes per day, enough to buy a pound of rice and a pound of beans. Milk and meat were out of the question for many families.

Price increases had taken a toll at the orphanage too. Jesús said the price of the tortillas I smelled toasting on the wood stove in the yard had doubled in recent months. The home is dependent upon donations from abroad to meet the boys' needs, so every day is full of question marks. Just before I arrived, the padre had inspected the boys' shoes, and found feet protruding from a dozen pair. Though his boys are orphans, they are also normal kids, and shabby clothes hurt self-esteem. "Sure, that's the way the poor live," he said, "but I'm going to change the lives of these kids. That's my purpose in being here, to make them unpoor."

The padre said that in some ways the political climate in El Salvador had improved since the 1992 peace accord that ended the war. The level of killing was reduced, and there had been some progress in replacing the "death squad police force" with civilians, though he said the new force remained almost as sinister. He said some corrupt judges had been fired, and a law limiting the amount of land one person can own had freed some land for distribution to campesinos and former combatants. But there was a long way to go implementing the provisions of the peace agreement, and frustrated landless peasants had begun squatting on excess holdings of the rich, though usually they were forcibly evicted. Jesús said unemployment hovered around 50 percent and many others were seriously underemployed.

"But what I fear most" the padre said, "is that another revolution is brewing, not an ideological struggle as in the eighties, not a class war fought in the inter-est of the poor, but a criminal revolution by a generation of young people born in war, living in the streets, often without parents and homes, tutored by fathers and uncles and former combatants in killing, devoid of hope or social restraint. A whole Salvadoran generation has been raised on violence," he said. "Political decisions made in San Salvador and Washington in the eighties are bearing bit-ter fruit."

This priest's passion and determination somehow reminded me of an ances-tor, a determined European colonizer and exploiter of resources in some lonely "outpost of progress," as Joseph Conrad put it. Except that with this man, all is reversed. He is spending his life, his inheritance, his retirement fund, even losing his health and risking his life in the particular lonely outpost he has chosen, giv-ing every ounce of time and energy to undo what the exploiters have spawned, working to turn back the clock, back to a time when his beloved country had not been destroyed by thievery and foreign domination and war. Of course he knows that is not possible, but he invests his days as if it were. "Something's got to hap-pen here," he said. "Because these people have suffered long enough, and they're still suffering."

Padre Jesús told me to be careful as I traveled. "Vaya con Dios," he said. Go with God. Somehow I felt more secure as I drove out the gate. I drove south across the mountains toward Izalco, the spectacular upstart volcano which took its name from the town nearby. Of course in Salvador, most every city has its own volcano, with which the city shares its name. But Izalco is different. Izalco is a modern volcano. On February 23, 1770, a small hole opened, and dust and smoke began to spew. A crater formed, and a mountain grew, reaching a height of 4,000 feet within a few weeks, and eventually 6,000 feet. Mariners guided their ships by the fiery glow of the "lighthouse of the Pacific," which erupted almost continuously for two centuries.

In 1957, its fury apparently spent, Izalco grew calm except for occasional puffs of smoke. But 40 years is too short a time for volcanic rock to decay to plant-supporting soil, so unlike its wooded older neighbors, this towering cone remains barren and black. I descended at an ear-popping rate from the mountains toward Izalco and the Pacific, down a road cut deep through volcanic rock, past bamboo houses and outlandish gardens and coffee plantations, thriving in far more ancient volcanic soil.

Of course I wanted to see this spectacular site for intrinsic reasons. But I also wanted to visit the volcano and the town because of their prominence in one of my favorite Central American novels, The *Ashes of Izalco*, published in 1989 by Nicaraguan writer Claribel Alegría and her South Dakota-born husband Darwin Flakoll. *Ashes of Izalco* is a story of violence and vision in Central America, set amidst 1960s repression, before the emergence of revolutionary struggle lead by the FMLN. But the story is deliberately told from a perspective insulated by social position and wealth, narrated by Carmen, a young Salvadoran woman married to a Californian, living in Washington, DC. Returning to Santa Ana when her mother dies, Carmen finds that her mother has left to her the diary of another North American, Frank Wolff.

Thus the novel acquires a second narrator, and a second time frame, a period of extraordinary violence, including the 1932 slaughter of rebels led by Farabundo Martí. Some of the peasants were publicly executed in the Izalco plaza, under a shower of ashes from a simultaneous outburst of the volcano. Wolff, a recovering alcoholic writer from Oregon, had come to El Salvador to find an old friend, Virgil Harris, a veterinarian and evangelical preacher. But he also finds Carmen's mother, Isabel Rojas, the wife of a conservative doctor.

Alegría and Flakoll skillfully interwove not only the two parallel narratives, but also the various structures of violence – the volcano, the matanza, and the more subtle violence of sexism and social repression. But the novel also examines vision, and the levels of consciousness upon which vision depends. In the end, the apparently conservative Virgil consciously sacrifices himself for the peasants, thus clarifying for Carmen the conclusion reached by her mother and her brief lover Frank Wolff, that we must not live for self alone.

I left the hulking lifeless cone behind and headed for the capital, again navigating through a massive road rebuilding project. Though the dry season had just begun, the dust was asphyxiating; workers wore kerchiefs over their faces to protect their lungs. Back on CA-1 at last, I found a fine divided four-lane into the capital.

San Salvador is built next to San Salvador volcano, known in Nahuatl as Quetzaltepec, mountain of the sacred quetzal. San Salvador last erupted in 1917, the same year the earthquake destroyed Guatemala City. The most recent earthquake in San Salvador killed over a thousand people in 1986. The city was previously leveled in 1854 and 1873, so few colonial buildings remain.

As I entered the city, the Pan American Highway became Alameda Franklin D. Roosevelt, then Rubén Darío, honoring the Nicaraguan father of modern Central American poetry. But just after the Plaza of the Americas, with its big statue of El Salvador del Mundo, Jesus astride the globe, I turned onto the Boulevard de los Heroes and headed for the fringe. Padre Jesús had warned me that el centro was especially dangerous at night, so in deference to his wishes I took a room in the Happy House, a modest hotel in the suburbs just a couple of blocks from the famous Camino Real, the international hotel which in the 1980s served as headquarters for businessmen and bankers, politicians and journalists, diplomats and spies. If the massive U.S. Embassy, far out of proportion to this tiny country, was their workplace, the Camino Real was where they slept and drank.

With the passing of the Reagan era, the war had wound down at last, and business was now a little slow around the high-rise hotel. But the neighborhood still profited from a string of nice little restaurants, from traditional Salvadoran to Chinese, Greek, Mexican, and seafood. I'm sure such neighborhoods exist in Guatemala City too, but I didn't find them downtown, nor would I find them in central San Salvador. I had a nice dinner of the Pacific fish boca colorado, far from the filth and hustle, the crime and grime, the world of the groveling poor. Ah it's nice to be "rich," to be privileged, to escape to a neighborhood with music instead of blasting buses, to inhale the fragrance of flowers rather than choke on exhaust. Perhaps this explains why the rich have fought so hard to maintain their privilege, at the expense of other people's rights.

In the afternoon I changed some money at a bank across from the Camino Real, a bank guarded by five well-armed men. Then I sneaked into the Camino Real to make a phone call and visit the men's room. I am delighted to report that the granddaddy of all the cockroaches I saw in Central America was basking in florescent glow on the gleaming tiled wall of the men's room of this $100 per night hotel. There was nothing to match it in any of the $5 places I'd stayed. I guess you get what you pay for.

Still chuckling, I headed for the city center. I wanted to see Rosario church and the Cathedral, where Padre Delgado and Archbishop Romero lie. Besides, I'm always drawn to the center, as the place of action and life. Those things I found in downtown San Salvador, but not in the healthiest of forms. Whole streets around the plaza had been commandeered by the unemployed, merchants of the "informal sector," street vendors of everything from socks to bananas to floor mats. Vendors of rock and roll and rap were engaged in a deadly battle of decibels that assaulted everybody else in the market place, more offensive even than the reek of urine. These retailers at the bottom invest their capital at the wholesale level, say a ten-roll pack of toilet tissue, or even a pack of cigarettes, and retail their goods one unit at a time, hoping to make a couple of cents on each transaction. But the formal economy wasn't thriving either. Many shops were virtually empty, and even the smallest of restaurants and stores stationed a rifle-toting guard at the door. Why was it that with all those guns, the capitals of Guatemala and El Salvador didn't feel safer?

I found the plaza where Father Delgado issued the cry for liberty, now a stinking market place. Constitution Monument, in the center of Plaza Libertad across the street, features Lady Justice, arm extended over a long-dry fountain. An electrical cord stretched from one corner of the plaza to the other, supported in the center by her scales of justice. Scores of unemployed men stared blankly past a marketplace preacher who confirmed that they had no hope on this earth. Across the street, the cathedral where Oscar Romero lies was closed for post-earthquake repair. A small circle of people watched a boa constrictor-handling herbalist who used the snake to gather a crowd, described the medicinal benefits of his herbs and seeds and barks, then sold small bags to those still grasping for some kind of hope. His competitor in another corner had a smaller snake, but a motorcycle battery-powered microphone, and a bigger crowd.

Around the corner a string of pawn shops advertised "compro oro," gold bought. In place of conquistadors enslaving people to dig for gold, pawn brokers offer petty prices for heirlooms and wedding rings. A delirious old woman, naked from the waist down, washed herself in the median with a dirty rag. A boy of seven or eight darted among speeding cars with inches to spare, peddling an armful of wash clothes to drivers at stoplights.

Next morning I left San Salvador by 7:00, hoping to beat some of the rush. I couldn't wait to get out. To some extent it's always that way with me and cities, but by this point in my journey, I couldn't take much more smoke and congestion and human despair. I headed again for the relative sanity of the countryside, but it took over an hour to escape the city traffic. "Congestion" in all its contexts kept asserting itself; even at that early hour the streets were jammed with buses and cars and market carts and people. At least at the street level, the air pollution was as bad as anything I'd ever seen in Mexico City. Congested lungs and sinuses, plugged and itching, gasped for fresh air, a commodity in short supply in the most densely populated country of North America.

Unfortunately any improvement in the standard of living for the poor here will presumably mean increased fossil fuel consumption, which means even more pollution. And given the Catholic Church's staunch opposition to birth control, the future here portends ever more people in a small and finite space. People simply weren't meant to live in such concentration, especially in the midst of worn-out internal combustion engines.

*A snake-handler and herbalist marketing medicinal herbs on the plaza in San Salvador (top), and an ox-cart entering the Pan American Highway.*

So it was good to reach banana groves, and finally Cerro Pavo, Turkey Hill, 25 miles beyond the city smog. From the hilltop town of Cojutepeque, the capital was but a hazy mirage, huddling below its volcano as Salvadoran cities must do. I entered a little cafe for coffee and pineapple bread. A skinny dog lay on the floor beneath my table, crunching a chicken bone. In the open-air Instituto Henry Ford across the street, a dozen boys pecked away at manual typewriters, preparing for a technical future.

Even beyond Cojutepeque, population remained dense. I passed one prone body beside the road (asleep or passed out, I hoped, instead of dead) and thousands of upright bodies, waiting, moving, cutting through the traffic. My roving eyes were open wide, watching for movement, chickens and children darting between speeding cars. Men stirred piles of corn dumped on the highway shoulder to dry, waiting for a truck to stop and haul their gunny sacks of grain to town. Women offered kilo bags of beans for sale. Animals of all kinds were on the road, oxen carting corn or hay, emaciated dogs scrounging for something to eat.

All across Guatemala and El Salvador I'd been moving mostly east, and would continue so through Honduras. I topped a ridge and passed San Vicente off to the right, sprawled in the Jiboa valley of Río Alchuapa, below its own twin-peaked volcano, San Vicente, or Chinchontepec. Beyond San Vicente population thinned at last, but now, far from the capital, poverty actually seemed to increase by the mile. And predictably, the road began to disintegrate. The farther from the capital I got, the more frequent and fresh were the hand-painted signs of the FMLN.

Everything that can be taken from the earth was for sale beside the road here: bananas and mangos, birds and snakes, armadillos and iguanas, bottles of a yellow liquid that might have been orange juice, even what looked like a dead rat. Those who have no corn land or livestock turn directly to nature, exploiting dwindling resources to put tortillas on the table. One man, crazy, drunk or desperate, lay on his back in the middle of my lane, extending a can of Coke in each hand, the most dramatic marketing strategy I've seen. I slowed and crossed to the other lane. He hurled a frantic curse as I clattered by.

I picked up a woman named María, who lowered her basin of tortilla masa from her head, gathered her skirts, and edged suspiciously into the car. After a few miles she responded tersely to my questions, but continued to hug the door like a teen-ager on her first date. I don't know if she feared cars in general or this rattling Dodge in particular, strangers in general or this gringo in particular. But she appeared unsure of the wisdom of accepting the ride until the moment she climbed out. Like all the hitch-hikers I'd carried, María offered to pay. She smiled at last when I refused money.

Then came El Salvador's biggest river, the Lempa. So important this river is, and such a sad history. As I approached, instead of birds, armadillos and iguanas, the poor beside the road now offered fish from the river, holding them up as I passed, one or two or a whole string, hoping to snag a passing driver. The Lempa is perhaps a quarter mile from bank to bank, though the bed is partly gravel bars. But it takes a major bridge to span it, and without such a bridge, the country is bisected, the eastern third cut off from the rest. The FMLN took that into account in 1981 when they blew the Pan American bridge into the river. Without the bridge the army couldn't move.

Eventually the bridge was rebuilt, a temporary span on steel pilings, which 14 years later seemed to have become permanent. The old "first world" bridge, the pride of the Salvadoran highway, lies in ruins, reminding the powerful not to take for granted the passivity of the people. Freshly-painted on the eastern pier are the bright red, man-high letters, FMLN. The conditions so many people died to change have changed but little, and rebellion could rekindle in a moment.

The Lempa is also remembered for another reason. Today the bodies in the river were alive – bathers, and women doing the family wash. But in 1981 the Salvadoran Army dumped hundreds of dead civilians in the mountain river upstream. Bloated bodies floated down, congregating at the dam just above the highway. I stopped to remember, then proceeded to San Miguel.

San Miguel was probably my favorite city in El Salvador. It's a long way from the capital, and with a population of about 170,000, this third largest city seemed to retain more sanity. For whatever reasons, San Miguel was cleaner, better maintained, and it seemed to me, a little happier.

Yet the great gulf between rich and poor was evident here too. On the edge of town I passed a Mercedes Benz dealership, gleaming cars worth more than the average Salvadoran could earn with a life-time of work. In the plaza, middle-aged men offered their services as lustradores, shoe shiners. As in Guatemala City and San Salvador, I couldn't find a comedor on the plaza; the choices for lunch were street vendors in the market or North American fast food places. I munched peanuts and fruit as I walked the downtown streets.

Just beyond San Miguel is the road to San Francisco Gotera. Up this road lies Nuevo Gualcho, the resettlement community where my South Dakota friend Michael Sprong had delivered artificial limbs to war amputees. On north from San Francisco are the ruins of the former village of El Mozote, completely annihilated by the Salvadoran Army in 1981. In his first months in the White House, Ronald Reagan not only ordered a surrogate war against the Sandinista government of Nicaragua; his stepped up funding to military regimes in Guatemala and El Salvador gave them the green light to wipe out rebels. U.S. Special Forces at the Army School of the Americas in Panamá, now quartered at Fort Benning, Georgia, began training and equipping elite special forces in the latter two countries to take the lead in eliminating what Reagan perceived as communist insurgencies. One result, in December 1981, was the obliteration of El Mozote.

The Morazán province in northeastern Salvador was named for Francisco Morazán, the Honduran statesman who first attempted to unify Central America in the 1830s. Morazán was an FMLN stronghold. By late 1981 the Salvadoran government had adopted the strategy of bombing and destroying civilian villages with suspected rebel sympathies. In early December the army launched a scorched earth offensive, one goal being to take out rebel Radio Venceremos. Though by most accounts El Mozote wasn't even a rebel town, it was in the way. On December 11, Col. Domingo Monterrosa's elite Atlacatl Battalion (the name obscenely usurped from a hero of Indian resistance against the conquistadors) murdered an estimated 926 civilians in El Mozote — men, women and children. Many of the young women and girls were raped first, and after a long day of killing, the soldiers burned the town. One woman escaped and hid in the maguey.

Rufina Amaya witnessed the slaughter, and told anyone who would listen what happened. The U.S. State Department immediately attacked her credibility. But Raymond Bonner and Susan Meiselas of the *New York Times* and Alma Guillermoprieto of the *Washington Post* walked into Morazán from Honduras and wrote first-hand accounts of the destruction. Bonner interviewed Amaya, and guerrilla leaders gave him a handwritten list of about 700 names of victims. The atrocities were reported in the U.S. papers on January 27, 1982. The next day, Ronald Reagan certified that the Salvadoran government was "making a concerted and significant effort to comply with internationally recognized human rights," and the Democrat-controlled Congress went along with continued funding of the Salvadoran Army. Not until 1993 did exhumation of the bodies begin. Twenty-three of the first 25 skulls recovered were children.

El Mozote was not the only such massacre of civilians by the Salvadoran Army. There were many others, most on a smaller scale. Killing children was justified on the grounds that if their parents were suspected of opposing the military regime, the children might one day become guerrillas, so better to kill them now.

As I neared the border, the road became almost impassable, as in the border regions of Guatemala. Car-sized potholes could sometimes be dodged, but some could neither be missed nor spanned. I simply dropped in, hoping to emerge from the other side still moving. Other cars were swerving across the road as I was, like a rink of bumper cars, except that the object was to avoid crashes and keep going. At one point I drove in the ditch for over a mile as the best possible alternative.

Just before the border I met a pedestrian in an American flag t-shirt that said "Ollie North." What a strange world. I figured he must have been hard up for a shirt, or if he was making a statement, he was either brave or ignorant to wear such a shirt in FMLN country.

At last I arrived at El Amatillo and crossed the Río Goascorán into Honduras. To get out of El Salvador I paid three more officials, bringing Salvador's grand border take to a mere $10. But I hadn't seen anything yet. Now I was entering Honduras.

# HONDURAS

*"In Honduras, a mule is worth more than a congressman."*

~ Sam Zemurray, president, United Fruit Company

I won't indulge in details that by now would be boring. But the Honduran frontier took another hour and a half of my time, a week off my life, and $45 from my pocket. Four more desk drones wanted their cut. Their only product is frustration, and anybody's brother-in-law with sunglasses, a rubber stamp, and a sticky palm could fill the job. Border crossings are easier by bus, but if you want to enter by car, be prepared to pay. The charge for non-Central Americans to drive the 85 miles to the Nicaraguan border on a fair two-lane road was $20. For the other $25, I asked for explanations and receipts, but got scowls and smirks. Perhaps the "Banana Republic" was feebly fighting back.

The first few miles I rumbled over familiar pot-holes. I passed a warning sign for land mines, a legacy of the late wars. As on the Nicaraguan border, many of the mines would be washed away by Hurricane Mitch in 1998, replanted down grade to await an unsuspecting farmer or child. The road smoothed out at last, and I cruised down the 23 cents per mile Honduran autopista at the unfamiliar speed of 55. Enjoying the road and the countryside, I mentally as well as literally put the border behind me.

I was in ranch country, not the Atlantic Coast domain of banana lords. The first substantial town is Nacaome, on the river of the same name. The river looked clean and inviting; people were bathing in the afternoon heat. A dog chased a pig across the cobble-stoned street next to the plaza. The side streets were quarried stone, but the principle streets in the center were what are known in Nicaragua as "Somoza bricks," the interlocking paving stones produced there by one of the many industries controlled by the dictator.

The Pan American Highway misses Belize, the tiny country on the east coast. It bisects every other country in Central American, and the capitals of all but Honduras. I could have crossed this corner of Honduras in two hours if I'd wished, but I was in no hurry.

At the little crossroads town of Jicaro Galán I was tempted to turn left and drive the 92 kilometers to Tegucigalpa. But the capital is a good two hours off the Pan Am, so I resisted the urge. Had I gone, I fear I would have found conditions similar to those in Guatemala City and San Salvador, including the remnants of the bloody 1980s crackdown on the left. As in El Salvador and Guatemala, there is an elected government, but as in those countries, the military was the real power in Honduras for decades. While the smoldering conflict never flared to open war in Honduras, the same poverty and political repression engendered the same resentments and the same struggles for economic and political justice.

An estimated 200 civilians were slain by the army or their operatives during the eighties, though most of the disappeared are unaccounted for. Sixteen officers, some connected to the secret intelligence unit, Battalion 3-16, were indicted on charges of human rights violations in connection with murder, torture and disappearances, but none had been brought to trial. In Jicaro Galán I picked up a newspaper which reported that in the capital the 300,000-member Coordinating Committee of Popular Resistance was preparing a "trial by the people" of accused officers. In 1999 the truth would leak out at last about torture cells and mass graves at El Aguacate, the air base illegally built with U.S. tax money in 1983 for the Nicaraguan Contras. The base was shared with the Honduran army. One grave, 500 yards long, held the remains of Nicaraguans kidnapped and executed by Pres. Reagan's "Freedom Fighters."

When I began studying Central America and reading Central American literature years ago, it struck me as strange that I couldn't find the poetry and fiction of Honduras. I found a gold mine of literature from across the region, but where were the poets and the story-tellers of Honduras? The more I looked, the more apparent it became that potential leaders of this country had withered on plantations in this quintessential "banana republic," the land where exploitation and repression have been so profound that whole generations have lived and died with their potential unrealized.

The *Statistical Abstract of the World* said that of the Central American nations, Honduras was tied with El Salvador for second lowest literacy rate, 73 percent, though ahead of Guatemala's 51 percent. According to the *United Nations Statistical Yearbook*, Honduras and Nicaragua had the highest rates of infant mortality, about seven per 1,000 births, and the lowest per capita incomes in the region. Internal development was not a priority of the rulers of either nation for most of the 20th century. When the Sandinistas triumphed in Nicaragua in 1979, reversing these deplorable statistics was top priority. Unfortunately, fighting U.S.-backed Contras siphoned off half the national budget. In Honduras, meanwhile, the massive infusion of U.S. aid went mostly to generals, doing little to improve this country's social statistics.

The banana republics were more than a century in the making. A Spanish priest first brought bananas from India to the Caribbean in 1516. In 1870 Minor Keith had them planted along the right-of-way of the railroad he was building through Costa Rica. Keith's enterprise eventually became the United Fruit Company, and by the turn of the century, banana interests were well on their way to regional domination.

In Honduras, the 2 cent per stem export tax on bananas was canceled in 1912 by Manuel Bonilla, the first president boosted to power by banana money.

According to Canadian scholar Alison Acker, this lost tax would have doubled Honduras' income between 1912 and 1950. Acker's book, *Honduras: The Making of a Banana Republic*, details a century of control and exploitation of Honduras, first by U.S. fruit companies, and increasingly by the U.S. military.

Marine Gen. Smedley D. Butler, recipient of two Congressional Medals of Honor, capped a 33-year career of fighting insurrectionists and guerrillas, including invasions of Mexico, Nicaragua, Panamá, and Honduras, with a repentant 1935 book, *War is a Racket*. Butler devoted his remaining energy to opposing further foreign intervention. "I spent most of my time being a high-class muscle man for Big Business, for Wall Street and for the bankers," he wrote. "In short I was a racketeer for capitalism ... I helped make Honduras 'right' for American fruit companies in 1903."

The 1954 invasion which overthrew elected Pres. Arbenz in Guatemala was staged in Honduras. Troops rode to Guatemala City on banana company trains. In their *Central America Fact Book*, Tom Barry and Deb Preusch detail the similar use of Honduran territory in the 1980s to train, quarter and equip the Contras for attacks on Nicaragua. Honduras was run by generals, and the country was for rent. In spite of not being at war, Honduras in 1982 was the region's second largest recipient of U.S military aid, getting over $31 million a year. U.S. Agency for International Development statistics show that by the end of Reagan's first term, annual military aid to the top client states, Honduras and El Salvador, had soared from $10 million to $274 million, a 2,700 percent increase. Over the years, thousands of Honduran military officers were trained at the U.S. Army School of the Americas in Panamá, and during the Contra war, over 70,000 U.S. troops were dispatched to Honduras.

Domination by foreign fruit companies had long prevented internal development. According to Acker, in 1986, trans-national corporations controlled 82 percent of the 50 largest companies in Honduras. Acker concludes that the militarization of Honduras added five casualties: human rights, democracy, sovereignty, the economy, and social harmony.

The misery of Tegucigalpa and of Honduras would be multiplied in 1998 by Mitch. The hurricane killed at least 10,000, many of them never found. A fifth of the nation's homes, 60 percent of its infrastructure and 70 percent of its crops were destroyed. Scores of bridges, miles of road and several entire communities washed away. Forty inches of rain dumped on the central mountains wreaked havoc. The Choluteca River, which heads in the mountains above the capital, flushed the homes and the people from the valleys of this mountain city, swept them down and dumped them into the Gulf of Fonseca below the town of Choluteca, just beyond the Pan American highway.

Though maintaining the highway no doubt benefits the economy of this corner of Honduras, it was also a necessary feature of U.S. foreign policy, needed to move troops and hardware to the Salvadoran and Nicaraguan borders. The more I thought about it, my anger at paying 23 cents a mile to drive on a road financed by my tax dollars faded away. Given what this country has suffered at the hands of my country's government and corporations, I was lucky nobody was shooting at me.

I descended from the mountains to the Pacific Ocean, the first time the highway had actually met the coast, which it would not do again until near Panamá City. But this was not the open ocean yet; it was the Gulf of Fonseca, the harbor shared by three countries, El Salvador, Honduras, and Nicaragua. The gulf was a place of great tension and conflict throughout the eighties, patrolled by mutually hostile forces, each determined to prevent the shipment of arms to enemies in the struggle.

I pulled off at the little town of San Lorenzo, passing the shady plaza with its big cement alligator. A big flesh and blood sow lumbered slowly across the street, teats almost dragging the paving stones. Toward the docks the atmosphere changed from typical Central America to typical waterfront: salt-crusted wooden structures, sea gulls, canneries, shipping concerns, hotels and bars to serve the needs of seafarers and other travelers.

It was very hot in San Lorenzo, and I found what I needed, the shaded pier of the Hotel Bienvenidos Mira Mar, where I peered out across the Pacific over a very cold Imperial, served with bocadillos (appetizers) of seafood ceviche , chips, and an incendiary salsa that made the icy beer taste even better. I visited with a young waiter named Noi about his town.

Noi said about 8,000 people live in this shipping and fishing town, where fishermen bring in shrimp year around. He said San Lorenzo is a few degrees cooler near the end of the rainy season in September. The town seemed well-maintained and prosperous, but even in the shade and with a bit of breeze, it was devilishly hot. I finished my drink and said good-bye to Noi, who was just getting off work. Somebody picked him up in a rusty Toyota, the door of which would not open. He climbed through the window and away they rumbled.

This part of Honduras is relatively flat and relatively prosperous ranch land. It once was forested, but now was growing beef for burger chains. I passed the post of the Second Battalion, the "Volunteers of God," they call themselves. Western-hatted cowboys on horses pushed herds of Brahmans across the road, bringing them in from pasture for the night. Houses here were bigger than I'd seen outside the cities, often of adobe or brick, with tile roofs. There were few vehicles besides the occasional ranch truck, but most everybody I saw was clean and well-dressed, looking healthy, prosperous and even happy.

Like all generalizations, this one is probably full of holes. But the overwhelming look of hopelessness and resignation which I found so common in parts of Guatemala and Salvador I didn't see here, at least not on this limited stretch of ranch country road. No doubt Honduras' escape from the large-scale slaughter of the eighties is a factor. In the neighboring countries, farming and business, small town life and social order were disrupted for most of a generation, devastating lives and families, rending the social fabric; here the rural and small-town traditions have endured with less interruption.

I crossed the Río Choluteca on a long steel suspension bridge and entered the town of the same name, a shady and delightful small river city which I found inviting despite the stifling heat. The low-lying neighborhoods of Choluteca too would be flung into the Pacific by Mitch, as well as the entire town of Morolica a few miles up river. The big new bridge would be rendered useless by a major shift in the river's bed, severing the American Artery. Mitch's deadliest stroke would fall just across the border in Nicaragua, where Casitas Volcano's crater would burst, burying seven villages, 4,000 people and 30 square miles with rocks and mud. Just as in North Dakota, where plowing coulees and filling the river bed with silt worsened the great flood of 1997, deforestation and mountainside cultivation doubled Mitch's fury.

But this day, Choluteca and her river were calm, all movement slow. Though the sun was dipping toward the Pacific, both temperature and humidity hovered at ninety, and scores of people languished in the placid waters of the Choluteca.

I cruised around the town, then headed east again, up the Choluteca valley past flowering mimosas and 10-foot poinsettias in full bloom, climbing back to the cool mountains and pine forests, through the little towns of El Chincheote and San Francisco and a series of smaller mountain settlements before San Marcos de Colón.

I picked up two elderly hitch-hikers on this stretch of road. First was María, taking a big pan of tortilla masa to make and sell tortillas on the streets of San Francisco. Later I stopped for Antonio Espinoza. Antonio was trudging up the mountain road to San Marcos, a gunny sack of corn over his stooped shoulder, which he was taking to the market to be ground. Then he would hitch-hike back home and his wife would make tortillas for dinner.

Certainly, María and Antonio were not wealthy people. In the United States, an elderly person who must hitch-hike or walk to town as one of several steps in the process of putting food on the table would be considered abjectly poor. But poverty was not their self-definition. They were well-groomed, dignified, polite, and proud. When we arrived in San Marcos where I intended to spend the night, Antonio insisted on riding around town with me, showing me his town and the three hospedajes where I might sleep. When we had completed the tour, I dropped him off at a grinder's stall at the market.

I settled on the Hotelita Esperanza, partly because I liked the name, hope, and also because it was small and homey. Strangely, a cop of some sort showed up immediately and wanted to see my passport as I checked in. At least he was friendly. For $5 I got a room with shower AND a shower curtain, a luxury I'd almost forgotten existed, and a well-worn towel featuring Garfield the cat. The hotel's rules were penciled on the wall. There were three, all sensible enough: 1. Leave by 11 am; 2. Turn off the light when you go; 3. Don't spit on the walls. I went out to case the town before dark.

The San Marcos parque was unusual, surrounded by a tall stone wall. It was swept meticulously clean of litter, the long arching strokes of brushy brooms still visible by twilight. Besides the usual monuments to local heroes, I found a colorful memorial to Honduran independence. Hand-lettered signs were attached to two trees, one healthy, the other dying, exhorting people to take care of their trees.

I left the park and walked on up the street. Men lounging in open doors talking with neighbors glanced up and said good evening. A few kids played in the streets, and someone somewhere set off an occasional firecracker. Otherwise, the town grew calm as darkness fell. Suddenly I realized why. There were no cars on the streets. From where I stood I saw two cars and a pickup parked beside the street. But the horns, the fumes, the mad rat race of the capitals was far away.

I found two real restaurants on my walk, both up the hill on the west edge of town. I picked the Parrillado Candeleja, a big adobe place with rough-hewn beams and a corrugated steel roof. I ordered the special and got a huge plate piled with nine vegetables and meats, more than I could possibly eat. I did what I could, then amused myself watching the teen-aged waitress, who was totally captivated by TV, a soap opera called "María en el Barrio." A pretty blonde in a miniskirt sobbed incessantly over a sick mother. But suddenly the weeping stopped; the power had failed.

Instantly the waiter struck a match, and soon candles glowed on the occupied tables. In the quiet candle light I imaged finding my way by starlight several blocks back to the hotel. How nice it would be to experience this town as it must have been a century ago. Then, as suddenly as they had gone, the lights and TV returned, dragging us back to the late 20th century. "This is a normal occurrence about 8:00 most evenings this time of year when everybody turns on 'María' at once," a man at the next table explained. "The power is hydro," he said, "and the dry season has begun." The problem would get worse in the next few months, he assured me. But he and his companion didn't seem to mind any more than I. The waitress, however, was delighted to have María back. María, by now, had dried her tears.

I stayed for a second beer, now curious about María, and about Honduran TV. Throughout a commercial for Boots cigarettes, the blunt message in Spanish, "Smoking causes cancer," was prominently displayed. Smoking was still uncommon across the region.

I paid my bill and went out. The South Dakota stars sparkled in the Honduran sky; the Southern Cross was riding high. It was good to be in a place where life seemed healthy, where children chased and laughed in the streets, where men sipped an evening drink or laughed in doorways, where women chatted conspiratorially in the shadows. I saw one drunk, and some guy walked the streets, now long after dark, blowing a whistle. In this clean town with cool mountain air and genuine people, I felt happiness, not only in these folks, but in myself. Though close to the frontier, the town seemed little affected by the country's long and troubled history, or by the baseness of the border that lay just ahead.

To the northeast, near the Nicaraguan border, things must be different. For more than a decade the border area, which the Contras called the "Nicaraguan Province of Honduras," festered with Contras and U.S. soldiers. Crime and prostitution were rampant. Today Honduras reports more cases of AIDS than all the other countries of Central America combined. Nicaragua has the fewest cases of AIDS.

Early next morning I went in quest of coffee. A man on the street directed me to a place I would otherwise never have found. A plain adobe wall, a doorway I had to stoop to enter, an unmarked comedor, and Margorina, a woman of about 60 with two little tables on her patio where she served sugary coffee, eggs, tortillas and frijoles, a standard Central American breakfast for a dollar. The only other diner was Margorina's parrot, who gobbled bits of tortilla she stuffed between the bars of his cage, then called for more.

I was just five miles from the border, so I arrived before it opened. Honduras is on central time, but Nicaragua on eastern, so it was already 9:00 in Nicaragua when the usual hour and a half process began, the typical time required to vault the hoops of a Central American frontier. By now I was resigned to the fact that borders are an industry, an industry which produces nothing and accomplishes little beyond the redistribution of money. Unfortunately they continually spawn new generations of unemployed young men, understudies in insolence and graft. Between crumbling roads and border crossings, I'd come to dislike the latter most.

I shelled out another $5 to exit, a rat in a maze, seeking the stamp of another raft of officials: exit, administration, police, secretary and guide. None wore a uniform or identification; none produced a receipt. I tried to keep in mind how nice I'd found the Honduran people as I grimaced my way through the gauntlet.

# NICARAGUA

*"How many of you love it as much as I do?"*

~ *Augusto César Sandino, 1926*

The land of poets – not only Rubén Darío, the father of modern Latin American poetry, but Sandinista Pres. Daniel Ortega, Comandante Tomás Borge, and Father Ernesto Cardenal. Among the other greats are Clarabel Alegría, Daisy Zamora, revolutionary martyr Leonel Rugamo, editor Pablo Cuadra, and Rigoberto López Pérez, who shot the first Somoza. The observation of Salvadoran guerrilla poet Roque Dalton is true in Nicaragua: "Poetry, like bread, is for everyone."

Nicaragua is the only country besides Vietnam to ever drive U.S. forces out. Their country is the largest in Central America, but Nicaraguans number only about five million. The voting age in Nicaragua is 16, and the median age not much higher. Under the Somoza dynasty (1932-79) internal development was as retarded as in Honduras. There is still no east-west highway across the country to link the Atlantic coast to the Pacific. Most Nicaraguans remain poor; per capita income is about $400, well below the regional average.

Hurricane Mitch dealt the country a major setback in October 1998. Besides the thousands dead, 400,000 were left homeless, without food, water and sanitation. Crops and infrastructure were destroyed, including stretches of the Pan American Highway. But Nicaragua has perhaps greater hope, and greater long-term economic potential than its northern neighbors – more tillable land and natural resources, the lowest population density, and a people hardened by repression but strengthened by their brief experiment in collective progress.

Entering Nicaragua was remarkably different from the three previous countries. Yes, it was expensive, $7 for visa and entry permit and $20 to import the car. But every official wore the clean, neatly-pressed and clearly-marked blue uniform of Nicaraguan immigration. The officials were young and lean, a generation raised on Sandinista ideals. I was treated with complete courtesy by all, receiving both explanation of standard fees and receipts for every Cordoba paid. After Guatemala, El Salvador and Honduras, I almost didn't mind coughing up the dough, since it appeared it wasn't merely lining the pocket of a frontier leech. Also absent in Nicaragua was the tacky border industry, the "guides," they call themselves, the money changers and the hustlers. The legacy of the Sandinista revolution was apparent in the absence of corruption at the border.

Unlike the rest of Central America, in Nicaragua, CA-1 actually runs more south than east. The first stop is El Espino, where it became apparent that hitch-hiking is a way of life. I had given occasional rides in every country, but in Nicaragua there were hitch-hikers everywhere. Apparently the Sandinista ideal of sharing caught on, that and the fact that like their cousins to the north, most Nicaraguans not only will never own a car, but can hardly afford a cheap bus ticket.

My first passengers were a young mother and her two small children, bound for the health clinic in Somoto. Then, just beyond Palacaguina I left the highway for a rocky 25-mile dirt road side trip through the Isabella Mountains of Jinotega to the town of Yalí. On the road to Yalí and back, I picked up eight people. From each I learned something which pieced together how Nicaragua had changed since my earlier visit. A pair of students hitching home from the technical institute in Estelí told me about the defunding of universal free education. A young woman with a bag of tortillas said there was no work to be had in the mountains. There were five others, from children to grandparents, each engaged in some enterprise which took them a few miles through the hills.

One rider was Alfredo, a nurse fighting malaria in the Isabellas. "I was trained as a brigadista in the Sandinista era," Alfredo said. "For five years since the war I have continued to travel these mountains, helping people who are sick." Alfredo carried a worn leather bag of chloroquine and pamphlets, teaching people how to avoid malaria, treating those who didn't. Alfredo had no transportation and no expense account; when no ride was offered he walked. His pay was $30 per month.

The excursion into the Cordillera Isabella was a visual feast. The hills were lushly green, pine forests and bean fields. One little house was shaded by an arching poinsettia 12 feet tall. The mountain streams are cold and rocky, the people hardy and handsome. In place of the burro of Mexico and the ox-cart of Salvador and Honduras, the beast of burden was the horse, the transportation of those lucky enough to ride instead of walk. In Yalí, I would find horses still as common as pickup trucks on the dirt streets of the plaza, and much quieter. The pollution they produce can be stepped around, and it enriches the soil instead of fouling the air.

Yalí is a mountain valley town of several thousand people, a town where I spent a week in 1985 during the U.S.-funded war. Just a few miles from the major Contra camps on the Honduran border, the town was under frequent attack for most of a decade. Contras burned schools and health clinics throughout the region, and civilian casualties were high. In 1985 I heard the stories of a dozen mothers whose sons or daughters were kidnapped or murdered by the rebels. I met the mother of Jaime Rivera, the director of adult education who had been tortured and murdered. "His only crime was that he taught people to read," his mother said.

My earlier visit to Yalí, as an observer with Witness for Peace, was among the most intense encounters of my life. In church one Sunday morning, bursting mortar shells shook the building, chunks of plaster raining down. I visited dozens of fresh graves with women who called themselves Mothers of Heroes and Martyrs. Under protection of civil guards, my colleagues and I helped a farmer named Ramón hoe his beans. I worked a day in the town plaza, helping repair the damage from a mortar blast. I took shelter from an afternoon cloudburst in the one-room home of 83-year-old Carmen Torrez Rivelo, who had served as a colonel under Gen. Augusto Sandino.

I found the dirt-street town pretty much as I'd left it, picturesque, primitive, proud and poor. The church had a new roof, and the plaza was green. Ten years of tropical rain had softened the graves, if not the hearts of the fathers and mothers. Five years of peace had healed some of the wounds to people, landscape and town. The people were still extremely poor, but more meat and eggs supplemented tortillas and coffee and rice and beans. The Sandinista-built Ché Guevara Institute still educated secondary students in technical skills. The elementary school was crowded with students. The orphans I'd met in 1985 were nearly grown.

I parked on the plaza and set out to find the people I remembered – Ramón, Julio and Catalina Rodriguez, who shared their home with me, and Torrez Rivelo, whose proudest memory was fighting beside Sandino to drive out the Marines in 1932. Ramón and Julio were at work in their fields, and Sr. Torrez Rivelo I found at rest in the cemetery. But I did have a nice long talk with Catalina.

Catalina recognized me at once. She couldn't recall my name at first, but she ushered me into the little sitting room with a sweeping gesture and the classic Spanish welcome: "Mi casa es su casa," my house is your house. The room held the same three home-made rocking chairs, a refrigerator, and a little glass cabinet. Family portraits and magazine pages adorned adobe walls. She murmured over each of the decade-old photos I'd brought – of the town, of us together, of her friends – then deposited them with her other treasures in the cabinet. Sra. Rodriguez hadn't changed a bit, and I told her so. "The change is here," she said, a wrinkled hand on her shriveled breast.

Catalina embraced the end of killing, but mourned the needless losses of her town. She described the continuing struggle to stay alive. "The road is still no better," she said, "and many still lack enough to eat." Indeed, I'd found the road to Yalí the same as in 1985, though now free of land mines. The same 30x30-foot cinder block building still served as health clinic for the town and surrounding countryside. The only outside help for Yalí was school and medical supplies and salaries for health care workers from the European Union.

Catalina had no faith in the new Nicaraguan government. She was sad that the Sandinista Front had splintered, and saw little hope that things would get better. Her eyes glittered with fond recollections, blazed in anger, and moistened with sadness as we rocked in the big home-made chairs.

One of Catalina's surviving sons emigrated to Miami, Florida, and once he flew her there for a visit. But she didn't like Miami, the congestion, the flatness,

*Carmen Torrez Rivelo, who served as a colonel under Gen. Augusto Sandino in 1932.*

*One of many murals in Estelí (top), and a chunk of the disappearing rain forest beside the Pan American Highway.*

the crime, the heat. In Miami, she said, the only way to stay cool was to be inside with air conditioning. In her mountains the windows and door were open, and the air cool and fresh.

I promised to visit Catalina again, hopefully before another 10 years rolled by, and walked down the hill to the Manuel Engalo Elementary School. I'd brought a bag of pencils and crayons from home, which I delivered to two teachers on lunch-time playground duty. They said the student population had swollen from about 300 during the war to 774, taught by 24 teachers. The facility appeared well-maintained. When I arrived, several young girls were mopping the tiled sidewalk. When I left, they were sprawled on the tiles, engaged in serious games of jacks. Some of the boys played basketball, others chase and tag, the universal boys' game. I had lunch at the Comedor Rivas on the plaza, visited Col. Torrez Rivelo at the cemetery, and headed back to the highway at Condega.

The Pan American Highway in Nicaragua had its share of potholes, though not as many as Guatemala and El Salvador, and men were shoveling asphalt into the holes. Ahead, two trucks groaned up a mountain slope, one loaded with tomatoes, the other with fire wood, men clinging to the side boards of each. The tomato truck inched out to pass on the narrow road, and when the two came abreast, tomato men tossed big red fruits to the wood men. One splattered and bled its juice across the highway.

South of Condega, a tractor disked a field, a rusted yellow Minneapolis Moline just like the 1948 Grandpa Wilson plowed with when I was a boy. I realized with shock that I hadn't seen a tractor since central Mexico. I had so internalized underdevelopment that the absence of technology had become normal.

Daylight lasted much later in the eastern time zone, and I arrived in Estelí well before dark, rumbling over Somoza brick streets to the plaza. Across from the cathedral I found ancient petroglyphs, carved into boulders at Las Pintadas, an archeological site five miles west. Half a dozen boys played baseball in the street with a stick and a sock-wrapped rock. How I wished I'd remembered the bat and balls my son Walter suggested I bring. I could have made those boys happy.

For more than a century Estelí has been a stronghold of progressive politics, and since the seventies, a dedicated Sandinista town. Estelí suffered heavy losses during the insurrection against Somoza, and some buildings still bore bullet holes and scars of war. The streets were bumpy, the Somoza bricks uprooted for hasty barricades still in need of realignment.

More prominent than scars were the murals ablaze with revolutionary slogans, proclaiming death to Somocismo, promoting Sandinista values of campesino pride, education, health care, and land redistribution – the socialist ideals which convinced Reagan the Sandinistas were communists who must be overthrown. But politics aside, the murals also demonstrated Nicaragua's wealth of artists as well as poets. In fact, that night a youthful artist would hit the Omni, now caked with the earth of seven nations. In the morning I found an elaborate finger-drawn monster on my hood, the work signed by "chica mala," bad girl.

I went to the Hotel Nicarao, a place recommended by my indispensable traveling companion, Lonely Planet's *Central America on a Shoestring*. The Nicarao was named for the Indian chief who led the resistance when the Spaniards arrived. When I opened the car door a toothless and skinny young man was breathing down my neck, asking for money for bread. I had no change or small bills, and for some reason, at the moment compassion fled, and I refused him. He vanished, and immediately my callous denial gnawed at my soul. I got a room and went back out. I looked for him all evening, but never saw him again.

I visited the Gallery of Heroes and Martyrs, a Sandinista museum run by the Mothers of Heroes and Martyrs, a 1,200 member organization of women who'd lost one or more children in the battles against Somoza and the Contras. The museum was filled with artifacts of struggle and pictorial histories of the insurrection, the triumph, and the Sandinista revolution which followed. I reviewed the lives of Augusto Sandino, and of Rigoberto López Pérez, the young poet who killed the first Somoza, not only with words, but in 1956 with a bullet. There was Carlos Fonseca Amador, who founded the Sandinista National Liberation Front, revolutionary poet Leonel Rugama, and the many local heroes of the struggle. By the end of the war, the dead were very young.

I talked with five of the Mothers, of whom Gloria was most vocal. "After the Sandinistas lost at the ballot box, things grew much worse for the average Nicaraguan," Gloria said. "The Chamorro government imposed austerity measures, trying to pay off the war debt and secure loans from the International Monetary Fund." Gloria said most workers earned about 14 Cordoba's ($1.65) per day, and professionals such as teachers and nurses not much more, up to $50 a month. She perched on the edge of her bench, agitated and determined, jabbing her finger for emphasis.

"A gallon of milk and a pound of the worst meat cost 10 Cordoba's each," another woman put in, "together more than an average daily wage." Gloria said free health care and medicine went out the window after the Sandinistas, that if you went to the hospital you had to buy your own medicines and even syringes. And with 18 percent of the total GNP going to foreign banks to service the debt incurred to fight the Contras, neither was education any longer a guaranteed right. A third woman said that many of their men had followed the highway north to the U.S. or south to Costa Rica and Panamá, looking for work. But amazingly, these women who had made the ultimate sacrifice of children to the struggle remained hopeful that somehow things would change.

Was their optimism justified? I don't know. After all, Arnoldo Alemán would be elected president in 1996 with cash raised among former Contras and Somocistas in Miami, promising to restore their confiscated property if elected. But of one thing I was pretty sure. The unflinching faith of people like Gloria, the commitment to the fight for justice, whatever the outcome or the price, makes tyrants shudder, makes anything possible.

I had a cerveza at the Rostecería El Colonial on the plaza, where Pedro

Madregeño and his three sons entertained with traditional Nicaraguan songs. Pedro picked a battered guitar, the two older boys played backup, and a sweet-voiced boy of 12 kept rhythm on maracas and sang the lead. I gave them $2 for their songs. Then I strolled to the Restaurante El Chaparrál (the oak grove) for supper. El Chaparrál had "atmosphere," split bamboo walls, a palm roof and cowboy decor. Two couples dined in the thatched shadows. A candy vendor rested his rack on a table, amusing himself by tossing a folded straw at a Pepsi bottle.

Obviously few Nicaraguans or other Central Americans could afford to eat in restaurants, a measure of the region's economic depression. Most eat at home, in the market or the street, or not at all. Witnessing such pervasive grinding poverty, I had begun to lose the pleasure of travel, of seeing the sights, and especially of eating in restaurants, though the food was cheap and usually good. At least on this, my second trip to Nicaragua, I was confronting only poverty, and not death accomplished with my tax dollars. Yet I could not escape the violence of poverty, the constant reminder that here, I was fabulously rich, cruising down the road in my 15-year-old Omni, eating $2 dinners, sleeping in beds with sheets. I couldn't stop seeing my children's faces in the hungry eyes of kids in the shadows. I couldn't escape the great teacher's injunction to sell our goods and give to the poor.

Nevertheless, walking back to my hotel I suddenly realized that something else was missing in Nicaragua, something I had almost begun to feel was normal, or at least inescapable – the soldiers and cops and armed guards and guns with which Guatemala and El Salvador were crawling. In Nicaragua I'd passed a small army base near Condega, and I'd seen a policeman or two. But nowhere in Nicaragua had I yet seen a rifle-toting guard.

I was up early as usual, had pan dulce y café, and hit the road for Managua. The American artery was already clogged, not so much with vehicles, but with people, school girls in their standard white blouses and blue skirts, men with straw hats and machetes heading for the fields, people of all ages bearing all sorts of burdens, bound for the market place.

It's a hundred miles down the highway from Estelí to Managua. As I headed south I searched the hills in vain for the old Somoza bomber I'd seen in 1985, shot down during the insurrection, left on the mountainside as a monument to triumph. Perhaps the Chamorro government had it removed, part of a systematic campaign to obliterate reminders of the Sandinista era.

Half way to Managua the road descends to a second Río Grande Valley, and the early morning air grew hot. The valley is flat, partly irrigated rice country, and the odor of pesticides permeated the air. I crossed the river on a 1938 U.S.-funded steel bridge.

Just past Sebaco a flatbed truck was parked beside the road. On the bed was a full load of wood – half of a single log. The giant trunk was a scrap of what was once a 12-foot diameter tree. The driver sprawled asleep on the ground in front of his truck. Just down the road a boy held out for sale two parrots on a stick.

Next was Darío, a town which honors Nicaragua's greatest poet. In his turn of the century poem "To Roosevelt," Rubén Darío wrote: "O men with Saxon eyes and barbarous souls/ Our America lives. And dreams. And loves./ And it is the daughter of the sun. Be careful."

I picked up a pair of school girls at Las Maderas. The name means "the woods," but the woods were gone. I hauled the girls as far as Tipitapa on Lake Managua, where I exchanged them for a young woman heading to Managua for what she feared would be another fruitless search for work. Managua is Nahuatl for "near the water," and it is. Across the lake, Momotombo Volcano steams, its geothermal power harnessed for energy. Managua was home to a million people, 20 percent of the country's population. Tens of thousand of refugees from war had become permanent squatters amidst the earthquaked ruins of the city.

In 1855, Tennessee adventurer William Walker arrived in the heart of Nicaragua on one of Cornelius Vanderbilt's Atlantic to Pacific gold rush ships. Walker aligned himself with the liberals in an internal power struggle, helping them defeat the conservatives at Granada. Walker had himself elected president, reestablished slavery, declared English the official language, and was recognized as legitimate by U.S. Pres. Franklin Pierce.

In 1857 Walker was finally driven out by a combined Central American force. In a moment of cooperation brought about by Walker's expulsion, long-time rival cities, conservative Granada and liberal León, agreed on Managua, half way between, as the new compromise capital of Nicaragua. Three years later Walker tried once more to conquer Central America. He was captured in the Honduran port of Trujillo and executed by firing squad.

I cruised into Managua on the autopista named for Pedro Joaquín Chamorro, the newspaper editor whose assassination in 1978 unified the middle class with the FSLN in opposition to Somoza. His widow, Violeta Barrios de Chamorro, was now president. I parked in front of Rubén Darío National Theater on the shore of Lake Managua, near the Huellas de Acahualinca, 10,000-year-old footprints of people and animals fleeing volcanic fury, permanently fixed in lava rock at the edge of the lake.

Adjacent to the Darío Theater is the Plaza de la República, with its shrines to the insurrection, the triumph and the revolution. Of course the ghost of Augusto Sandino lurks everywhere in Nicaragua. His silhouette stands on more than one hill, and his phantom image used to appear on bank notes held up to the light, such as the 100 Cordoba note I carried in my wallet from 1985 until May 1990, when the U.S. ended its surrogate war against Nicaragua. But the new government was still battling Sandino's spirit; it had recalled those bills and replaced Sandino with the Spaniard Cordoba, for whom the currency is named.

At the center of the plaza is the tomb of Carlos Fonseca Amador, founder of the Sandinista Front for National Liberation, the man who picked up the torch from Sandino in 1961 and carried it into the modern era. Fonseca fell in the struggle in 1976. The inscription reads that Carlos is "of the dead who never die." Nearby is the monument to Santos López, the living link between Sandino and the Sandinistas. López joined Sandino as a boy during the San Albino mine rebellion, was promoted to colonel on his 17th birthday, survived Somoza's purge of Sandinistas, and lived to help Fonseca and Borge revive Sandinismo in the mountains in the sixties.

Across the plaza I lurked in the doorway of the cathedral, severely damaged by the 1972 earthquake and never rebuilt. A steel superstructure holds the walls up, preserving the possibility of restoration if one day there might be money for more than tortillas and beans. Next to the cathedral ruins is the National Palace, where Edén Pastora and a small band of guerrillas held the National Assembly hostage in 1974 until ransom was paid and political prisoners were freed.

So this was el centro. But Managua is an extreme manifestation of William Butler Yeats' famous lament, "Things fall apart; the center cannot hold." When the city fell to the quaking earth in 1972, the commercial center which surrounded this plaza was not rebuilt. Somoza pocketed the international reconstruction aid, leaving the city in ruins. Only two skyscrapers remain: the pyramidal Intercontinental Hotel, and the Bank of America. A few multi-story apartment buildings also survived, most badly damaged and condemned, but some still inhabited. In the eighties, tens of thousands of refugees had fled the Contras to the city seeking food and safety, so the old city center was again encircled by people, squatting in barrios which festered with crime and squalor and despair.

Being almost at sea-level and at 12 degrees latitude, Managua is hot. Always. Now that the dry season had begun, it was perhaps a bit less humid than in the "winter" months of April to October, but ruthlessly hot, at least for a South Dakotan with a coat in the trunk and memories of frost still lingering in his fingertips. Sweat poured from my pores when I moved. Managuans seemed to take it all in stride.

I got a room in the Casa de Huéspedes Santos, near the Cine Dorado. Like most places in Nicaragua, it has no precise address. In fact, most streets in this sprawling, half-destroyed city seemed not even to have names, let alone numbers. If you want to tell someone where you live, it's in relation to a landmark, such as "two blocks from the lake and three blocks east of Restaurante Conche." The Santos is in the middle-class Martha Quezada neighborhood, between the Intercontinental Hotel and the baseball stadium. On the way to the Santos I'd stopped at the stadium to confirm that a game was on that evening.

To be perfectly frank, the Santos was a dump. My room on the second floor was constructed of an odd assortment of plywood panels and particle board, all bearing the stains of a leaky roof. In fact the room smelled as if a decade of rainy seasons were accumulated in one breath. I turned on the shower and it dripped twice. But it did have a curtain, just in case water pressure returned. The room came with an oily, rattling fan that stirred the air a bit. From outside, the door locked with a tiny padlock that any kid could bust with a screwdriver. Inside the lock was a screwdriver, at least the shaft of a former screwdriver, which slid into a hole in a scrap of pipe.

The place was actually below even my questionable standards, but I thought, what the heck. It was only $3, I was just sleeping there, and I was close enough to the stadium to walk to the game. I could tolerate it, and it was undoubtedly better than the accommodations of many in the barrio just up the street. The Santos also had a shady courtyard, and housed people from several countries, including a Chinese man who didn't speak a word of Spanish or English, but stared over my shoulder for half an hour as I wrote, fascinated to watch the letters and words appear on my little Apple screen. I wondered how he possibly navigated the streets of Managua, with no street signs and no oral communication. There was also a student from Sweden and a pair of guys who'd quit their jobs in Northern Ireland and set out to see the world. And just outside my window were banana and lemon trees with fruit almost close enough to grasp.

When I felt hungry I walked around the corner to a little seafood place, the first packed restaurant I'd seen anywhere in Central America. Of course the clients sipping seafood soup at almost $2 a bowl weren't the poor. They were office workers and professionals. In fact, I was the only person in the place in sneakers and jeans. Also the only gringo. Outside, a clot of boys waited to beg coins from exiting diners. An elderly policeman, armed only with a night stick, kept them at bay, also keeping watch over the automobiles of the new Nicaraguan bourgeoisie.

To get a professional opinion on economic and political conditions, and especially their impact on health care, I drove to the southeast edge of the city, to the sprawling barrio of Villavenezuela, the poorest neighborhood in Managua. I wanted to visit Los Chavalitos (little children's) Clinic. More than 100,000 people lived in Villavenezuela, the community served by Los Chavalitos. The houses were mostly one-roomed structures of rusty tin, most with no windows, no electricity, no running water, and no sanitation. A majority of the residents were unemployed, and many of the employed worked in the notorious "informal economy," selling fruits, vegetables, grain and cooked foods at the Ivan Montenegro market.

I learned about Los Chavalitos Clinic from Dr. Karla Fuentes, a Nicaraguan physician in residency in Omaha, Nebraska. North Americans had helped build and equip the facility. I knew it was near Ivan Montenegro Market, but of course it had no precise address. After asking directions three or four times, I was closing in. But after weeks in the underdeveloped world, I still hadn't shaken all my preconceptions; I could easily have missed the 40x40-foot cinder block building. But Los Chavalitos was freshly painted in pastel blue, and the sign of the International Rotary Club, a clinic sponsor, announced that I had found it.

I was welcomed by Dr. Patricia Largaespada, a young general practitioner who handled consultations and referred patients to seven specialists who volunteered time after hours at their regular hospital jobs. "The spirit of sharing time and energy for very little or no pay still lives in Nicaragua," Dr. Largaespada said. Los Chavalitos was open daily, and now treated adults as well as children.

Dr. Largaespada said that after declining in the Sandinista era, infant mortality was on the rise again, seven percent in the country as a whole, but undoubtedly higher in neighborhoods as poor as Villavenezuela. Facing a crushing war debt, the Chamorro government was forced to institute austerity measures to qualify for international loans, and Dr. Largaespada said one casualty was the free health care the Sandinistas had instituted. Thus, though doctors volunteered their services, the clinic had to pass part of the cost of medicine to patients, many of whom could not pay. I asked Dr. Largaespada what she saw as solutions. Her answer would probably apply to the entire region. "Work," she said. "With work people would have money. Without work there is no money. Without money there is no food, no health care, nothing." But the mystery remains: How to put millions of people back to work at legitimate wages.

Back at the Santos, I had just gotten comfortable in a big rocker and turned on my laptop, when into the courtyard came a muchacha, selling lottery tickets. I didn't buy one, but she was fascinated by my computer, a luxury they didn't have at her school. She slowly pecked out all four of her names: Iseada María López Medina. She wouldn't let me work for the next 20 minutes, insisting next that I type my name. I wasn't sure if her reaction to my having only three was condescension, or only pity. Then she typed out her school subjects, as follows: español, geografía, moral ciencia, matemática, and cuentionari. I never did figure out whether the latter had to do with stories (cuentos) or accounts (cuentas). She said there were 52 students in her third-grade classroom when they all showed up, all managed somehow by Señorita Asunción López (who probably earned about one-tenth the U.S. minimum wage for her efforts). Iseada said that "moral science" involves learning to accept other people, and helping others when you can.

By now it was almost 6:00, so I walked to the Rigoberto López Stadium for baseball. It turned out the game didn't actually start until 7:00, so I watched the game in progress in the plaza. A dozen boys played baseball with what looked like a ragged tennis ball, which they hit with a board. General admission to the real game was just a dollar, and behind home plate where I would sit, a dollar and a half. But it was out of the question for these boys to actually go in and see professionals play their national sport. They had to remain outside, playing an imaginary game with imaginary equipment, no doubt dreaming of something better, not of being inside as multi-million dollar players striking for more, perhaps not even dreaming of being poorly paid players barely making ends meet, but simply being on the inside as spectators of the game they loved, played with real bats and balls.

As I waited at the gate the Irish guys from my hotel wandered by. They decided to join me for the game. Paul and Brendan were from Warren Point, County Dowan, in Northern Ireland. Paul was a quantity surveyor (construction estimator) and Brendan a mainframe computer technician. They decided to quit their jobs and see as much of the world as they could while they were young. They flew to Boston to visit Paul's brother, where they saw a Red Sox game. So this was their second exposure to baseball, and by now they had the game pretty well figured out. From Boston they had flown to Venezuela, toured Colombia, took a boat to the Panamá Canal, worked their way through the canal and up to Costa Rica on a yacht, and continued northward by bus.

We watched the Condega Boers beat the Managua Caraza team by a score of 6-2, part of a tournament celebrating the centennial of baseball in Nicaragua. Though baseball began here in the 1890s, it was popularized by U.S. Marines who invaded in 1909. At least we left something positive behind, something which still holds us and our Nicaraguan neighbors together in spite of all our government has done to drive us apart. Unfortunately, since most Nicaraguans can't afford a dollar ticket, the game was not well-attended.

I left early in the morning, driving through Masaya, the "city of flowers," and on to the little pueblo of Niquinohomo, the birthplace of Augusto Sandino. I'd been told Sandino lived in a house on the plaza opposite the church, but there was no official marker to indicate which of the little adobe houses was his. It might have been one of several which bore his name: "Sandino vivo," "Vota FSLN," etc. I followed my usual practice of asking a couple of people on the street, and getting the same answer from both, I was satisfied.

The plaza at that early hour on Saturday morning was almost empty, except for one elderly man and two young men who had already been drinking, or were still a little drunk from the night before. I asked them what they knew about Sandino, and they all wanted to talk at once. The young men launched into bravado about being fighters like Sandino, about kicking the gringos out. The old man silenced them. "You don't know anything," he told them. "I remember when Sandino used to eat in that comedor," he said, pointing to the closed door of a non-descript building across from the church. "I remember the time he broke his leg." I eyed the guy hard, trying to figure out if he was old enough to have known the people's general, but I couldn't decide. He told good stories, for a drunk, but it was too early in the morning to breathe alcoholic air, so I left them and went for my own look at Sandino's house.

After descending from the northern mountains, the highway through Nicaragua is a simmering strip of crumbling asphalt down the coastal plain. By 9:00 it was hot again. I passed sugar cane fields and cattle ranches, steaming in the morning sun. Then, just before the fruit country north of Rivas, I picked up a hitch-hiker named Martha, an unemployed cashier on her way to San Juan del Sur on the Pacific to visit her mother. She paid for her ride with a running commentary on everything we passed for the next 30 kilometers, identifying every tree, the mangos, papayas, zapotes, granadillas (passion fruit) and plátanos (like bananas but bigger and used mainly for cooking). I learned from Martha that what I called the mimosa tree was here the carambolo, the beans of which make a honey-like liqueur. Martha was an encyclopedia of the natural world, domesticated plants and animals, the names of rivers and streams, even the sugar cane press and boiler that bathed us as we passed in the syrupy smoke of almost-burning sugar cane juice. What a shame for such sweeping knowledge to be unemployed except to satisfy the curiosity of passing gringos.

The highway skirts Lake Nicaragua, the largest fresh-water body in Central America. Martha got out at La Vírgen, where she hoped to catch a ride down the old route of Cornelius Vanderbilt's stage line to San Juan. This was the last leg of Vanderbilt's route, which in the 1850s carried not only William Walker, but many a prospector who steamed up the Río San Juan and across Lake Nicaragua, rode overland to the Pacific, then sailed again to the gold fields of California. Control of the route was coveted not only by rogues like Walker, but also by the U.S. government as a potential canal site. After Walker was finally executed in Honduras in 1860, the U.S. Marines formed the habit of periodically invading Nicaragua when U.S. control was threatened, maintaining the option of one day digging a canal here, the only place in the Americas that could be ditched without moving mountains.

When I let Martha out, Leonardo got in. Leonardo was an electrician on his way to la frontera to do a wiring job. Not only nurses, but even electricians have to hitch-hike here. As I had learned to expect near borders, the road fell apart, and I dodged craters the last few miles. But the fact that I arrived at the frontier with a Nicaraguan passenger, one there to do a real job that needed doing, didn't facilitate my passage. Once again, getting out of one country and into another took the standard hour and a half, and cost me the average $25 − $5 to leave Nicaragua, and $20 to enter Costa Rica.

# COSTA RICA

*"The problems of the rainforest are microcosms of the problems*
*of the world ....They reflect the tensions and interplay between the*
*powerful and the powerless, the rich and the poor, the north and the south."*

~ *Chris C. Park, Tropical Rainforests*

Rich Coast, Christopher Columbus dubbed it. And by Central American standards, so it is. Certainly in natural beauty Costa Rica is rich, though as elsewhere, much of that beauty has been stripped away. Only a quarter of the country's primary forest remains, but now Costa Rica is developing an environmental ethic and a progressive policy of resource preservation.

Compared to many countries of the region and of the Earth, Costa Rica is also rich in progressive political values. The country has thrived, partly because following a military coup in 1948, Costa Rica abolished its army, and has invested its resources in more productive ventures. In fact, except for the 1948 military uprising and one other brief challenge, democracy has prevailed here since 1889, among the best records in the hemisphere.

Costa Rica is not necessarily a workers' paradise, but neither is the appalling poverty of its northern neighbors so widespread here. Education has been free and compulsory since 1869, and Costa Rica boasts a literacy rate of 93 percent. Per capita income is second in the region only to Panamá.

Costa Rican men and women often kiss when they meet on the street, and when you thank someone for a service, instead of de nada (for nothing), they say con mucho gusto (with much pleasure).

At the Costa Rican border I drove through what looked like a car wash, but which left every surface dripping with a sticky, smelly pesticide. At least they didn't fumigate inside, as in Guatemala. Though employing twice as many bureaucrats as necessary to accomplish the task, the border crossing into Costa Rica was at least coherent. Various required stops – passport, fee payment, vehicle permit and mandatory duplicate auto insurance – were arranged at logically sequential windows. Was I still in Central America? I set my watch to central time once again, and hit the road.

As in southern Nicaragua, the Pan American Highway follows the Pacific coast, a plain that was mostly ranches. The cattle were Brahmans, the big, white, hump-shouldered India import. The road was a path through bushy-headed grass, seven feet tall. In the first 20 miles I stopped twice for passport checks, and braked once for a bright green iguana which streaked across my lane. Once I almost left the road, gawking at a flock of long blue-tailed birds.

The first Costa Rican I met was Manuel Salvador Ojuando, a vaquero, a cowboy on the 18-kilometer-wide Fernando Pinto finca, just south of the rushing Ajogado River. I'd stopped to photograph a big cement Brahman bull mounted on a rock in the pasture, surrounded by real Brahman cows, and Manuel asked for a ride. Lean, handsome and strong, Manuel had worked here over 20 years, his whole adult life, one of 20 men who maintained a herd of 3,000 cows. Manuel said that all the ranches in the area are big, but the Pinto was the biggest, old and very famous. Though like workers of all kinds across the region, Manuel's pay is insufficient to provide transportation beyond the bus, he was clearly proud of his station in life. I had no doubt he was a skilled and valuable worker. I let Manuel out near his home in Liberia, the biggest town in northern Costa Rica.

The Guanacaste mountains had risen to my north, and twice I glimpsed the Pacific Ocean on the south. The highway was relatively straight, flat and fine, but the looming mountains beckoned. I hoped to spot some of the 50 species of hummingbirds that live in Costa Rica, and I'd read that the country is home to 800 other birds too, more than either North America, Europe or Australia. Flora and fauna in general are famously diverse here, with 200 mammals, 150 amphibians, 200 reptiles, 10,000 plants, including 1,400 trees, and 35,000 insects. Strategically located between the North and South American continents, Costa Rica has a high percentage of the species of both.

I pushed on through Bagaces and Cañas, but when I came abreast Costa Rica's most active volcano, Arenal, I yielded to temptation. I headed up the valley of a rushing mountain stream toward the cloud forest preserve at Monteverde. Astride the continental divide, Monteverde includes both Pacific and Caribbean slopes, so I hoped to find much of Costa Rica's diversity here. Maybe I would see the sacred quetzal at last, or the Costa Rican national flower, the Cattleya skinneri orchid.

This would prove my second longest detour from the Pan American highway, some 22 miles north. The road was not built with Omnis in mind. Had I known how bad it was, I probably wouldn't have risked the trip, so it's fortunate I didn't know. The dirt road was littered with rocks and boulders, hauled in to control erosion and to make it passable by four-wheel drive in the rainy season.

The higher I climbed, the more breath-taking the view. But I had little chance to gape; dodging rocks proved a full-time job, and one I struck while peering after another of the long-tailed blue birds gauged a substantial bulge in the floor board. I pulled off at the next wide spot to inspect the damage, and to identify the azure-hooded jay in my bird book. Behind me summits of grassy green rolled all the way to the hazy blue Pacific, and then to infinity. Ahead the road snaked toward yet higher peaks, bigger boulders, and the billowing clouds in which the forest stood. At under 15 miles an hour, it took an hour and a half to reach the mountain top.

Monteverde is a Quaker settlement, founded in 1951 by a community of North American immigrants just above the town of Santa Elena. The Quakers contributed significantly to the development of Costa Rica's leadership in forest protection. Besides visiting the Monteverde Cloud Forest Biological Reserve, I wanted to meet some of those far-sighted pioneers.

One of the Quaker couples, Marvin and Flory Rockwell, opened the Pensión Flor Mar many years ago, the words borrowed from their first names, but in Spanish also meaning flower and sea. I found their pensión and got a room with meals, served family style. At dinner were a bus load of health-care workers from Cartago, Costa Rica, a social worker from Seattle named Marcia, a physician from Albuquerque named Jeff, and me.

Dulce Wilson, a local teacher who was helping out at the pensión, told me that shortly after some of the Quaker men had been released from prison as Korean War resisters in 1950, nine families emigrated from New Hope, Alabama to Costa Rica. They pooled their resources and bought 1,500 hectares (3,750 acres) in the cloud forest, setting aside the upper third of their land to protect their watershed.

In 1972, Wilford "Wolf" Guindon joined forces with scientists George and Harriet Powell to begin expansion of the original 1,300 acre Quaker-owned cloud forest reserve to about 7,000 acres. Thus the Reserva Biológica Bosque Nuboso Monteverde was formally established, owned and operated by the Tropical Science Center in San José. The Monteverde Conservation League was formed in 1985 to operate the reserve, and in 1988 the MCL began a campaign whereby school groups could simultaneously raise consciousness and funds to expand the reserve through the International Children's Rain Forest Project. It was from my friend Sandy Pederson, whose L. B. Williams Elementary School in Mitchell, South Dakota raised money to add four acres to the reserve, that I first heard about Monteverde.

Dulce told us that the best naturalist and guide around was Tomás Guindon, the son of Wilford and Lucky, the first boy born in the Quaker community, in 1953. Marcia called Tomás and arranged a hike for the next morning. When I turned in, a giant praying mantis was engaged in its evening devotions in my room. Ten miles north, Arenal volcano was rumbling and spitting out rocks.

The next morning it was light by 5:00. Marcia, Jeff and I had a big early breakfast and went to meet Tomás. We hiked the three kilometers up the mountain and entered the Cloud Forest Reserve.

Tomás lived up to his reputation as a guide. Slender, bearded and muscular, this self-educated naturalist pointed out how the mixed species flocks of birds move together through the forest, providing a dual symbiotic advantage to every species: Insects rousted by one bird are the natural prey of another, and the bird families alert each other to the presence of species-specific predators.

Tomás said we probably wouldn't see a quetzal, since they are reclusive except during nesting season in the spring. His crow-footed eyes squinted into epiphyte-laden trees, searching the foliage for birds. His voice a low gentle drone that blended with the forest sounds, he recognized by sight and call each of the dozens of birds, the Wilson's warbler, the bush tanager feasting on blueberries, the myriad hummingbirds, the wood creeper, the prong-billed barbet, whose haunting call reminded me of the laughing loon, the gray-breasted wood wren, the azure-hooded jay, the crested caracara, the five-colored blue-crowned mot-mot (the national bird of Nicaragua) and many more. He called the birds in their languages, and they replied.

Tomás also knew the names of every plant we saw in the dripping forest. He pointed out several of the 317 orchids which grow here, the begonias, the impatiens, which he said are a natural antihistamine for insect stings, and the edible melastomas. The largest trees are the oaks, with trunks over four feet in diameter. Also common are balsas, zapotes, and strangler figs, trees whose trunks consist of multiple interwoven strands. We saw the elephant's ear begonia, giant philodendrons, 25-foot hydrangias, and dozens of ferns, including the monkey tail. Tree-like ferns and bamboos stood 50 feet tall. Mosses and liverwort covered the leaves of other plants like fur. This was the wettest year in half a century, Tomás said, and the epiphytes, non-parasitic plants which grow on other vegetation, were enjoying life.

Tomás pointed out a coati, the long-bodied, long-tailed, flexible-snouted relative of the raccoon. He conversed with a family of howler monkeys, the first I'd encountered since 1988 at Tikal. Their mournful shriek was like the noon whistle in a far-off South Dakota farm town. We saw two howlers up close, vaulting from branch to branch, foraging in the canopy. We crossed the tracks of foxes and weasels, and Tomás described their diets and habits. He told us about the sloth, who comes down from his lazy leaf-munching pursuit of happiness once a week to defecate, his metabolism so slow he's in danger of starving with a full stomach because bacteria in his system can go to sleep. He pointed out the fresh tracks of peccaries, the same wild "pigs" that inhabit the brush country of south Texas. We followed them all morning but never caught up. He described the eco-system that is still in balance here, supporting ocelots, tapirs, and even the elusive jaguar, the top of the cloud forest food chain.

Tomás explained how the cloud forest differs from the rain forest. The cloud forest is high in the mountains, as opposed to the tropical lowlands. Trees in the cloud forest receive about 150 inches of measurable precipitation each year, supplemented by constant fog and mist which also water plants through leaves. So trees don't bother to develop deep roots. Swept by nearly constant strong trade winds from the Caribbean, trees on the continental divide are dwarfed and sculpted to the west. The load of epiphytes (vines, ferns, orchids, bromeliads and mosses) which overburden the trees with weight and wind resistance, conspires with the wind to bring the trees down after a century or so. Thus, most trees are smaller here than in the rain forest, and the regenerative cycle is much faster. However, the mountain slopes are also more vulnerable to erosion, so deforestation takes its toll in soil destruction faster in the mountains than in the lowland selva.

Tomás showed us the spider wasp, the two-inch orange and blue insect which

*The cloud forest at Monteverde (top), and the Pacific Ocean from the Guanacaste Mountains.*

lays its eggs on a spider, which takes them underground to hatch. He picked up a millipede, let us smell the almond odor of hydrogen cyanide which it emits to warn its predators of its toxicity, and showed us how to tell its sex. The male, which this one was, has legs in pairs all along the writhing muscular body, but on the sixth axle from the back, one pair of wheels is missing, sex organs in its place. The female has her organs on her back, and thus, the full complement of legs.

We tramped through the dripping forest to the continental divide, where the Caribbean slope unfolded. At the summit, the forest is shortest, the "elfin forest," permanently combed westward by prevailing winds. There we stood one moment in clouds, the next in dense fog. Then suddenly the fog swept away, and we gazed upon the Children's Rain Forest Sandy had hoped I'd see. I took a picture for her students. At the top of the world I picked my way to the origin of a crystal mountain stream to drink, slipped on a precarious rock and went in.

As we walked, Tomás also talked of the history of Monteverde, of his Quaker forbears who came to the Cordillera Tilarán in 1951, attracted as much by the newly-demilitarized government of Costa Rica and the chance to avoid military taxes as by the beauty and economic potential of life in these mountains. Early on, the Quakers set up a bi-lingual school, to which they also invited other area children. They immersed themselves in the local culture, giving their children Spanish names with Spanish spelling and pronunciation. Now some of the Quakers have become Seventh Day Adventists, but Tomás said the two religious communities coexist cooperatively.

Tomás also told us about the struggle to establish Holstein and Jersey dairy farms and a successful cheese factory. He described the all-day trips to San José once or twice a year in a four-wheel-drive truck with chains. He remembered when stretches of the Pan American Highway were still unpaved toward San José in the late fifties. By the mid sixties the highway was paved all the way, and the trip was down to three hours. But now, even in Costa Rica the road had deteriorated while traffic increased, and the trip was back to five hours, he said.

As we descended from the mountain top, we talked soberly about forest destruction, and about the hope to preserve some of what remains. Tomás said that in Costa Rica, the dry forest, mostly on the west coast and easily accessible from the Pan American Highway, was the first to go. The rain forest came under attack next, and the cloud forest, protected by the mountains, was the last to be cut. For a day I had trudged through a wide expanse of what remained, had experienced nature in her complex simplicity. I had imagined for a day that this magnificent ecosystem was not on the verge of collapse to man's heedless ambitions and needs.

I asked Tomás one last inescapable question: Wonderfully foresighted as the decision to preserve this forest was, did the community ever have second thoughts about creating a reserve which would attract visitors from around the world, spurring development of a tourist industry in their tranquil mountains? "Yes," Tomás said, "especially some of the older people had second thoughts. On the other hand, the decision simultaneously saved a big chunk of pristine forest, and gave the children and grandchildren of Quaker founders the chance to stay in the mountains they love."

We descended from cloud nine to the pensión, the sun hanging low. We devoured a late lunch, and I headed for San José, with Marcia hitching a ride. The first thing I did was somehow take a wrong fork, which was both good and bad. It was good because we saw some new country, and especially because a flock of bright green parrots streaked across our path and lighted in a tree, dazzling us with their iridescent beauty. It was bad because the new route was several miles farther and had even bigger boulders. One I failed to dodge gouged a hole in the Omni's exhaust pipe. Fortunately my Oklahoma farmer brother Jim had thrown a roll of baling wire in my trunk as I came through Hennessey. I crawled under the car and wired up the muffler so the next big rock wouldn't complete the job.

Twenty-five miles and two and a half hours later we finally hit asphalt again at Juntas. We stopped at a bar on the plaza for pop. A drunk with a broken beer bottle in his hand blocked the door. When the bartender had finally relieved him of his toy, we quickly downed a couple of "Kolas," an artificial orange-colored drink which resembled cherry flavor, and rejoined the Pan American Highway. By now it was getting late. The central time zone sun was on the horizon, and long before we crawled into San José, it was dark. I got a room in a downtown hotel, the Rialto on Calle 2, had something quick to eat, and wrote awhile before falling into bed.

November 20: My 22nd wedding anniversary. 4 a.m.: Awakened from a fitful four-hour sleep with the discord of Hades rumbling in the street below, I flipped from side to side, pulled the sheet over my head, imagined lambs leaping a wooden stile in perfect somnambulant order, endured the Righteous Brothers somewhere in the street wailing "can't live if living is without you," the hotel clerk rapping on the next door, calling "quatro y media," 4:30, somebody getting up, showering, packing, slamming. 5 a.m.: Gave up on sleep, dragged myself out, staggered to the window.

Lights twinkled and flashed to infinity in a purple dawn. San José is cosmopolitan, in some ways elegant. And unlike most of the places I'd been since Texas, you can even drink the water. But it is a city, and I was tired of cities, the sagging beds, the traffic, the noise, the grime, the over-the-shoulder glance. All these weeks on the road, nearly 5,000 miles. But the end of the road was near, over a few more mountains, around a few more bends. Maybe tonight I would find another quiet place in some small town to sleep, and in a few days reach the end of my road.

Across the street in a yawning vacant lot, an itinerant market of fruit sellers and a vendor of flashing Christmas ornaments of every imaginable gaudy configuration were going strong. Music blasting. Buses roaring. The streets already full of people, hurrying, catching buses, laughing and snarling at the early morning hour.

San José proper has only a quarter million people, but the metro area is near-ly a million. Like three other of Costa Rica's five largest cities, it is on the central plateau, elevation 3,800 feet. And it is south, just 10 degrees from the equator, farther south than Caracas, Venezuela, South America's northern-most capital. This combination of factors makes for a perennially mild climate – like most of the cities of Guatemala and Costa Rica, perpetual spring.

I remembered the busted muffler. Exhausted as I was, I had to go down and patch it. Somewhere I had a tin can, and more baling wire. I'd met a man at Monteverde who wanted to buy the Omni, so today might be our last together. We had grown intimate, the Omni and I, and it would be hard to part. On the other hand, selling the car in San José would add a dimension of freedom, and in some ways, simplify the journey.

I would throw everything I had in the big duffel bag in the trunk and catch a bus on south. In just a few days I would get on a plane and scream back into the north wind, defying pot holes and mountains and curves and smoking buses and dormant burros and everything else waking and sleeping far below on the Earth, and in a few hours, magically transported, land in the arms of my lover, the embrace of my children, the oh so sweet and wonderful bed in the quietest place on earth, where the only voice of the night is the wind, or if the night is calm, the yap of the coyote chasing a kill, or the hoot of the great horned owl in the woods. If I could just make it home to Frog Creek Road, where rush hour is noon on Sunday when the Pleasant Valley Lutheran Church lets out, I would never again need to roam. At least not for awhile.

By 5:30 it was light enough to work. I put on my dirty exhaust pipe-fixing jeans and hit the street. I was celebrating my anniversary in style. Little did I know that the rest of the day, and the next, would be two of the most Kafkaesque of my life. The first couple of hours went fine. I patched the pipe, changed clothes, had pan dulce and cafe leche at a little restaurant on Parque Central, then called home my anniversary love to Norma.

In the center of the plaza, I noted a plaque in a recently constructed dome, commemorating "3000 years of Jerusalem as the eternal capital of Israel." Why here? Zionists must wield influence in San José. A man in a wheelchair whirred along in the busy traffic. A filthy teen-aged boy in pink-bowed thongs loped vacant-eyed across the plaza and into the streets, flailing his arms, howling inces-santly, an animal in a trap. Men in suits and dirty jeans, women in mini-skirts and maid uniforms, rushed to work. The sun was warm, and I was feeling happy and sad on my anniversary. I sat down on a bench by the cathedral to wait for Victor.

I'd met Victor on Saturday at the Flor Mar at Monteverde. He was part of the group of health care workers from Cartago. On my left at dinner was Neil, a transplant from Scotland married to a Costa Rican nurse, and on my right was Victor. I assumed that Victor, like others in the group, was a professional of some sort at the hospital. In the course of conversation I mentioned my project, and that I was hoping to sell my car and fly home in a few days. Victor was very interested, and before we left Monteverde, said he wanted to buy the Omni. He said he could get the money next morning, no problema, and would meet me at 9:00. At 9:30 Victor came.

Neither Victor nor I knew the bureaucratic process involved, but he said he'd consulted a lawyer, who told him the deal would be easy. We walked across town, but the lawyer was not in. To make a long story a bit shorter, by the time we found a lawyer and the agreement was written, it was 3:30. We had to go to the aduana, (customs) to transfer the title, pay a tax, and get the vehicle stamp on my passport fixed.

When the customs clerk had pecked out the papers, it was almost closing time. We still hadn't learned the amount of the tax, and I had no money in hand. The agent in charge rolled a big steel gate shut behind the car, inventoried its features, and said to come back in the morning.

I protested, said I'd come for information, had received no money, and wanted to take my car back out. He said I had entered a one-way street, and refused to open the gate. Victor and I dragged my gear from the Omni, piled it beside the street, and caught a taxi to the Hotel Azul Sur. It was near the Tracopa bus station, from which I hoped to depart for Panamá early next morning. With great trepidation, I left everything, camera, computer, tapes and all in a shabby hotel room, and headed out with Victor to Cartago, 20 miles away. He assured me he could get the money that night.

I had looked forward to Cartago. Established in 1563, Cartago was the colonial capital of Costa Rica until it moved to San José in the 1820s. Earthquakes undid the city in 1841 and again in 1910, and most of the colonial buildings were destroyed. But long before the fall, Cartago was home to Costa Rica's patron saint, La Negrita. In 1635, a century after the Virgin had visited Juan Diego in Mexico City, she appeared black-skinned in Cartago. The church of Nuestra Señora de Los Angeles was built on the site, and the shrine to La Negrita. On August 2, pilgrims walk from San José, bringing as offerings models of body parts miraculously healed by the saint. While Victor made phone calls from a booth, I lurked amongst the twice-quaked walls of the 1575 cathedral across the street, thinking about miracles. A mature tree reaches to the heavens from the sanctuary.

After phone calls, we made the rounds of people Victor knew. By now it was clear he didn't have the money, and was desperately trying to shake down his friends. He probably assumed he could turn a quick profit on the car, pay back the loan, and have money in his pocket. No one loaned him money with no collateral, no car in sight, no guarantee of return. So we caught a bus to Victor's house for the night. He said for sure he could get the money from the bank at 8:30 next morning. I would miss the early bus to Panamá. I hoped my possessions in San José would be safe.

It turned out Victor didn't live in Cartago, but rather in the dismal, sprawling barrio of Paraiso, paradise. When we got off the bus and began to walk again, the first houses we passed were not bad looking, concrete block or frame structures, a few with cars in front. The farther we walked, the smaller and more haphazard the houses. When we finally turned onto Victor's street, the last street on the dark edge of town, we had left the last vehicle behind, the long dead hulk of an aged Chevy wagon.

Victor's house was a 20x20-foot corrugated steel structure behind a sagging barbed wire fence. Victor shared the house with his mother and a nephew. Plywood partitions formed three little rooms. I was frustrated and hungry, exhausted by pavement-pounding and too little sleep. When Victor offered a bed, I gladly took it. I fell asleep, resigned that the sale was off, that I would waste another day undoing this day's work. But hopefully sometime tomorrow I would retrieve my car and again hit the road.

At 5:30 Victor turned on a blasting radio, took the dining chairs off the table, and served eggs and bread and coffee. To his cup he added two heaping tablespoons of brown sugar. His mother seemed dazed, confused, hard of hearing, and unhappy about my presence. They whispered together and she quickly dressed and left the house on some unknown errand, perhaps some long-shot quest for funds. Soon she returned, and with mother and nephew now in tow, we left the house in a cold drizzle, I in my short-sleeved shirt. We joined a trickle of people which became a river, flowing toward the bus stop. Dogs barked and dug holes in front yards. In the absence of car tires and fire hydrants, they marked the tin walls of houses.

At the bus stop Victor's mother realized she was wearing her old muddy shoes, and refused to get on the bus until Victor made the mile-long round-trip for her good ones. When he finally returned we caught a standing room only bus for Cartago.

At 9:00 Victor had been turned away at the bank, and was back at the pay phone, making more calls. I shivered in the cold windy drizzle with mother and nephew, thinking fondly of my jacket in San José.

At 10:00 we were at the hospital, where I now discovered Victor's job was in the kitchen. I told him we'd have to call it off, but he had one last hope, a doctor he wanted to check. He disappeared down the hall, and I never saw him again. I searched the hospital and inquired about Victor, but people knew only that he was a dish-washer, and that he wasn't there.

At 11:30 I called Neal, the Scottish engineer I'd met at Monteverde, and asked for help. He met me at the cathedral ruins and accompanied me to San José to try to reclaim the car. But it was impounded, and customs had the title and sale agreement, which could not be undone without the missing Victor. They now told me the import tax would be greater than the value of the car. The head man said there was nothing he could do, that I could reclaim the car after 60 working days. I would later learn from the U.S. Embassy that in 10 days, on December 1, the Costa Rican government would impose a new tax structure. The import tax on my $600 car would be $6,395. The government would sell the car at auction and pocket the money. A pretty smooth racket. But short of extending a long and now distasteful stay in San José, there seemed nothing I could do. People had told me San José could be expensive, but I had no idea it would cost me two distressing days and my car.

I said good-bye to the ever-faithful Omni, inconspicuous in a dusty sea of others which shared its fate. Back at the Hotel Azul, I learned that Victor had been there while I was at customs; I'd just missed him. I crammed my hundred pounds of gear — clothes, computer, recorder, books and tapes, gifts bought in Mexico and Guatemala, tools brought in case of a breakdown, and all the other incidentals one has when traveling by car — into a large suitcase, my army duffel bag, a backpack and a briefcase.

I'd brought the duffel bag for just such an eventuality, even magic-marking over my army service number, RA 15929883 with the letters PAZMUNDO — world peace. But I had hoped to fill the bag in Panamá City at the end of my journey, not several hundred miles and a couple of long bus rides away. It would have been better to dump the car on the black market in Panamá, or even to drive to the Panamá City airport, take out my bags, leave the key in the ignition, and walk away. I experimented with methods of shouldering the four bags, barely possible for a non-Herculean human such as myself.

By now it was dark again, and I walked once more to El Centro, getting lost on the way in yet another capital nearly devoid of numbers and street signs, where addresses are given in so many meters from some landmark everybody is supposed to know. A hundred meters allegedly equals a block, but asking distance is like asking about the weather, and the answers about as reliable.

In spite of my foul mood, I had to admit that compared to downtown Guatemala City, Managua, or San Salvador, San José was clean, light, and relatively safe, alive and working. It has a pedestrian-only zone in the center, and there are fewer bile-belching buses here, though if you blow your nose after a day on the streets, your handkerchief will be black. I had something to eat and walked back to my room at the Azul Sur (southern blues) where I observed the three rules for nights in flop houses: 1. Avoid looking closely for movement on the walls when flipping on the light; 2. Keep all bags closed when not in use; 3. Shake out clothes, especially underwear and socks, before dressing.

After two nightmarish days in San José, I was ready for a change — like a nice long bus ride out of the country. At dawn I lugged my four bags past another reminder of how little old-growth forest is left to save — three semi-trailers loaded with four-foot logs, waiting to catch the train to the Pacific, and from there probably to somewhere in Asia. Perhaps they would eventually return to North America as furniture or knickknacks. On the other side of the block I caught the 7:30 bus for the all-day ride to David, Panamá. The bus carried me out of San José, back through Cartago, and into the high mountains, far above the blight and chicanery of the city.

Leaving my car behind, I was free of the constant reminder that this journey and this book, including its consideration of environmental values, required traveling 5,000 miles one way, enough to fuel a Central American family for a very long time. I would have ridden the bus as on previous trips, but buses neither go where you want nor stop when you want them to. My only defense for the car was that I hadn't hidden from the contradiction.

When I bought my ticket for David, I had requested a window seat, but got an isle seat instead. My seat mate, Carlos Eduardo Gamboa Ruiz, had been over this road many times, and was kind enough to let me have the better view. Eduardo was presidente of the Agropecuaria Harradura, or Horseshoe Finca, a 350-acre diversified plantation and ranch just north of the Panamanian border. He lived in San José, but was riding down to the ranch to check on his men.

Though not air-conditioned, the bus was relatively comfortable and the windows clean. The day was cloudy and not too hot to enjoy the ride. The conversation was pleasant, and the mountains spectacular, especially the big mountains, the highest pass of which is known as the Cerro de La Muerte, or Death Pass, elevation 3,491 meters, about 11,000 feet. Besides not having to drive, and thus having more leisure to observe, I now had a constant and informative fellow traveler who told me much about what we passed. Now I was traveling as Central Americans do, at least those who can afford a $13 ticket. That is to say, slow, public, not quite so comfortable as a car, and requiring walking and carrying at the beginning and end of the journey. But the bus also means companionship.

Companionship can be bad as well as good. Across the isle, a man with wild eyebrows and a wild mind babbled incessantly and loudly to the old lady beside him, who obviously didn't want to be bothered. We climbed higher and higher, and the curves grew sharper. Suddenly the wild man stopped talking, and began puking in a plastic bag. At least sickness shut him up. After about 15 minutes he opened the window and hurled the bag of vomit out the window onto the highway.

We passed through what once was cloud forest like Monteverde, now eroded hillsides with scattered secondary forest and brush. Estimates vary, but the United Nations Food and Agriculture Organization reported in 1982 that the highest deforestation rate in the world was in Central America. In 1988, the World Wildlife Fund estimated that by the year 2,000, over half of Central America's forests would be gone. However, that projection proved optimistic. Already, only half the forest remained in Nicaragua and Honduras, a third in Guatemala and Mexico, and almost none in densely-populated El Salvador. Perhaps a quarter of the primary forest remained in Costa Rica.

Globally, forests are logged, bulldozed, and burned at the rate of at least 40,000 square miles, an area the size of Kentucky, each year. Another 40,000 square miles of forest are damaged by logging, slash and burn agriculture, road building, and oil and mineral extraction. Rainforest Action Network's 1996 estimate of damage and destruction is even higher, 120,000 square miles, or 78 million acres – three Kentuckies per year. In 1990, the U.S. National Academy of

Sciences said that at the current rate of destruction, the world's remaining rain forest will be gone by the year 2,030, at the latest. Besides the loss of bio-diversity, oxygen production and carbon sequestration, forest peoples are dying at an alarming rate. In Brazil, for example, several million people once lived in rain forest, but fewer than 200,000 remain.

We passed two fincas named for the sacred Maya bird, "Mirador de Quetzal," and "Finca de Quetzal," both carved from the ancient cloud forest the quetzal requires in order to survive. Gone were the aromatic lauraceae trees which produce the olive-sized avocados that are the quetzal's favorite food. Guernsey milk cows grazed among giant flowering shrubs and the rotting stumps of fallen giants, monuments to what is lost. Murky reddish water creased its way down deepening ravines.

Yet, bathed in the soft morning mist, lavender and pink, everything appeared beautiful none-the-less, especially if one didn't compare the mountains to how they used to be. We passed frequent gullies, land-slides and wash-outs, but Mother Nature was working hard to repair the damage, four-foot elephant ears arching over the shoulder, and impatiens growing wild in the ditch, symbols, perhaps, of nature's attitude toward man's encroachments. But nature too is as busy breaking down as building up, so farmers sharpen fence post tops to shed the rain.

At last we passed the over-look to San Isidro de El General, the first city south of Cartago. We began a rapid hair-pinned descent, tacking our way down the mountain, past a pair of tall and pure mountain waterfalls, back into the range of coffee and bananas, then palms and oranges, and finally 50-foot rubber trees, exotic magenta flowers and mangos, and the agricultural town of San Isidro, named for the patron saint of animals. On May 15 farmers bring their animals to town to be blessed. The Río San Isidro looked cold and clean, apparently descended from still-forested mountains. On its bank we passed a low hovel called the Texas Bar.

The road straightened out in the lowlands, the bus picked up speed, and the babbler resumed. We rumbled through sugar cane and corn, the towns of Brujo (the sorcerer) and Paseo Real, and past the turn-off to the Boruca Ruins. The ever-curious Omni would have wished to stop, but the big bus was in its rut; it knew only its routine course, every day southeast to David, every night back to San José. We rumbled past the ruins, now in the valley of the big Río de General. In spite of the clear mountain tributaries which fed it from the north, it was foaming chocolate, full of soil and nutrients formerly held in balance by the forest, plunging blindly to deposit its burden in a growing delta of the Pacific.

On the coastal plain we passed the Finca Gracias Adios (thanks to God) where the fence posts, which Eduardo told me were Amera negras, had sprouted and grown into trees, forming a hedge similar to the bois-d'arc hedges once planted by farmers in Kansas. Nature was regenerating what man had killed for his needs.

After Palmar I watched for the strange and unexplained spherical stones I'd read about, finally spotting a perfectly round four-foot boulder in a front yard we passed. The flat land was heavy with pineapple plantations, most flood irrigated, the closest thing to monoculture since Nebraska corn and Kansas wheat. Perfect pyramids of pineapples stood for sale beside the road. The other crops were oil palms and malena trees, the latter planted and harvested for paper pulp, Eduardo said. Forty-foot bamboo grew around houses made of the same, an integrity Frank Lloyd Wright might have enjoyed.

The nearness of the border was signaled by the once again deteriorating highway. The legibility of my notes declined as we bounced past Piedras Blancas, Río Claro, and Buenos Aires, where we stopped for lunch at La Flor de Sabana. I had a big plate of rice with fresh Pacific shrimp, which I enjoyed in spite of sharing a table with the regurgitator of words and breakfasts. He babied his stomach with a big glass of milk, flavored with a tablespoon of salt. When he finished his milk he bought two pineapples for the road for 25 cents each.

The rest of the way to the border we bounced through holes beside the muddy Río General. At last we came to Neily, the last town in Costa Rica. Eduardo debarked as rain began to fall, and the bus crawled on to the Panamanian border.

Crossing by bus was quick, uncomplicated and free. Without a car, entering Panamá was almost as easy as passing a Western European frontier. The bus got fumigated outside, I got stamped out of Costa Rica without questions about my lost car, and stamped into Panamá the same way. In 20 minutes the few of us remaining on the bus were bound for David. At border crossings cars and possessions are a burden. It is better to be traveling with the poor.

# PANAMÁ

*"If we shrink from the hard contests where men must win*
*at the hazard of their lives and at the risk of all they*
*hold dear, then bolder and stronger peoples will pass us by,*
*and will win for themselves the domination of the world."*

~ *Theodore Roosevelt, president of the United States,*
*The Strenuous Life, 1900*

I was in the last of nine countries, nearing the end of my road. Rolling through sugar cane, flat pasture land and papaya groves, we crossed two more arched steel bridges built in the 1930s with U.S. help. Just before La Concepción, the clouds burst, as if they knew the meaning of the name. Just what the riders of the 25th annual Vuelta Cyclista, the bicycle race we now overtook, had not been hoping for. Seemingly undeterred, they streaked down the highway at near traffic speed, ribbons of water rising from their tires, dissipating in fans of spray. What was fast for bicycles was a little slow for a bus on a good road, but they had a police escort, so we dawdled at bicycle speed the last 15 miles to David. People lined the highway, huddled under umbrellas. They cheered the leaders, and all Panamanian cyclists, whatever their position. Where bicycles remain a major mode of transportation, the ability to ride one fast has broad appeal. In a monsoon, I preferred the bus.

Apparently the rain had not just begun. Deforestation is almost complete in the "developed" corridor along the Pan American Highway, and ditches and streams were rusty red and full. Unlike the rest of Central America, the brief dry season would not come to Panamá until January; the rainy season here is nine months long. Panamá City, on the "dry" Pacific side, gets just 70 inches, while parts of the Caribbean coast get over 10 feet of rain a year.

The bus passed the big Carta Viejo rum distillery, where sugar cane not bound for refineries goes, and at last we pulled into David. I wondered how many of the houses were dry, since most have corrugated steel roofs, many almost flat. Flags were everywhere. Banners spanned the streets, the most clutter I'd seen since election week in Mexico. Apparently this bike race was a big deal. Fortunately for me and my four bags, the rain had almost stopped.

I got a room for $3.80 in the Pensión Costa Rica, next to the bus station. The Costa Rica was cavernous and sprawling, a one-story labyrinth, perhaps 60 cubicles along curving corridors, small concrete boxes with bed and ceiling fan. In the shared shower down the hall a Colombian biker was washing his wheels. I followed the bike in the shower, then wandered down to the plaza to take care of business and find some supper.

The plaza in David is big and shady, the church small. In lieu of dominating cathedral and municipal palace, I found lively businesses, some even air-conditioned. Capitalist enterprise seemed to rule here, in place of religion and bureaucracy which so dominate the northern neighbors. In one corner of the plaza a digitized Lucky Strike clock said it was 7:15 — eastern time again. I found a travel office still open, bought a plane ticket from Panamá City to Sioux Falls, and called to say I'd be home Saturday night.

About the only restaurant still open was Chinese, so I had chop suey with lots of good fresh vegetables, and a Panamá cerveza. The beer was in a double-sized bottle, but below three percent alcohol, appropriate for a climate where a major daily intake of liquid is necessary. I wanted to leave for Panamá City early next morning, and that bus departed from a different station, so I asked a young man for directions. "Come on, Papá," he said. "I'll show you."

Thursday, November 23: In the U.S. it was Thanksgiving Day. At home my family would celebrate with friends, but without me. I was on a bus to Panamá City, the next to last stretch of the road. I imagined Norma and Walter and Laura giving thanks that I would soon be home. I was grateful for that too, and that I had a home to go to, a family, a job, comforts, food — all those things most North Americans take for granted, things which in Central America are daily question marks.

When I'd called home last night, there were two pieces of bad news: My father had cancer, had begun chemo-therapy, and would have surgery soon. My brother Paul had a motorcycle crash in Eugene, Oregon, that day. A car pulled out, and he sailed over the car and hit the street. His helmet probably saved his life, but he was undergoing surgery. On Thanksgiving Day I was thankful my father and brother were still alive, and prayed they'd be O.K. The completion of my journey now seemed urgent.

I would catch a plane in 48 hours — Panamá City to Miami to Minneapolis to Sioux Falls — where my family would be waiting for me. From South Dakota to Panamá had taken six weeks. In 12 hours I would miraculously transmute home — a first-world concept perhaps akin to walking on water for some fellow passengers on this relatively fast Central American bus, streaking along at almost 50 miles an hour on one of the best stretches of road south of Texas. Yes, the road offers escape, but escape is best with the promise of return.

The land south of David is flat, with a rippling surf of hills. Ever-present Brahmans, bizarre humped shoulders and sagging throats, grazed placidly in verdant pastures, at home here as in the tropics of India from whence they came. Watered daily by rains which feed the frequent streams, they are shaded from tropical sun by acacias and other surviving trees. Their constant companions the egrets were at their sides, or riding on their backs, pecking at grubs. Two calves butted playfully like a pair of boys.

The bus was built for Panamá, the windows heavily tinted to keep out the sun, a sun this morning veiled by an overcast sky. Yet it was already warm, or still warm I should say – the overnight temperature must have been in the 70s – and I opened my window for breeze.

The paper currency in Panamá is the American greenback, but here it's called the Balboa. The coins are the same value and size as in the U.S., but more-highly decorated, the dime, the quarter and the half-dollar all bearing the image of the Spanish explorer Balboa, looking as if "with wild surmise – Silent, upon a peak in Darien," the first European to gaze upon the continent's Pacific shore. Keats had Balboa confused with Cortés, but he captured what the man must have felt.

After Canadian dollars, Mexican pesos, Guatemalan quetzals, Salvadoran colones, Honduran lempiras, Nicaraguan Cordoba's, and Costa Rican colones, it was somehow comforting to have dollars in my pocket once more. At least I knew how little things cost without elaborate calculations, as in Costa Rica, where a dollar buys 190 colones, and a $10 hotel costs 1,900. On the other hand, the dollar also symbolizes U.S. domination of Panamá, a country established in 1903 so the U.S. could dig a canal.

The countryside was dotted with homes, some concrete block with tin roofs, others bamboo and thatch. A barefoot young woman in shorts and tank top swung a machete through the dewy grass. But she was merely cutting the lawn, not mowing hay. In Panamá they don't "make hay while the sun shines"; it shines all year, except when it's raining, and "the grass is always greener."

Crossing endless swollen muddy streams, I was homesick again for the Missouri, the biggest and among the cleanest of rivers I'd crossed. How fortunate to live by the great river, above the cities which pollute it and use it for trade. How sad so few clean rivers remain. If man has degraded the rivers of Panamá this much in half a century, what does the future hold, even for the Missouri?

We stopped a few minutes in San Juan, where the rest room doors said "Ellos," and "Ellas," those males and those females. For 15 cents I bought a comb to replace the one I must have left in the Omni. I could again smooth my hair with a tool finer than fingers.

We were now in Guaymí country. Most of the women we passed wore long, colorful skirts; a man with sharp, dark features took a silent seat across from me. The landscape evolved to small mountains again, most stripped of their forest. Eroded hillsides were brushy with random second growth, dotted with cattle. The land quite simply has been raped, little done to reclaim it or preserve its sustainability. In the gullied hills and opaque streams I saw parts of my native Oklahoma, farmed out, washed down, eroded, blown away – unproductive, with little apparent future. But perhaps in Oklahoma less was lost, and there are greater efforts to reclaim. Here a generation ago stood pristine rain forest, and now the land lay ravaged.

I thought about the role of the Pan American Highway in this destruction. Like the Amazonian highway now being built, it made intrusion possible, and the removal of resources. Most of the deforestation has occurred in my life-time, in the half-century since the road was finished. Highways are marvelous links that bind us together, allow us to know each other, to visit, migrate and trade. But they also allow us to haul away what the Earth has produced, and too rarely have we considered the balance of assets and liabilities.

The sky cleared, the sun instantly blazed and I slid my window shut. I had chosen a seat on the right again, to watch for town signs and for glimpses of the Pacific. I now half regretted my choice. Through Panamá the journey is much more east than south, and the sun, even through tinted glass, was scorching.

The bus rolled on, through alternating stretches of hills and ranches, sugar cane and fruit, to Santiago. Just beyond Santiago, at the turn-off to Atalaya, I was the farthest south I'd ever been, or would be on this trip. Here the North American stretch of the Pan American Highway reaches its most southerly point, eight degrees, five minutes from the equator, below substantial parts of two South American countries, Colombia and Venezuela. From Santiago, the highway angles northeast to its end at Cañita. Like some indecipherable omen, exactly at this southern pole, a scissor-tailed fly-catcher, the state bird of my native Oklahoma, flitted past the window, flying south. Was I to follow?

After Divisa and Aguadulce, we stopped at a little restaurant in Penonomé, where I had a tamale, fried plátanos and a Balboa cerveza, all for a Balboa. We briefly skirted the Pacific at San Carlos, climbed back into hills one last time to La Chorrera, then descended to Ciudad de Panamá. The great first-world bridge came into view, the Bridge of the Americas. Built in 1962, it stretches across the Panamá Canal, the longest steel arch bridge in the world. As my family ate turkey in South Dakota, my bus crawled over the mile-long span to the last capital of the continent. Below me lay a city of half a million. Several ocean vessels chugged toward us from the Atlantic. Four dozen yachts bobbed in the harbor, impatient to go east. Far out in the Pacific a score of ships lay anchored, waiting their turn.

"Welcome to la Ciudad de Panamá!" the bridge proclaims. Historic den of thieves and pirates, marauders and scoundrels. Long-time home of the School of the Americas, where the U.S. Army trained thousands of soldiers, terrorists and assassins. The bus stopped in a sprawling ghetto just outside Casco Viejo, also known as San Felipe, the third colonial capital of Panamá, my destination. The first person I met was a screaming, horn-blasting hyena cab driver. I paid the fare to nearby Hotel Central on Independence Plaza, but his other rider was bound for a closer hotel in San Felipe, so he dropped us both there and sped away. I carried my four bags the last three blocks to the Central.

Of all the cheap hotels I'd patronized in Central America, this was the first with real class. Built at the turn of the century in the heyday of canal construction, it was then the finest in town. It faces on Parque Catedrál, also known as Constitution Plaza and Independence Plaza. Two blocks north is Palacio de las Garzas, where Pres. Manuel Noriega used to live. Just across the plaza is the cathedral where Noriega holed up until U.S. forces blasted him out with rock music, the same strategy they'd try on David Koresh and the Branch Davidians at Waco.

Here on this plaza, Panamanian independence from Colombia was declared on November 3, 1903. Theodore Roosevelt, the New York city boy and Harvard graduate who failed as a rancher in North Dakota in 1884 and as a mayoral candidate in New York in 1886, got appointed Secretary of the Navy in 1897. He rode his exploits as "Rough Rider" into the New York governor's mansion in 1898, became William McKinley's vice-president, and ascended to the presidency with McKinley's assassination in 1901.

As president, Roosevelt made a deal with Philippe Bunau-Varilla, engineer of the French canal company, agreeing to recognize a military coup against Colombia as legitimate. The Panamanian junta declared independence and was immediately recognized by the Roosevelt government. The U.S. Navy blocked Colombian forces from intervention. Two weeks later the new regime signed the pre-arranged treaty with the U.S., granting the U.S. "sovereign rights in perpetuity over the Canal Zone."

I recalled that back in South Dakota, the "Shrine to Democracy" features Theodore Roosevelt. Mount Rushmore sculptor and Ku Klux Klan member Gutzon Borglum especially admired Roosevelt, the man who two weeks before achieving the presidency defined his ruling strategy: "Speak softly and carry a big stick." Roosevelt established for U.S. relations with Central America a tone of hegemonic control and a policy of frequent intervention – a mode slightly altered by the next Roosevelt, but to which the U.S. would return again and again, especially under the next rough rider, Ronald Reagan.

Now shabby, the Central Hotel is regal and imposing, a four-story structure spanning half a block, a grand open courtyard in the middle, balconies on every room. My room was the biggest I'd had, at least five times larger than at the pensión in David. High ceiling, a big ceiling fan, and a private bath, all for $8. Of course two blocks away is a neighborhood most gringos wouldn't walk through at night.

In mid-afternoon I walked the neighborhood of San Felipe, first to the Paseo de las Bóvedas. From the old sea wall I peered across the harbor at the ships and the Bridge of the Americas. Below is the Plaza de Francia, honoring not only the 22,000 workers from France, Guadeloupe and Martinique who died of malaria and yellow fever during the 1880s French attempt to dig the canal, but also Carlos J. Finlay, the Cuban doctor who in 1881 figured out how mosquitoes transmitted yellow fever, a discovery without which the canal might never have been completed.

From there I strolled across the peninsula to Palacio de las Garzas (herons), the Panamanian "White House." But I couldn't get within a block; every street leading to the palace was obstructed by two tiers of riot-equipped soldiers and police. I took some pictures, and was just asking a man what was going on, when distant thunder rumbled across the plaza. A throng of men and women erupted

*Panamá Viejo, the 1519 capital of Panamá, burned by English pirate Henry Morgan in 1671.*

*The Bridge of the Americas across the Panamá Canal (top), and San Felipe, the third Spanish capital of Panamá, built in 1673.*

around the corner of the cathedral, banners waving, chants reverberating across the park. It was a demonstration by workers from 49 trade unions, including some from the canal, demanding better pay for themselves, and the cancellation of an announced doubling of pay for government ministers.

Leaders also insisted that the Yankees had a secret plan to annul the Carter-Torrijos treaty, scheduled to return the Canal Zone to Panamá on the last day of 1999. The clamoring crowd demanded that the treaty be fulfilled. Probably they didn't know yet about the time bomb of buried and leaking mustard and chemical weapons the U.S. had tested and stored in the Zone from 1923 to the 1970s, and planned to abandon. In 1997 the U.S. would ratify the Chemical Weapons Convention, and on the last day of the millennium former Pres. Jimmy Carter would be on hand here to turn over the canal to new Panamanian Pres. Mireya Moscoso as promised. But the Pentagon still had not turned over records of chemical weapons tests and storage and disposal sites to the Panamanians, as the treaty required.

The demonstration took a strident anti-U.S. tone: the Yankees should leave their military bases as promised and go home. This particular "Yankee" planned to do just that, and soon, but I determined that for the moment, if anyone should ask, I would be Canadian. Yet, I mixed with the crowd, taking pictures, recording sound, talking with demonstrators, and not a single person was so much as rude. Nobody seemed to view me personally as an enemy. Typical of Central Americans, I thought — able to separate the individual from the country and the policy, always ready to give the benefit of the doubt, to be hospitable to guests. This attitude was especially remarkable since to arrive at Independence Plaza, the demonstrators had just marched through El Chorrillo, the working class neighborhood destroyed by U.S. forces in 1989 to clear their path to Noriega. I asked a woman how things had changed since then. "Nothing has changed," she said. "We're just as hungry now as under Noriega."

Independence Plaza rumbled for an hour with chant and speech and song. I briefly left the demonstration, reentering the major edifices fronting the plaza. A well-attended mass was in progress in the cathedral, worshippers reciting well-worn phrases, apparently oblivious to the rage outside. Across the plaza, the Central Hotel bar echoed with rowdy men and cumbé music. Both groups were ensconced in safe and ancient rubrics, aloof from the noisy conflict between. Three segments of Panamanian society on one small piece of historic real estate, absorbed by separate rituals, borne along by divergent visions, each with its own sounds and motion, three distinct worlds. Yet, without doubt, many immersed in each insular rite would move as readily in the others.

In the gathering twilight teenaged boys played basketball on an asphalt court with Los Angeles Lakers backboards. A half dozen young people in an empty store-front assembled eight-foot Christmas ornaments of chicken wire and newspaper, covering them with brilliant paint and glitter. A band of boys spun their tops in the band shell in the plaza center. One wore a Lakers t-shirt, another

Michigan State. One looked Oriental, another African, the rest mestizo, about the local mix. The black boy's Spanish bore the Caribbean imprint so prominent here. As in David, most restaurants in San Felipe were Chinese, so I had that cuisine once more, then went up to my balcony to write. The air was cooler now, the evening fine. Tomorrow would be the last short leg of my journey to the end of the road.

As I had every morning for many weeks, I rose early my last full day in Central America. At 6:50 I paused with everyone else in the street for the national anthem, wafted through the morning air from an unseen crackling loudspeaker. Everyone was still, but no one seemed enthused. I got coffee and a paper, *El Panamá America*. The front page covered the demonstration I'd witnessed the night before, and reported 28 years later that when Ché Guevara was killed by U.S. agents in Bolivia in 1967, his head and hands were brought to Panamá for positive identification by U.S. authorities.

I caught a bus to the Tocumen airport 20 miles south of the city to rent a car. I had too many places to go my last day to do it all by bus. Anyway, I couldn't possibly board a crowded city bus to the airport tomorrow with a duffel bag, a suitcase, a briefcase and a backpack, and a taxi to the airport would cost $20. It would be more efficient to rent a surrogate Omni for the day.

Every city bus is elaborately painted here, inside and out, old U.S.-style school buses decorated top to bottom and stem to stern with the most fantastic murals imaginable, each with its own theme − bizarre fire-breathing dragons, scenes of Panamá Viejo, Jesus at the last supper. On one, even the mud flaps were works of art. I mounted a flying dragon and headed east, past pineapple stands where colossal fruits were 40 cents − overhead and transportation added to the country-side cost of a quarter − and out to the suburb of Tocumen.

I picked up what I thought was a Toyota Tercel, and continued southeast in air-conditioned first-world comfort toward Chepo. Suddenly I realized how long it had been since I'd seen an American-built car. Toyotas and Mitsubishis and Datsuns and Isuzus were everywhere. What few Fords and Chevrolets I'd seen were aging. While the U.S. pursued Theodore Roosevelt's vision of domination, managing and changing governments in Panamá, Japan had been selling them cars, lots of cars. To varying degrees, I realized, Japan had come to dominate car sales in Mexico and the other countries of Central America too. I wondered if we would ever learn.

I was not only a long way south, but now east of Miami, Florida as well. Apparently I was beyond where most map-makers have gone. Even my latest map showed the highway gradually petering out, the pavement ending at Chepo. What I found instead was a brand new two-lane concrete road, with shoulders no less, not just to Chepo, but extended a few kilometers beyond to Cañita. On both sides of the highway, the forest was newly stripped away, replaced by brush and haphazard development.

Near Cañita the pavement did crumble to gravel, and not far ahead, gravel would turn to dirt. I got out and gazed long down the narrowing trail, to where it bent in the underbrush. I took a photograph of the Pan American Highway's fading end, a kid on a bike laboring toward me. Ahead was 125 miles of dusty road to Yaviza, then the Darién, the roadless rain forest home of the Chocó Indians, and finally Colombia. In the "dry" season the Darién Gap can be traversed on foot, though the Chocó are less than thrilled about intruders. The rest of the year the journey can be made by canoe, with a knowledgeable guide.

Business interests in both Panamá and Columbia were pushing hard for completion of the highway through the Darién, but environmental and indigenous rights groups were resisting, arguing that completion of the road would constitute a death sentence for the remaining rainforest and for the autonomous native cultures, and would increase drug trafficking from South America. Environmentalists at Bio-Pacifico had proposed instead a ferry link to the Pan American Highway in South America.

As for me, I had reached the end of my road at last. With respect for what lay ahead, I would push no farther. Where explorers and pioneers have gone, forests have fallen, indigenous peoples have died, and the Earth's self-sustaining power is failing. To my south lay the last piece of North America where life is not yet wrenched from its natural balance by intrusion of the developed world. I did not wish to be a pioneer.

So this was it. Somehow, after 5,000 miles, the terminus seemed anti-climactic. I wished for a friend to share the moment. Instead, a tractor rumbled by, heading south with a load of concrete blocks, the advance guard of the unstoppable thrust into the wilderness. I turned around and headed back to Panamá City.

At the police check at Chepo, an off-duty cop named José Martinez asked for a lift to the city. He was unarmed, so I agreed. I asked José about the progress of the road, whether he thought it would be completed to South America. "Ciertamente," he said. "Certainly. I don't know when, but it will happen." We passed a load of logs heading north, which told me why.

José said that 20 years ago his home town of Chepo was surrounded by selva. Now the forest was cut down, and most of the men worked at the new maximum security prison which had taken its place. The trees were gone, with little to replace them, 500 men were unemployed in prison, and 200 others were employed to keep them there. If that's progress, I thought, I hope the rest of this road never gets built.

Back in the city I dropped José off at the barrio of San Miguelito. Then yielding to a sudden temptation, I braked for a batida at McDonald's. The milkshake was reviving. Everything under the golden arches, including the prices, was the same as in the U.S., except that the fast food wasn't quite so fast. In this land of incredible heat and humidity, slow movement is a necessity. But even in this air-conditioned oasis, nothing short of a fire could have altered the snail pace at which employees moved, a pace by now no doubt carried in the genes.

*A typical Panamá City bus (top), and the end of the Pan American Highway near Cañita.*

Refreshed by the new world indulgence, I drove to the old, Panamá Viejo. When Spaniards moved their colonial capital from Santa María on the Atlantic to the Pacific side of the isthmus in 1519, they named the new city Panamá, meaning "abundance of fish." Gold from Peru was brought by mule train to Panamá, then across the isthmus on the Camino Real to the Caribbean, and thence to Spain. The mule trains were preyed upon by cimarrones, escaped slaves, and the capital was repeatedly attacked by pirates. Finally English pirate Henry Morgan burned this second capital in 1671. By 1673 Spaniards had rebuilt at San Felipe a few kilometers west, but what remains of the half-mile-long old city on the bay is marvelous — massive stone walls, towers, the cathedral — an old world city in placid ruin amongst the palms.

San Felipe was in its prime when the California gold rush began almost two centuries later. U.S. investors replaced the Camino Real with a railroad across the isthmus, a rival to Vanderbilt's Nicaragua route. The railroad pre-dated even the French attempt at a canal by 30 years.

From Panamá Viejo I drove through the opulent sky-scraping new Panamá City, high-rise home of 104 international banks, by far the wealthiest and most modern of the Central American capitals, Dallas on a slightly smaller scale. Here is the business place of international shippers and bankers, not to mention drug money launderers who, according to U.S. investigators, filter the blood from $2 billion a year in Colombian drug money.

Between new Panamá and San Felipe where I was staying is the neighborhood destroyed by a more recent invader, the barrio of El Chorrillo. It was bombed and burned in Pres. George Bush's December 20, 1989 invasion to arrest his former CIA operative, Gen. Noriega. When the fires finally died, several blocks of El Chorrillo had ceased to exist. Unlike Panamá Viejo, a few of the devastated blocks have been rebuilt, but what remains continues its slow rot. This neighborhood, from which one could walk to either the presidential palace or to the Mecca of bankers in 10 minutes, was the most desperate slum I'd seen since Managua.

The official civilian death toll of "Operation Just Cause" is unknown. At a press conference after the invasion, Pres. Bush told reporters, "I just can't help you on the total numbers." According to the final Pentagon report, 202 Panamanian civilians were killed. A secret U.S. Army memo written nine days after the invasion estimated "a thousand civilian casualties." But Isabel Coro, a Panamá City woman whose father was among the dead, said at least 4,000 civilians were killed.

Five months after the invasion, Coro raised private funds to exhume more than a hundred bodies, including that of her father, from two mass graves in a Panamá City cemetery, Jardín de Paz. Other secret mass graves were later discovered. The U.S. government refused to set up a claims program for the survivors of the victims, because, according to another official Army document cited by Mike Wallace on CBS' "Sixty Minutes," it "would not be in the best interest of the Department of Defense of the U. S. because of the potentially huge number of such claims." In spite of all the killing, El Chorrillo is still crawling with the living, just as desperate for work, food, and a decent life now as in the days of Manuel Noriega.

My last three stops I began to feel like a regular tourist. Well, almost. I drove up the Canal Zone, past Albrook Air Force Base where the invaders landed, past the U.S. Army's Fort Clayton, to Miraflores Locks. The canal was finally built from 1904-1914, employing the labor of 75,000 men. Part of the cement was quarried at Yankton, South Dakota, and hauled by train and ship to Panamá.

Thirty-eight vessels traverse the canal on a typical day, paying an average $33,785 for passage, producing gross revenue of well over $1 million a day. Ships generally transit the 50-mile canal and its three sets of locks in 24 hours. Ship builders around the world designed vessels to fit the dimensions of the canal's locks, 110 feet wide and 1,000 feet long. The widest ships to navigate the canal were the USS New Jersey and its sister ships, with 108-foot beams; the longest was the San Juan Prospector, a 973-foot ore and oil carrier. The highest toll ever paid for passage was by the Crown Princess in 1993, $141,344.97. The lowest toll was levied on Richard Halliburton, who paid 36 cents to swim the canal in 1928.

On the way to the locks I picked up two African Panamanian men, locomotive operators who guide the ships through the locks. Even skilled workers in the richest country in Central America can be found riding the bus, walking, or hitchhiking to work. I watched a Russia-bound cargo ship lowered through the locks. It was loaded with Midwestern corn, perhaps from South Dakota.

Hoards of tourists from everywhere had flocked to Miraflores, but at my next stop I was alone. I got out of my rented car at the trail head in the Parque Natural Metropolitana, a rain forest preserve. At this moment I saw that I'd been driving, not a Toyota, but a Mitsubishi. Mitsubishi is the transnational corporation boycotted by the Rain Forest Action Network for its exploitation of rain forest and its disregard for rain forest peoples. With logging subsidiaries throughout the world, Mitsubishi was considered by RAN "the greatest destroyer of forest on earth." I slammed the door and plunged into the rain forest, steaming in self-irony.

The dominant trees are the cedro and cuipo, the latter a deciduous tree with a straight, 120' trunk. In spite of the afternoon heat, I saw numerous animals and birds in the thickets and the shade of branches. But I didn't see another person in the rain forest that hot afternoon, which is rather sad, given that there's so little forest left to experience, and so little time. On the other hand, in the solitude I encountered a blue-crowned motmot, who allowed me to creep close enough for a photograph and a good view of his brilliant lime-green back, yellow neck, orange breast, blue-green tail, blue head and tail tip, and unique featherless strip just before the end of his eight-inch tail.

I thought of all the birds I'd seen on my journey, as well as some I had missed. Five thousand miles northwest, in the prairie preserve in Winnipeg, a great flock of Canada geese had angled overhead, beginning their migration south with me, across the Dakotas and Nebraska, honking their way to their winter home on the Gulf of Mexico. Meadow larks and pheasants were among the birds on the plains. From Fort Worth on there was the great-tailed grackle, long iridescent tail and perpetual squawk. South of the Tropic of Cancer, wherever there were cattle I found their companion, the cattle egret, recent immigrant from the old world, striking white against the blacks and browns and grays of cows. And of course in every city I found the paloma, the pigeon, the unofficial bird of the world.

Throughout Mexico and Central America the black vulture was common, feeding on garbage heaps, circling over impending death, cleaning up carrion beside the road. As the forests dwindled, the quetzal declined, and as the death toll rose in the 1980s, the vulture thrived. In the cloud forest at Monteverde, there were red-crowned parrots, azure-hooded jays, motmots, and at least a dozen varieties of hummingbirds – the ruby-throated, broad-tailed, black-chinned, Cuban emerald, rufous, black-throated, and others. Over the bay of Panamá City the magnificent frigate bird floated, 90-inch wings and hollow bones, evolution's highest accomplishment in gliders, a bird that can stay aloft for weeks, not even lighting to feed, but swooping down to steal from the beaks of gulls and terns in flight. On the beach the spotted sandpiper darted about in the surf, pecking at tiny scraps the sea had brought. The one bird I most hoped to see, the quetzal, I had not seen, at least not alive. In the visitor center at Monteverde, a quetzal which had crashed into the window and broken its neck is mounted on the wall, its iridescent two-foot tail a graceful bow.

I stood in the shade in this other natural preserve at the far southeast extent of my trek, remembering what I had seen from the native prairie to the rain forest, thinking how quickly man in his need and greed and desire to control has conquered and ravaged the natural world from pole to pole. Suddenly a coati, the long-tailed cousin of the South Dakota racoon, lost his nerve and bounded from his hiding place in a cane grove beside the trail. He paused 10 feet away, curious and unafraid, then loped in raccoon fashion into the forest. Two giant butterflies flickered by, one black and the other orange, each with four-inch wings. I stumbled upon a green iguana sunning himself in the trail, and watched a dozen armies of red ants toiling down highways through the forest, each balancing a half-inch scrap of rubber tree leaf on his back, a favorite morsel borne to ant babies back home.

It was sweltering in the selva. I climbed to El Mirador, the highest hill, from which I could see most of Panamá City, the graceful Bridge of the Americas, and ships from around the globe. To the north was the Canal Zone forest, where during Vietnam, Army Rangers learned to kill and survive in the jungle. Even standing in the shade and the breeze on top, sweat continued to flow. What an utterly different world from the South Dakota winter to which I would return tomorrow.

Finally I escaped the tropical heat by driving to the sea. Though for 2,000 miles I'd been close to the Pacific much of the time, and had even glimpsed it in three countries, it was time to take off my clothes and wade in. The water was warm, the waves calm, the sky mercifully clouded. My feet were in the other element now, no longer on the North American continent I had traversed, but beyond it, linked by the great ocean not just to the Americas, but to every shore on earth. Surf splashed away the dust of nine nations. All borders had vanished.

Back at the Central Hotel, I went to the bar for a last cerveza. The music was cumbé, loud as always. Half-drunk men slapped and drummed on the bar in time with the Caribbean rhythm, the bongos and base fiddle and fast accordion reminding me somehow of bouzouki, the classical folk music of Greece with which my journey had begun in Winnipeg. I'd followed country and pop all the way to Texas, where country reached its crescendo at Billy Bobs. On to Austin for jazz and blues, to San Antonio for Tejano. Mariachis and salsa and Andean flutes in Mexico, the marimba and flutes again in Guatemala, the family guitar band and Nicaraguan folk in Estelí, and now a music and rhythm imported across the Atlantic from Africa. And everywhere, organs in the cathedrals, the unifying chords of Latin anthems, lulling alike from Winnipeg to Panamá.

I climbed the stairs and stepped out on the balcony for a last encounter with my guiding constellation, the Southern Cross, sparkling dimly over the bay. Tomorrow would be another early day, back to the airport to return the borrowed car and board the big airplane. Tomorrow night I'd be home in my own wide unsagging bed, happy my travels were over, hoping to make some sense of what I'd seen and heard.

I was at the airport by 7:00. I boarded an Airbus A300 Luxury Liner eight seats wide in 37 rows, the biggest bus of my journey, air-conditioned, uncrowded, clean. Five minutes after take-off we were high above Panamá, the Pacific visible on my left, the Atlantic on my right. Ships pass through the canal in 24 hours, but in five minutes more we had crossed. The San Blas Islands, where the Cuna Indians still live in relative innocence of the northern world, were tiny specks below. Somewhere down there, perhaps the woman who appliquéd the molas I bought at Miraflores Locks yesterday looked up from her work, wondering at the strange silver bird droning overhead.

# EPILOGUE

*"We abuse land because we regard it as a commodity belonging to us. When we see land as a community to which we belong, we may begin to use it with love and respect. There is no other way for land to survive the impact of mechanized man."*

~ *Aldo Leopold, A Sand County Almanac, 1949*

We flew over Cuba and the coral-reefed Florida Keys, over the ditched and drained brown Everglades. Down we floated, above big green signs I could almost read from the air, over freeways, smooth and eight lanes wide. Cars and trucks crawled by at 70 miles an hour. We touched down, taxied, and entered the terminal through an air-conditioned tube. I walked not on pavement or soil, but on supple carpet through the Miami airport. Tropical plants flourished behind glass, viewed from cool comfort by hurrying passengers. No coatis or iguanas lurked among the leaves. I drank greedily the refrigerated, purified water at the fountain, the first I'd found in weeks. It was good to be home in the modern world, so efficient, so marvelous and clean — yet so artificial, so cultivated, so tamed, so close to the brink of we know not what.

Norma, Walter and Laura met me at the airport in Sioux Falls. They were healthy and strong, and we drove in happiness to our warm home. As I had traveled from fall to eternal spring to sweltering summer heat, the world back home had assumed the monochromatic hues of winter, trees the exclamation marks against a sea of white. The sun was brilliant on the snow, and the wind was calm.

In the morning I trudged through snow-filled Indiangrass and flushed nine pheasants from their warm hiding place. I followed fresh tracks and droppings and found the beds of deer in the wild plum thicket west of the house. I carried out a bucket of North Dakota sunflower seeds, then pulled a chair close to the fire. As usual blue jays screeched in first for breakfast, then the nut-hatches, head-first hopping down the trunk of the ash. Then came the whistling chickadees and the lark sparrows.

After lunch I split some firewood, then resumed my mindless vigil by the stove. The slate-colored junco came just before dusk, then the woodpeckers, downy and hairy. The finches, purple and gold, came for a nightcap. Any day now the cardinals and the red-bellied woodpecker would return to our shared winter haven. It felt strange to be home, but very good. I had returned to balance with my universe, back in alignment with the brilliant South Dakota stars.

A strange dream recurred my first three nights home. I was walking south, somewhere in Central America, in a barrio of the poor. It was night, and I was lost. On the third night I loaned my passport to Tom, the friend with whom I stayed the night in San Antonio. He had entered El Salvador on my passport, and I was attempting illegal entry, over a wooded mountain. There were no birds in the mountains, and then I saw that the forest itself was withering.

I shuddered to wakefulness and lay long, remembering my journey. I recalled my last steps down the continent, venturing into the sea. Wading out from the shore, I had entered the other dimension from land. Having traced the American artery across eight boundaries and through the lives of Americans of many hues and tongues, I had left all frontiers behind, entering the realm of eternal motion, of constant flux, the medium where solid and stable give way to shifting and fluid. Perhaps there, better than anywhere else on my journey, I felt the universal, the connectedness not only of all mankind, but of all life.

Now I was home once more on my little particle of Clay County, South Dakota, USA, North America. But never again could home be bounded by the quarter-mile fence. Never again can I forget that my residence is Planet Earth, that I am brother of all the men and women, Papá to all the babies and boys and girls, son of all the aged, co-inhabitor of God's earth with the coati, the quetzal, the iguana and the industrious ant. I affect all, and they alter me. I had traveled from north to south, then peered west across infinity to the far east. If I had learned any thing at all on this humbling journey down the continent, it is that we are one.

I had witnessed the joy and the hope, but also the oppression and despair of fellow women and men whose lives are linked by the American artery. I had beheld the human struggle – for food, for land, for freedom from foreign domination, for dignity and right. I had lived many days among the poor, yet I could not tell why so many must work so hard, and suffer so much, for so little.

I had seen the devastation of great swaths of the continent – eroded topsoil, silted rivers, fallen trees, fouled air. I had felt the truth of Aldo Leopold's 1949 vision, and I knew that his understanding of the land applies to people and to all of life as well. The Earth and all her life is a vast cosmic community, not a commodity to be exploited. Our future is sustainable only as we give ourselves to this community, approaching one another and the Earth with respect and love.

I had seen, everywhere along this greatest of North American roads, man's greed, his exploitation of his fellow man, his failure to protect, his disregard for future generations. But also I had found women and men of global vision, building community, working to preserve and restore, respecting and nurturing the sustainable Earth, aware of balance.

On the fourth night I implored the ghosts to leave me. I promised a new journey, pursuing the intimations of my dreams.

# Notes

Sources Cited, in Sequence

**South from Winnipeg**
Cousteau, Jacques. (Scott Simon, Weekend Edition, Natl. Public Radio, 28 June 1997. Quoted from *A Sense of Wonder*. New York: Harcourt Brace Jovanovich, 1966).

Rifkin, Jeremy. Interview. "All Things Considered." Natl. Public Radio. 20 Oct. 1992.

Neihardt, John G. *Black Elk Speaks*. New York: Washington Square P, 1959: 24.

Laurence, Margaret. *The Stone Angel*. Chicago: U of Chicago P, 1964: 161.

Poitras, Lisa. "Resurrecting a Revolutionary: Interview with Maggie Siggins." Regina, Saskatchewan: *The Prairie Dog*. August 1996: 2.

**North Dakota**
McGrath, Thomas. "Beyond the Red River." *Selected Poems 1938-88*. Port Townsend, WA: Copper Canyon P, 1988: 128.

Allen, James Paul and Eugene James Turner. *We The People: An Atlas of America's Ethnic Diversity*. New York: Macmillan, 1988.

Robinson, Elwyn. *History of North Dakota*. Lincoln: U of Nebraska P, 1966.

Williams, Mary Ann Barnes. *Origins of North Dakota Place Names*. Bismarck: Tribune, P, 1966.

Gohlke, Frank. *Measure of Emptiness: Grain Elevators in the American Landscape*. Baltimore: The Johns Hopkins U P, 1992.

Kolstad, Mark. "Mexican Night." *South Dakota Review*. 33 (1995): 37-56.

**South Dakota**
Neihardt, John G. *Black Elk Speaks*. New York: Washington Square P, 1959: 5.

"Tribe selects supporter of Hawkins as chairman." Sioux Falls: *Argus Leader*. 10

Aug. 1995: D5.

Reese, M. Lisle. *South Dakota.* New York: Hastings House, 1952: Brookings 231.

Schell, Herbert. *History of South Dakota.* Lincoln: U of Nebraska P, 1966.

Sneve, Virginia Driving Hawk. *South Dakota Geographic Names.* Sioux Falls: Brevet P, 1973.

**Nebraska**
Brown, Dee. *Bury My Heart at Wounded Knee.* New York: Bantam, 1972: Standing Bear quote 333.

Flodman, Mildred. *Early Days in Polk County.* Lincoln: Union College P, 1966: 35.

Fitzpatrick, Lilian L. *Nebraska Place Names.* Lincoln: U of Nebraska P, 1960.

Perkey, Elton A. *Perkey's Nebraska Place Names.* Lincoln: Nebraska State Hist. Soc., 1982.

**Kansas**
Henry, S. T. *Highways of Friendship.* Washington, D.C: U.S. Dept. of Trans., 1924.

Lange-Kubick, Cindy. "Drivers beware: Journey on U.S. 81 can be fatal." Lincoln: *Journal Star* 25 Feb. 1996: A1.

Kramer, Arnold. *Nazi Prisoners of War in America.* Chelsea, MI: Scarborough House, 1991: POW statistics.

Rydjord, John. *Kansas Place-Names.* Norman: U of Oklahoma P, 1972.

**Oklahoma**
Guthrie, Woody. "Down In Oklayhoma." *Woodie Guthrie Folk Songs.* New York: Ludlow Music Inc., 1963: 214.

Berthrong, Donald J. *The Cheyenne and Arapaho Ordeal.* Norman: U of Oklahoma P, 1976.

Debo, Angie. *A History of the Indians of the United States.* Norman: U of Oklahoma P, 1970.

Shirk, George. *Oklahoma Place Names.* 2nd ed. Norman: U of Oklahoma P, 1974.

Ruth, Kent. *Oklahoma Travel Handbook*. Norman: U of Oklahoma P, 1977.

Henson, Lance. "The Ageless." *Keeper of Arrows: Poems for the Cheyenne*. Chickasha, OK: Rennaissance P, 1972.

Irving, Washington. *A Tour on the Prairies*. Philadelphia: Carey, Lea & Blanchard, 1835.

**Texas**
Asleep at the Wheel. "The Best of Asleep at the Wheel." Capitol Records, 1993.

"Texas County in Forefront in Executions." *New York Times*. 7 Aug. 1994: A31.

Carelli, Richard. "56 convicted killers were executed in 1995." Sioux Falls: *Argus Leader*. 30 Dec. 1995: A4.

Fort Worth Chamber of Commerce. "History of Fort Worth": 2.

"Baylor allows dancing." Sioux Falls: *Argus Leader*. 30 Jan. 1996: A5.

Whitehead, Fred and Verle Muhrer, eds. *Free Thought on the American Frontier*. Buffalo, NY: Prometheus Books, 1992: Brann quote 153.

Ferlinghetti, Lawrence. "A Buddha in the Woodpile." *These Are My Rivers: New and Selected Poems*, 1955-1993. New York: New Directions, 1994.

Killeen Chamber of Commerce. Killeen.

Austin Convention and Visitors Bureau. Austin, 1995.

Gomez, Tammy. *Seis Huesos*. Austin: Tejana Tongue Press, 1995.

Kerouac, Jack. *On the Road*. New York: Viking P, 1957: Dilley quote 306.

Pearsall Chamber of Commerce. Pearsall.

**Northern Mexico**
Kerouac, Jack. *On the Road*. New York: Viking P, 1957: 276.

Cassady, Carolyn. *Off the Road*. Ann Charters, ed. The Portable Beat Reader. New York: Viking P, 1992: 454.

**Central Mexico**

Bardach, Ann Louise. "Mexico's Rebel Poet." *Vanity Fair.* July 1994: Zapata quote 70.

"Ten police charged in deaths of 17 Mexicans." Sioux Falls: *Argus Leader.* 3 July 1995: A5.

Birnbaum, Stephen and Alexandra. *Mexico 1991.* Boston: Houghton Mifflin, 1990: Yanhuitlan 643.

**Southern Mexico**
Theroux, Paul. *Riding the Iron Rooster.* New York: Ivy Books, 1988: 180.

Bardach, Ann Louise. "Mexico's Rebel Poet." *Vanity Fair.* July 1994: Marcos quote 71.

de las Casas, Bartolomé. *A Short Account of the Destruction of the Indies.* New York: Penguin, 1992: 1511 sermon xxi.

Garrett, Wilbur E., ed. "La Ruta Maya." *National Geographic.* Oct. 1989: 474.

Castellanos, Rosario. *City of Kings.* Pittsburgh, PA: Latin American Literary Review P, 1992.

**Guatemala**
Menchú, Rigoberta. *I, Rigoberta Menchú.* London: Verso, 1984.

"Bettina Gray speaks with Luis Valdez" (videorecording). Princeton, NJ: Films for the Humanities and Sciences, 1992.

Seligson, Mitchell A. & John A. Booth. *Elections and Democracy in Central America.* Chapel Hill: U of North Carolina P, 1995 (Casualty statistics).

Saravia, Albertina, ed. *Popol Vuh.* Guatemala City: Publicaciones Turisticas, 1987.

"Arzú y Portillo encabezan la primera ronda electoral." Guatemala City: *Prenza Libre.* 13 Nov. 1995: 1.

"MINUGUA Becomes a Target Too." *Guatemala.* Oakland, CA: Guatemala News and Information Bureau, Dec. 1995: 3.

Swift, Richard. "NI Interview: Bruce Harris." *New Internationalist.* July 1995: 31.

"Unweaving the Web of Deceit." *Guatemala.* Washington, D.C.: Guatemala

Human Rights Commission/USA. July 1995: 4.

Priest, Dana. "Guatemalan on CIA Payroll Linked to Deaths." *Washington Post*. 23 Mar. 1995: A18.

**El Salvador**
Quemain, Jamie Suárez. "The Streets of San Salvador." Claribel Alegría and Darwin Flakoll, eds. *On the Front line: Guerrilla Poems of El Salvador*. Willimantic, CT: Curbstone Press, 1989: 87.

Reddy, Marlita A., ed. *Statistical Abstract of the World, 1994*. New York: Gale Research, 1994.

United Nations Statistical Office. *1992 Statistical Yearbook*. New York: United Nations, 1994.

Bernardi, Debra. *Fodor's Central America*. New York: Fodor's Travel Publications, 1987: Izalco volcano 206.

Alegría, Claribel and Darwin Flakoll. *The Ashes of Izalco*. Willimantic, CT: Curbstone Press, 1989.

Danner, Mark. "The Truth of El Mozote." *The New Yorker*. 6 Dec. 1993: 50+.

**Honduras**
Acker, Alison. *The Making of a Banana Republic*. Boston: South End Press, 1988: Zemurray quote 57.

Butler, Smedley. *War is a Racket*. Clackamas, OR: Emissary Publications, 1984.

Pearce, Jenny. *Under the Eagle*. Boston: South End Press, 1982: Butler quote 20.

Barry, Tom and Deb Preusch. *Central America Factbook*. Albuquerque, NM: The Resource Center, 1986: Statistics 265.

**Nicaragua**
Galeano, Eduardo. *Century of the Wind*. New York: Pantheon Books, 1988: Sandino quote 62.

Dalton, Roque. "Like You." *Clandestine Poems*. Willimantic, CT: Curbstone Press, 1990.

Brosnahan, Tom, et al., eds. *Central America: A Lonely Planet Shoestring Guide*. 2nd ed. Hawthorne, Australia: Lonely Planet Publications, 1994.

Darío, Rubén. "A Roosevelt." *Poemas*. Guatemala City: Editorial Piedra Santa, 1981.

Yeats, William Butler. "The Second Coming." M. H. Abrams, ed. *The Norton Anthology of English Literature*. Vol II. New York: W. W. Norton, 1968: 1582.

**Costa Rica**
Park, Chris C. *Tropical Rainforests*. London and New York: Routledge, 1992: 161.

"Rates of Rainforest Loss." Online. Rainforest Action Network. Internet. 5 Apr. 1996. Available: Magellan.igc.apc.org.ran.

**Panamá**
Roosevelt, Theodore. *The Strenuous Life*. New York: Century, 1902.

Shaff, Howard and Audrey Kari. *Six Wars at a Time: The Life and Times of Gutzon Borglum*. Sioux Falls, S.D.: Center for Western Studies, 1985: 197.

"All Things Considered." Natl. Public Radio. 1 Nov. 1995. (Drug money laundering)

"Victims of Just Cause." Narr. Mike Wallace. "Sixty Minutes." CBS. New York. June 1990.

Rainforest Action Network. Newsletter. San Francisco: RAN. Feb. 1996: 1.

**Epilogue**
Leopold, Aldo. *A Sand County Almanac*. New York: Ballantine Books, 1966: xviii-xix.

# INDEX

## ABOUT THE AUTHOR

Jerry Wilson is a native Oklahoman, now living on the South Dakota prairie. He has worked as a journalist, taught college literature and writing for 25 years, and has published numerous essays and short stories. He now serves as managing editor of *South Dakota Magazine* in Yankton, South Dakota.

For additional copies contact:

South Dakota Magazine
P.O. Box 175, Yankton, S.D. 57078
605-665-6655
800-456-5117